The Science-Backed Heart Healthy Diet for Beginners

Easy, Evidence-Based Guide to Lower Cholesterol, Reduce Blood Pressure, and Strengthen Heart Health
Tasty Recipes and 60-Day Meal Plan Included

Emily Reynolds

Table of Content

Discover Your Exclusive Free Bonus!

Thank you for choosing "The Science-Backed Heart Healthy Diet for Beginners"! We are thrilled to support your journey towards a healthier lifestyle with three exclusive free bonus.

Scan the QR code to download these valuable resources:

Bonus 1: The Complete Mediterranean Diet Cookbook for Beginners
Explore another book from the same author, guiding you through the complete Mediterranean diet for beginners.

Bonus 2: Anti-Inflammatory Diet for Heart Health
Discover recipes, directions, and plans to reduce inflammation and protect cardiovascular health.

Bonus 3: The Heart-Healthy Grocery Shopping Guide
A comprehensive guide to selecting the best heart-healthy foods at the grocery store.

Don't miss out on these incredible bonus! Scan the QR code to download your free resources and start your journey towards a healthier life and a stronger heart. Happy reading and good health!

Introduction

Welcome to Your Heart-Healthy Journey

Hello, and welcome to the beginning of a new chapter in your life—one where your heart health is front and center. I'm Dr. Emily Reynolds, and I'm thrilled to be your guide on this transformative journey. As a nutritionist and health coach, I've dedicated my career to understanding the profound connection between what we eat and how our hearts function. Through years of research and practical experience, I've seen firsthand how the right dietary choices can prevent, manage, and even reverse cardiovascular issues.

You may be here because you've experienced a wake-up call—perhaps a diagnosis or a family history of heart disease—or maybe you're simply looking to take proactive steps to ensure a long, vibrant life. Whatever brought you here, know that you're in the right place. This book is designed to empower you with the knowledge and tools you need to take control of your heart health.

A well-balanced diet isn't just about preventing disease; it's about feeling better every day, enjoying your meals, and living with the confidence that you're nourishing your body in the best way possible. When you commit to heart-healthy eating, you're not just choosing foods that benefit your heart—you're making a decision that can lead to more energy, better mood, improved digestion, and a stronger immune system. In short, you're investing in a healthier, happier you.

The journey you're about to embark on is supported by science and tailored to your needs as a beginner. You don't need to overhaul your entire life overnight. Instead, we'll take this step by step, making small, sustainable changes that add up to big results. My goal is to make this process as simple, enjoyable, and rewarding as possible.

How to Use This Book

This book is your roadmap to a heart-healthy lifestyle. It's filled with practical advice, delicious recipes, and actionable steps designed to make your transition to heart-healthy eating seamless and enjoyable. Here's how to make the most of it:

1. Start with Understanding: The first few chapters will walk you through the science of heart health. Don't worry—I've broken it down into clear, simple terms. Understanding the "why" behind the recommendations will help you stay motivated and make informed decisions.

2. Set Your Goals: Before diving into the practical tips, take a moment to reflect on your personal health goals. Whether you're aiming to lower your cholesterol, lose weight, or simply eat healthier, setting clear, achievable goals will keep you focused and committed.

3. Gradual Implementation: You don't have to make all the changes at once. This book is designed to be flexible, allowing you to integrate heart-healthy habits at your own pace. Start with small steps—perhaps incorporating more fruits and vegetables into your meals or swapping out processed snacks for whole foods.

4. Practical Tools and Tips: Throughout the book, you'll find tips and strategies to help you make heart-healthy eating a part of your daily routine. From grocery shopping advice to meal planning, I'll guide you through each aspect of this lifestyle change with simple, practical steps.

5. Delicious Recipes: At the heart of this book are the recipes—carefully crafted to be both heart-healthy and satisfying. Each recipe is designed to be easy to prepare, using ingredients that are both accessible and beneficial to your cardiovascular health. You don't have to sacrifice flavor for health; these meals prove that you can enjoy your food while taking care of your heart.

6. Staying Motivated: Changing your diet can be challenging, especially if you're used to certain habits. I've included motivational tips and personal stories throughout the book to help you stay on track. Remember, this is a journey, not a race. Celebrate your progress, no matter how small, and keep moving forward.

7. Tailoring the Plan to Your Needs: While this book provides a detailed guide, it's important to listen to your body and adjust the recommendations to suit your personal needs. If you have specific health concerns or dietary preferences, I encourage you to personalize the advice and make it work for you.

8. Beyond the Diet: While our focus is on diet, heart health is also influenced by other factors like physical activity, stress management, and sleep. I'll touch on these areas as well, offering a holistic approach to your well-being.

By the end of this book, my hope is that you'll feel confident in your ability to nourish your heart through smart, science-backed choices. This isn't just a diet—it's a sustainable lifestyle that will serve you well for years to come. Together, let's take the first step on your heart-healthy journey. Your heart will thank you for it.

Section 1: Mastering the Heart-Healthy Diet

Chapter 1: The Essentials of Cardiovascular Health

When it comes to living a long and healthy life, there are few things as crucial as taking care of your heart. Cardiovascular health is not just about avoiding illness; it's about embracing a lifestyle that promotes vitality, energy, and overall well-being. Understanding the essentials of cardiovascular health is the first step on your journey toward a heart-healthy life. In this chapter, we'll explore what cardiovascular disease is, the common conditions associated with it, and the vital role that diet plays in maintaining heart health. We'll also cover the symptoms and warning signs to watch for, and the global impact of heart disease, so you can see the bigger picture and why your efforts matter not just for you, but for people everywhere.

Understanding Cardiovascular Disease

The Basics: What is Cardiovascular Disease?

Cardiovascular disease (CVD) is a broad term that refers to a variety of conditions affecting the heart and blood vessels. These diseases are often the result of a combination of genetic, environmental, and lifestyle factors. The most common forms of CVD include coronary artery disease (CAD), heart failure, arrhythmias, and stroke. Each of these conditions affects the heart and circulatory system in different ways, but they all share a common thread: they hinder the ability of the heart and blood vessels to function properly.

Coronary artery disease, for example, is the result of plaque buildup in the arteries that supply blood to the heart. This buildup can lead to narrowed or blocked arteries, reducing blood flow to the heart muscle and potentially causing a heart attack. Heart failure, on the other hand, occurs when the heart is unable to pump blood efficiently, leading to a buildup of fluid in the lungs and other parts of the body. Arrhythmias involve irregular heartbeats, which can be too fast, too slow, or erratic, affecting the heart's ability to pump blood effectively. Stroke, a condition closely related to heart disease, occurs when the blood supply to part of the brain is interrupted or reduced, depriving brain tissue of oxygen and nutrients.

Understanding these conditions is critical because they all stem from similar risk factors and can often be prevented or managed with the right lifestyle choices. By taking steps to improve your heart health, you're not only reducing your risk of one specific condition, but potentially all forms of cardiovascular disease.

Common Types of Cardiovascular Conditions

To better grasp the importance of heart health, let's delve into some of the most common cardiovascular conditions:

1. **Coronary Artery Disease (CAD):** This is the most common type of heart disease and occurs when the arteries that supply blood to the heart become hardened and narrowed due to the buildup of plaque. This can lead to chest pain (angina), shortness of breath, or more serious conditions like heart attacks.

2. **Heart Failure:** Despite its name, heart failure doesn't mean the heart has stopped working. It means that the heart isn't pumping blood as effectively as it should. Over time, conditions such as high blood pressure or CAD weaken the heart, making it harder for it to fill with and pump blood.

3. **Arrhythmias:** These are problems with the rate or rhythm of your heartbeat. They occur when the electrical impulses that coordinate your heartbeats don't work properly, causing your heart to beat too fast, too slow, or irregularly. While some arrhythmias are harmless, others can be serious or even life-threatening.

4. **Stroke:** Often classified under cardiovascular disease, a stroke happens when blood flow to a part of your brain is blocked or reduced, preventing brain tissue from getting oxygen and nutrients. This can lead to brain damage, disability, or death.

5. **Hypertension (High Blood Pressure):** Often called the "silent killer" because it typically has no symptoms, hypertension is a condition in which the force of the blood against your artery walls is too high. This can lead to serious heart problems, including heart attacks, strokes, and heart failure.

6. **Peripheral Artery Disease (PAD):** PAD is a condition where the arteries that supply blood to your limbs, usually your legs, become narrowed or blocked. This can cause pain and cramping in the legs and increase the risk of heart disease.

Understanding these conditions is not just about learning medical terms; it's about recognizing how interconnected your heart health is with your overall well-being. By becoming aware of these conditions and their impact, you're taking the first step toward making informed decisions that can protect your heart and improve your quality of life.

The Role of Diet in Heart Health

Diet plays a pivotal role in maintaining cardiovascular health. What you eat directly influences your heart and blood vessels, affecting your risk of developing cardiovascular disease. A heart-healthy diet isn't about restriction or deprivation; it's about making choices that nourish your body and support your heart's needs.

The Impact of Nutrients on Heart Health

Your heart relies on a variety of nutrients to function properly. Here's a look at how different components of your diet can impact your cardiovascular health:

1. **Fats:** Not all fats are created equal. Saturated and trans fats, found in foods like red meat, butter, and fried foods, can raise your LDL (bad) cholesterol levels and increase your risk of heart disease. On the other hand, unsaturated fats, found in foods like olive oil, avocados, and nuts, can help reduce LDL cholesterol and are beneficial for heart health.

2. **Fiber:** Dietary fiber, particularly soluble fiber found in oats, beans, and fruits, helps lower cholesterol levels. It also aids in digestion and can help prevent heart disease by keeping your blood sugar levels stable.

3. **Sodium:** Excessive sodium intake can lead to high blood pressure, a major risk factor for heart disease. Reducing your sodium intake by limiting processed foods and using herbs and spices for flavor instead of salt can significantly improve your heart health.

4. **Antioxidants:** Found in fruits and vegetables, antioxidants protect your cells from damage caused by free radicals, which are unstable molecules that can contribute to heart disease. Eating a diet rich in colorful fruits and vegetables ensures you get a variety of antioxidants to support heart health.

5. **Omega-3 Fatty Acids:** These healthy fats, found in fatty fish like salmon and mackerel, as well as in flaxseeds and walnuts, have been shown to reduce inflammation, lower blood pressure, and decrease the risk of heart disease.

Building a Heart-Healthy Diet

To build a heart-healthy diet, focus on incorporating a variety of nutrient-dense foods that provide the vitamins, minerals, and other nutrients your heart needs to function optimally. Here are some key guidelines:

1. **Emphasize Whole Foods:** Whole grains, fruits, vegetables, lean proteins, and healthy fats should make up the bulk of your diet. These foods are rich in nutrients and low in unhealthy fats and added sugars.

2. **Choose Healthy Fats:** Opt for sources of unsaturated fats, such as olive oil, nuts, seeds, and fatty fish. Limit your intake of saturated fats and avoid trans fats altogether.

3. **Increase Fiber Intake:** Aim to include a variety of high-fiber foods in your diet, such as whole grains, beans, legumes, fruits, and vegetables. These foods help manage cholesterol levels and support overall heart health.

4. **Limit Sodium:** Be mindful of your sodium intake by reducing your consumption of processed foods and cooking with fresh ingredients. Use herbs and spices to add flavor without the need for salt.

5. **Incorporate Antioxidant-Rich Foods:** Eat a rainbow of fruits and vegetables to ensure you're getting a wide range of antioxidants. Berries, leafy greens, and brightly colored vegetables are particularly beneficial.

6. **Stay Hydrated:** Proper hydration is essential for heart health. Drinking enough water helps maintain blood volume, supports kidney function, and keeps your cardiovascular system running smoothly.

By making these dietary changes, you're not just protecting your heart—you're investing in your overall health and well-being.

Symptoms and Warning Signs to Watch For

Understanding the symptoms and warning signs of cardiovascular disease is crucial for early detection and prevention. Many heart-related conditions can develop silently, without obvious symptoms, which is why regular check-ups and being attuned to your body's signals are essential.

Common Symptoms of Cardiovascular Disease

Here are some symptoms to be aware of:

1. **Chest Pain or Discomfort (Angina):** This is one of the most common symptoms of heart disease. It may feel like pressure, squeezing, fullness, or pain in the center of your chest. It can last for a few minutes or come and go. If you experience chest pain, it's important to seek medical attention immediately.

2. **Shortness of Breath:** If you find it difficult to breathe during normal activities or while at rest, it could be a sign that your heart isn't pumping efficiently. Shortness of breath can be a symptom of heart failure, CAD, or other cardiovascular conditions.

3. **Fatigue:** Feeling unusually tired or exhausted, especially after routine activities, can be a sign that your heart is struggling to meet your body's needs. Fatigue is a common symptom of heart failure and other heart conditions.

4. **Palpitations:** If you feel like your heart is racing, pounding, or skipping beats, you may be experiencing palpitations. While palpitations can be harmless, they can also indicate arrhythmias or other heart issues that need to be evaluated by a doctor.

5. **Swelling (Edema):** Swelling in your legs, ankles, or feet can be a sign of heart failure, as fluid builds up when the heart doesn't pump blood effectively.

6. **Dizziness or Lightheadedness:** Feeling dizzy or lightheaded can occur if your heart isn't pumping enough blood to your brain. This can be a symptom of various heart conditions, including arrhythmias and low blood pressure.

7. **Nausea or Indigestion:** While these symptoms are often associated with gastrointestinal issues, they can also be signs of a heart attack, particularly in women. If you experience nausea or indigestion along with other symptoms like chest pain or shortness of breath, seek medical attention immediately.

When to Seek Medical Attention

If you experience any of the symptoms mentioned above, it's important to seek medical attention, especially if they are new, severe, or worsening. Early detection and treatment of cardiovascular disease can significantly improve outcomes and reduce the risk of serious complications.

The Global Impact of Heart Disease

Cardiovascular disease is a leading cause of death worldwide, affecting millions of people across all demographics. Understanding the global impact of heart disease can help put into perspective why taking steps to protect your heart is so important—not just for your own health, but as part of a larger effort to combat a major public health issue.

Heart Disease: A Global Epidemic

According to the World Health Organization (WHO), cardiovascular diseases are the number one cause of death globally, accounting for an estimated 17.9 million deaths each year. This represents 31% of all global deaths. Of these deaths, 85% are due to heart attacks and strokes.

The burden of cardiovascular disease is not limited to high-income countries. In fact, over three-quarters of cardiovascular disease deaths occur in low- and middle-income countries. This highlights the need for global awareness, education, and access to preventive measures.

The Role of Lifestyle and Diet

Many cases of cardiovascular disease are linked to lifestyle factors, including poor diet, physical inactivity, tobacco use, and excessive alcohol consumption. By addressing these factors through education and supportive policies, it's possible to reduce the global burden of heart disease.

As you embark on your heart-healthy journey, you're not just improving your own health—you're contributing to a larger movement toward better cardiovascular health for all. Every positive change you make helps build a healthier future for you, your family, and communities around the world.

Key Risk Factors and Prevention

When it comes to cardiovascular health, understanding the key risk factors is crucial. By identifying these risks, you can take proactive steps to protect your heart and prevent cardiovascular disease. While some risk factors are beyond your control, many can be managed or even eliminated through lifestyle changes. In this section, we'll explore the primary risk factors for heart disease, highlighting both those that are genetic and those that are lifestyle-related. We'll also discuss actionable steps you can take to reduce your risk and support a healthy heart.

Genetic vs. Lifestyle Risk Factors

Genetic Risk Factors

Some people are more predisposed to cardiovascular disease due to their genetic makeup. If you have a family history of heart disease, high blood pressure, high cholesterol, or diabetes, your risk of developing these conditions may be higher. This doesn't mean that heart disease is inevitable, but it does mean you need to be particularly vigilant about your heart health.

Family History: If your parents, siblings, or close relatives have had heart disease, especially at a young age, your risk of developing similar conditions is higher. This is because genetic factors can influence how your body processes cholesterol, how your blood pressure is regulated, and how your heart responds to stress and other factors.

Genetic Disorders: Certain inherited conditions, such as familial hypercholesterolemia, can cause extremely high cholesterol levels from a young age, significantly increasing the risk of heart disease. These genetic conditions require medical management and careful monitoring.

Ethnicity: Your ethnicity can also play a role in your risk of cardiovascular disease. For example, African Americans tend to have higher rates of high blood pressure and heart disease, while South Asians are at increased risk for diabetes and heart disease. These differences are thought to be due to a combination of genetic and lifestyle factors.

What You Can Do: If you have a genetic predisposition to heart disease, it's essential to be proactive about your health. Regular check-ups with your healthcare provider, routine screening for cholesterol and blood pressure, and a heart-healthy lifestyle can help you manage your risk. While you can't change your genetics, you can significantly influence how they affect your health by making smart choices.

Lifestyle Risk Factors

Unlike genetic factors, lifestyle risk factors are within your control. These include the choices you make every day about what to eat, how active you are, whether you smoke or drink alcohol, and how you manage stress. By addressing these factors, you can dramatically reduce your risk of developing heart disease.

Poor Diet: A diet high in saturated fats, trans fats, cholesterol, sodium, and added sugars can contribute to the development of cardiovascular disease. Eating large amounts of red and processed meats, refined grains, and sugary beverages increases your risk of heart disease by contributing to high cholesterol, high blood pressure, and obesity.

Lack of Physical Activity: Sedentary behavior is a major risk factor for cardiovascular disease. Regular physical activity strengthens the heart muscle, improves circulation, helps control weight, and reduces blood pressure and cholesterol levels. In contrast, a lack of exercise contributes to weight gain, high blood pressure, and increased risk of heart disease.

Smoking: Smoking is one of the most significant modifiable risk factors for heart disease. The chemicals in tobacco damage the lining of your arteries, leading to the buildup of fatty material (atheroma) which narrows the artery. This can lead to atherosclerosis, heart attacks, and strokes.

Excessive Alcohol Consumption: While moderate alcohol consumption might have some protective effects, excessive drinking can raise blood pressure, increase triglyceride levels, and contribute to the development of cardiomyopathy, a disease of the heart muscle.

Chronic Stress: Chronic stress contributes to cardiovascular disease in several ways. It can lead to high blood pressure, unhealthy eating habits, and physical inactivity. Stress can also cause the body to release hormones like adrenaline and cortisol, which increase heart rate and blood pressure. Over time, this can strain your heart and increase your risk of heart disease.

What You Can Do: The good news is that lifestyle factors are within your control. By adopting a heart-healthy diet, staying active, avoiding tobacco, moderating alcohol consumption, and managing stress, you can significantly lower your risk of cardiovascular disease. Even small changes can make a big difference over time, so start where you are and build healthy habits gradually.

The Impact of High Blood Pressure and Cholesterol

Two of the most significant risk factors for heart disease are high blood pressure (hypertension) and high cholesterol. Both conditions can be managed effectively with lifestyle changes and, when necessary, medication.

High Blood Pressure (Hypertension)

Blood pressure is the force of your blood against the walls of your arteries. When this pressure is consistently too high, it puts extra strain on your heart and blood vessels, increasing your risk of heart disease, stroke, and other health problems.

What Causes High Blood Pressure? High blood pressure can be caused by a variety of factors, including:

- **Diet:** A diet high in sodium (salt) can cause the body to retain water, leading to increased blood pressure. Diets low in potassium, calcium, and magnesium can also contribute to hypertension.

- **Weight:** Being overweight or obese increases the strain on your heart and can raise blood pressure.

- **Physical Inactivity:** Lack of exercise contributes to weight gain and can lead to high blood pressure.

- **Stress:** Chronic stress can lead to temporary spikes in blood pressure, which over time can contribute to sustained hypertension.

- **Alcohol and Tobacco Use:** Excessive alcohol consumption and smoking can damage the heart and blood vessels, leading to high blood pressure.

How to Manage High Blood Pressure Managing high blood pressure involves a combination of lifestyle changes and, in some cases, medication. Here are some strategies to help lower blood pressure:

- **Eat a Heart-Healthy Diet:** Focus on a diet rich in fruits, vegetables, whole grains, lean proteins, and healthy fats. The DASH diet (Dietary Approaches to Stop Hypertension) is particularly effective for lowering blood pressure.

- **Reduce Sodium Intake:** Aim to consume less than 2,300 milligrams of sodium per day, or less if advised by your healthcare provider. Cook at home using fresh ingredients, and read food labels to avoid high-sodium processed foods.

- **Exercise Regularly:** Aim for at least 150 minutes of moderate-intensity exercise each week. Activities like walking, swimming, cycling, and dancing can help lower blood pressure.

- **Maintain a Healthy Weight:** Losing even a small amount of weight can significantly lower your blood pressure.

- **Limit Alcohol and Avoid Smoking:** If you drink alcohol, do so in moderation. Quitting smoking is one of the best things you can do for your heart health.

High Cholesterol

Cholesterol is a fatty substance found in your blood. Your body needs some cholesterol to build healthy cells, but too much cholesterol can increase your risk of heart disease.

Types of Cholesterol There are different types of cholesterol, and understanding them is key to managing your heart health:

- **Low-Density Lipoprotein (LDL):** Often referred to as "bad" cholesterol, LDL can build up in the walls of your arteries, forming plaque that narrows the arteries and increases the risk of heart attack and stroke.

- **High-Density Lipoprotein (HDL):** Known as "good" cholesterol, HDL helps remove LDL from the arteries and transport it back to the liver, where it's processed and eliminated from the body.

- **Triglycerides:** These are a type of fat found in your blood. High levels of triglycerides can also contribute to the hardening and narrowing of arteries.

What Causes High Cholesterol? Several factors can contribute to high cholesterol, including:

- **Diet:** A diet high in saturated and trans fats can raise your LDL cholesterol levels.

- **Weight:** Being overweight or obese is linked to higher LDL cholesterol levels and lower HDL cholesterol levels.

- **Physical Inactivity:** Lack of exercise can contribute to weight gain and higher LDL cholesterol levels.

- **Genetics:** Some people are genetically predisposed to high cholesterol, regardless of their diet or lifestyle.

How to Manage High Cholesterol Managing high cholesterol involves making dietary changes, increasing physical activity, and sometimes taking medication. Here's what you can do:

- **Eat Heart-Healthy Foods:** Focus on foods that are low in saturated and trans fats. Incorporate more fruits, vegetables, whole grains, and lean proteins into your diet. Foods rich in omega-3 fatty acids, like fatty fish, flaxseeds, and walnuts, can help raise HDL cholesterol and lower LDL cholesterol.

- **Increase Fiber Intake:** Soluble fiber, found in oats, beans, and certain fruits, can help reduce LDL cholesterol levels.

- **Exercise Regularly:** Regular physical activity can help raise HDL cholesterol and lower LDL cholesterol. Aim for at least 30 minutes of exercise most days of the week.

- **Maintain a Healthy Weight:** Losing weight, if needed, can help lower LDL cholesterol and triglyceride levels while increasing HDL cholesterol.

- **Limit Alcohol and Avoid Smoking:** Moderation is key when it comes to alcohol, and avoiding smoking can significantly improve your cholesterol levels and overall heart health.

The Role of Obesity and Diabetes in Heart Health

Obesity and diabetes are two closely linked conditions that significantly increase the risk of cardiovascular disease. Understanding their impact on heart health and how to manage these conditions is crucial for preventing heart disease.

Obesity

Obesity is defined as having a body mass index (BMI) of 30 or higher. Excess body weight, particularly when it's concentrated around the abdomen, is a major risk factor for heart disease. Obesity can lead to high blood pressure, high cholesterol, and insulin resistance, all of which increase the risk of heart disease.

Why Obesity Affects Heart Health

- **Increased Workload:** Carrying extra weight puts additional strain on your heart, as it has to work harder to pump blood throughout your body.

- **Fat Accumulation:** Excess fat, particularly visceral fat (fat around the organs), can lead to inflammation and the buildup of plaque in the arteries.

- **Risk of Diabetes:** Obesity is a leading cause of type 2 diabetes, which is itself a major risk factor for heart disease.

Managing Obesity If you are overweight or obese, even a modest weight loss can have significant benefits for your heart health. Here's how to get started:

- **Set Realistic Goals:** Aim to lose 5-10% of your body weight to start, which can significantly improve your heart health.

- **Adopt a Healthy Diet:** Focus on portion control, eating nutrient-dense foods, and reducing your intake of high-calorie, low-nutrient foods.

- **Increase Physical Activity:** Regular exercise is essential for weight loss and maintaining a healthy weight. Aim for a combination of aerobic activity and strength training.

- **Seek Support:** Consider working with a healthcare provider, nutritionist, or weight-loss group to help you stay on track.

Diabetes

Diabetes, particularly type 2 diabetes, is a major risk factor for cardiovascular disease. High blood sugar levels can damage blood vessels and the nerves that control the heart. People with diabetes are more likely to have other conditions that raise the risk of heart disease, such as high blood pressure and high cholesterol.

Why Diabetes Affects Heart Health

- **Blood Vessel Damage:** High blood sugar levels can lead to atherosclerosis, or the hardening of the arteries, which increases the risk of heart attack and stroke.

- **Increased Cholesterol Levels:** Diabetes often leads to an imbalance of cholesterol levels, with higher LDL cholesterol and triglycerides and lower HDL cholesterol.

- **Increased Blood Pressure:** Diabetes is frequently accompanied by high blood pressure, which further increases the risk of heart disease.

Managing Diabetes If you have diabetes, managing your blood sugar levels is crucial for protecting your heart. Here are some strategies:

- **Monitor Blood Sugar Levels:** Regularly check your blood sugar levels to ensure they stay within your target range.

- **Follow a Diabetes-Friendly Diet:** Focus on foods that are low on the glycemic index, such as whole grains, legumes, and non-starchy vegetables. Avoid refined sugars and limit carbohydrate intake.

- **Exercise Regularly:** Physical activity helps regulate blood sugar levels and can improve insulin sensitivity.

- **Take Medications as Prescribed:** If you're on medication for diabetes, take it as directed by your healthcare provider.

Smoking, Alcohol, and Their Impact on the Heart

Smoking

Smoking is one of the most harmful habits for your heart. The chemicals in tobacco smoke damage your blood vessels, reduce the amount of oxygen in your blood, and increase your blood pressure and heart rate. Smoking also contributes to the buildup of plaque in your arteries, which can lead to atherosclerosis, heart attack, and stroke.

Why Smoking Is Dangerous for the Heart

- **Damage to Blood Vessels:** Smoking causes the lining of your arteries to become sticky, allowing plaque to build up more easily.

- **Reduced Oxygen Supply:** Carbon monoxide in tobacco smoke binds to hemoglobin in your blood, reducing the amount of oxygen that can be delivered to your organs and tissues.

- **Increased Blood Pressure:** Nicotine raises blood pressure, which puts additional strain on your heart.

How to Quit Smoking Quitting smoking is one of the best things you can do for your heart health. Here's how to get started:

- **Seek Support:** Talk to your healthcare provider about quitting smoking. They can provide resources, medications, and support to help you quit.

- **Identify Triggers:** Recognize the situations that make you want to smoke and develop strategies to avoid or manage them.

- **Stay Positive:** Quitting smoking is challenging, but it's worth it. Focus on the benefits, such as improved heart health, better lung function, and increased energy.

Alcohol

Moderate alcohol consumption might have some protective effects on the heart, particularly red wine, which is rich in antioxidants. However, excessive alcohol consumption can lead to high blood pressure, heart failure, and stroke.

The Risks of Excessive Alcohol Consumption

- **Increased Blood Pressure:** Drinking too much alcohol can raise blood pressure, which is a major risk factor for heart disease.

- **Cardiomyopathy:** Excessive drinking can weaken the heart muscle, leading to a condition called cardiomyopathy, which affects the heart's ability to pump blood effectively.

- **Weight Gain:** Alcohol is high in calories and can contribute to weight gain, which increases the risk of obesity and heart disease.

How to Drink Responsibly If you choose to drink alcohol, do so in moderation. This means up to one drink per day for women and up to two drinks per day for men. Consider alcohol-free days each week to give your body a break and reduce your overall intake.

Preventive Measures: What You Can Control

While some risk factors for heart disease are beyond your control, many can be managed through lifestyle changes. Here's a step-by-step guide to taking control of your heart health:

1. **Eat a Heart-Healthy Diet:** Focus on whole foods, including plenty of fruits, vegetables, whole grains, lean proteins, and healthy fats. Limit processed foods, added sugars, and sodium.

2. **Stay Active:** Aim for at least 150 minutes of moderate-intensity exercise each week. Find activities you enjoy, such as walking, swimming, or dancing, to make it easier to stay active.

3. **Maintain a Healthy Weight:** If you're overweight or obese, work toward a healthy weight by combining a balanced diet with regular physical activity.

4. **Quit Smoking:** If you smoke, seek support to quit. Your heart health will improve significantly once you stop smoking.

5. **Limit Alcohol:** If you drink alcohol, do so in moderation. Avoid binge drinking and consider alcohol-free days.

6. **Manage Stress:** Practice stress-reducing techniques, such as mindfulness, meditation, deep breathing, or yoga. Managing stress can help lower blood pressure and reduce your risk of heart disease.

7. **Monitor Your Health:** Regularly check your blood pressure, cholesterol levels, and blood sugar levels. Work with your healthcare provider to address any concerns.

By taking these preventive measures, you can significantly reduce your risk of cardiovascular disease and take control of your heart health. Every small step you take toward a healthier lifestyle makes a big difference over time, leading to a longer, healthier life.

Chapter 2: The Science of Heart-Healthy Eating

In the journey toward better heart health, what you choose to eat is one of the most powerful tools at your disposal. The foods you consume can either support your cardiovascular system or contribute to the development of heart disease. In this chapter, we will explore the science behind heart-healthy eating, focusing on specific nutrients that play a crucial role in promoting heart health. By understanding these nutritional powerhouses and how they work, you'll be equipped to make informed, beneficial choices that support a healthy heart.

Nutritional Powerhouses for Heart Health

The term "nutritional powerhouses" refers to foods and nutrients that provide significant health benefits, particularly for your heart. These are the stars of a heart-healthy diet, offering essential vitamins, minerals, and compounds that work synergistically to protect and strengthen your cardiovascular system. Let's dive into some of the most important nutritional powerhouses for heart health.

Omega-3 Fatty Acids: Sources and Benefits

What Are Omega-3 Fatty Acids?

Omega-3 fatty acids are a type of polyunsaturated fat that is essential for human health. Unlike some other fats that the body can produce, omega-3s must be obtained through diet. They are vital for various bodily functions, including maintaining the structure and function of cell membranes, supporting brain health, and, crucially, protecting your heart.

Types of Omega-3 Fatty Acids

There are three main types of omega-3 fatty acids:

1. **Eicosapentaenoic Acid (EPA):** Found primarily in fatty fish, EPA is known for its anti-inflammatory properties and its role in reducing blood clotting, which helps prevent heart attacks and strokes.

2. **Docosahexaenoic Acid (DHA):** Also found in fatty fish, DHA is crucial for brain health and supports overall heart function by lowering triglycerides, reducing blood pressure, and improving arterial function.

3. **Alpha-Linolenic Acid (ALA):** ALA is found in plant-based sources such as flaxseeds, chia seeds, and walnuts. While ALA is beneficial, the body must convert it into EPA and DHA, a process that is not very efficient. Therefore, direct consumption of EPA and DHA from fish or supplements is often recommended for heart health.

Benefits of Omega-3 Fatty Acids for Heart Health

Omega-3 fatty acids offer numerous benefits for heart health:

- **Lowering Triglycerides:** High levels of triglycerides—a type of fat found in your blood—can increase the risk of heart disease. Omega-3s are effective in reducing triglyceride levels, which is critical for maintaining a healthy heart.

- **Reducing Inflammation:** Chronic inflammation is a key factor in the development of atherosclerosis, a condition characterized by the buildup of plaque in the arteries. Omega-3s help reduce inflammation, thereby lowering the risk of heart disease.

- **Preventing Arrhythmias:** Omega-3s help stabilize the electrical activity of the heart, reducing the risk of irregular heartbeats, or arrhythmias, which can lead to sudden cardiac death.

- **Lowering Blood Pressure:** Regular consumption of omega-3s has been shown to lower blood pressure in people with hypertension, reducing the strain on the heart and arteries.

Best Sources of Omega-3 Fatty Acids

To ensure you're getting enough omega-3s, include the following foods in your diet:

- **Fatty Fish:** Salmon, mackerel, sardines, and trout are excellent sources of EPA and DHA. Aim to eat these types of fish at least twice a week.

- **Flaxseeds and Chia Seeds:** These plant-based sources are rich in ALA. You can add them to smoothies, yogurt, or oatmeal for a nutritional boost.

- **Walnuts:** A handful of walnuts provides a good dose of ALA, along with other heart-healthy nutrients.

- **Algal Oil:** This plant-based supplement is derived from algae and is a great source of DHA, making it a good option for vegetarians and vegans.

Incorporating these omega-3-rich foods into your diet is a simple yet powerful way to support your heart health.

The Role of Dietary Fiber in Reducing Cholesterol

What Is Dietary Fiber?

Dietary fiber, often simply referred to as fiber, is a type of carbohydrate that the body cannot digest. Unlike other carbohydrates, fiber passes through the digestive system relatively intact, providing various health benefits along the way. Fiber is classified into two main types: soluble and insoluble.

- **Soluble Fiber:** This type of fiber dissolves in water to form a gel-like substance. It is particularly effective in lowering cholesterol levels and improving heart health.

- **Insoluble Fiber:** This type of fiber does not dissolve in water and adds bulk to the stool, aiding in digestion and preventing constipation. While it's important for overall health, it doesn't have the same cholesterol-lowering effects as soluble fiber.

How Fiber Reduces Cholesterol

Soluble fiber plays a key role in reducing cholesterol levels, which is crucial for preventing heart disease. Here's how it works:

- **Binds to Cholesterol:** Soluble fiber binds to cholesterol particles in the digestive system, preventing them from being absorbed into the bloodstream. Instead, these cholesterol particles are excreted from the body through waste.

- **Lowers LDL Cholesterol:** By reducing the absorption of cholesterol, soluble fiber helps lower levels of low-density lipoprotein (LDL) cholesterol, often referred to as "bad" cholesterol. High levels of LDL cholesterol can lead to the buildup of plaque in the arteries, increasing the risk of heart attack and stroke.

- **Improves Blood Sugar Levels:** Soluble fiber also helps regulate blood sugar levels by slowing the absorption of sugar into the bloodstream. This is particularly beneficial for people with diabetes or those at risk of developing diabetes, as high blood sugar levels can damage blood vessels and increase the risk of heart disease.

Best Sources of Dietary Fiber

Incorporating more fiber into your diet is a straightforward and effective way to support your heart health. Here are some of the best sources of dietary fiber:

- **Oats:** A bowl of oatmeal is a great way to start the day with a dose of soluble fiber. Oats contain beta-glucan, a type of soluble fiber that is particularly effective at lowering cholesterol levels.

- **Beans and Legumes:** Lentils, chickpeas, black beans, and other legumes are rich in both soluble and insoluble fiber. They make a heart-healthy addition to soups, salads, and main dishes.

- **Fruits:** Apples, pears, oranges, and berries are all high in soluble fiber. Enjoy them as snacks or add them to your meals for a sweet and nutritious boost.

- **Vegetables:** Carrots, Brussels sprouts, and sweet potatoes are excellent sources of soluble fiber. Including a variety of vegetables in your diet ensures you're getting the fiber you need to support heart health.

- **Psyllium:** Psyllium husk is a concentrated source of soluble fiber that can be taken as a supplement or added to foods like smoothies and cereals. It's particularly effective for lowering cholesterol levels.

By making fiber-rich foods a regular part of your diet, you can take a significant step toward improving your cardiovascular health.

Antioxidants and Their Protective Effects

What Are Antioxidants?

Antioxidants are compounds found in certain foods that help protect your cells from damage caused by free radicals. Free radicals are unstable molecules that can cause oxidative stress, leading to inflammation and the development of chronic diseases, including heart disease.

How Antioxidants Protect the Heart

Antioxidants play a crucial role in protecting your heart by neutralizing free radicals and reducing oxidative stress. Here's how they contribute to heart health:

- **Preventing Oxidative Damage:** Free radicals can oxidize LDL cholesterol, leading to the formation of plaque in the arteries. Antioxidants help prevent this oxidation, reducing the risk of atherosclerosis (hardening of the arteries) and heart disease.

- **Reducing Inflammation:** Chronic inflammation is a key driver of heart disease. Antioxidants have anti-inflammatory properties that help reduce inflammation throughout the body, including in the arteries and heart.

- **Supporting Healthy Blood Vessels:** Antioxidants help maintain the health and elasticity of blood vessels, ensuring that blood flows smoothly and reducing the risk of hypertension (high blood pressure).

Best Sources of Antioxidants

To ensure you're getting enough antioxidants, incorporate a variety of antioxidant-rich foods into your diet:

- **Berries:** Blueberries, strawberries, raspberries, and blackberries are packed with antioxidants, particularly anthocyanins, which have been shown to protect against heart disease.

- **Dark Chocolate:** Rich in flavonoids, dark chocolate can help improve blood flow, lower blood pressure, and reduce the risk of heart disease. Choose dark chocolate with at least 70% cocoa content for the most benefits.

- **Green Tea:** Green tea is a powerful source of catechins, a type of antioxidant that helps protect the heart by reducing inflammation and improving cholesterol levels.

- **Leafy Greens:** Spinach, kale, and other leafy greens are high in antioxidants, including vitamin C, beta-carotene, and flavonoids, all of which support heart health.

- **Nuts and Seeds:** Almonds, walnuts, and sunflower seeds are rich in vitamin E, an antioxidant that helps protect the cells in your heart and arteries from oxidative damage.

Including a wide range of antioxidant-rich foods in your diet is a delicious and effective way to support your heart health and overall well-being.

Healthy Fats: Unsaturated vs. Saturated

Understanding Fats

Not all fats are created equal. When it comes to heart health, the type of fat you consume is more important than the amount. Fats are essential for your body's functioning, but it's crucial to choose the right kinds.

Saturated Fats

Saturated fats are typically solid at room temperature and are found in animal products like butter, cheese, red meat, and processed foods. While your body needs some saturated fat, too much can raise LDL cholesterol levels, increasing the risk of heart disease.

Unsaturated Fats

Unsaturated fats, on the other hand, are considered heart-healthy fats. They are usually liquid at room temperature and are found in plant-based oils, nuts, seeds, avocados, and fatty fish. Unsaturated fats are divided into two categories:

- **Monounsaturated Fats (MUFAs):** Found in olive oil, avocados, and nuts, MUFAs can help reduce LDL cholesterol levels and lower the risk of heart disease.

- **Polyunsaturated Fats (PUFAs):** Found in fatty fish, walnuts, and flaxseeds, PUFAs include omega-3 and omega-6 fatty acids, which are essential for heart health.

The Impact of Healthy Fats on Heart Health

- **Lowering LDL Cholesterol:** Unsaturated fats help reduce LDL cholesterol levels, which can lower the risk of atherosclerosis and heart disease.

- **Reducing Inflammation:** Both monounsaturated and polyunsaturated fats have anti-inflammatory properties that help protect the heart and blood vessels.

- **Supporting Heart Function:** Omega-3 fatty acids, a type of polyunsaturated fat, are particularly beneficial for heart health, as they help regulate heart rhythms and reduce the risk of arrhythmias.

Best Sources of Healthy Fats

Incorporate these sources of healthy fats into your diet to support your heart health:

- **Olive Oil:** A staple of the Mediterranean diet, olive oil is rich in monounsaturated fats and antioxidants. Use it for cooking, in salad dressings, and as a dip for whole-grain bread.

- **Avocados:** Avocados are a great source of monounsaturated fats, fiber, and potassium, all of which support heart health.

- **Fatty Fish:** Salmon, mackerel, and sardines are rich in omega-3 fatty acids. Aim to include these in your diet at least twice a week.

- **Nuts and Seeds:** Almonds, walnuts, chia seeds, and flaxseeds provide a mix of monounsaturated and polyunsaturated fats, along with fiber and other heart-healthy nutrients.

By choosing healthy fats and limiting saturated fats, you can take an important step toward protecting your heart and improving your overall health.

Micronutrients: Potassium, Magnesium, and Their Benefits

What Are Micronutrients?

Micronutrients are vitamins and minerals that your body needs in small amounts to function properly. While they are required in smaller quantities than macronutrients (like carbohydrates, proteins, and fats), they are no less important for your health. Potassium and magnesium are two micronutrients that play a particularly important role in heart health.

Potassium

Potassium is an essential mineral that helps regulate fluid balance, nerve signals, and muscle contractions. It is crucial for heart health because it helps counteract the effects of sodium and keeps blood pressure in check.

Benefits of Potassium for Heart Health

- **Regulating Blood Pressure:** Potassium helps relax blood vessel walls and excrete excess sodium through urine, both of which help lower blood pressure.

- **Supporting Heart Function:** Potassium is vital for the electrical signaling that regulates your heartbeat. Adequate potassium levels help prevent irregular heartbeats (arrhythmias).

Best Sources of Potassium

To ensure you're getting enough potassium, include these foods in your diet:

- **Bananas:** Known for their high potassium content, bananas are a convenient and heart-healthy snack.

- **Sweet Potatoes:** Rich in potassium and fiber, sweet potatoes are a nutritious and versatile addition to your diet.

- **Spinach:** This leafy green is packed with potassium, along with other important nutrients like magnesium and vitamin K.

- **Avocados:** In addition to being a good source of healthy fats, avocados provide a significant amount of potassium.

Magnesium

Magnesium is another essential mineral that plays a critical role in heart health. It's involved in over 300 biochemical reactions in the body, including those that regulate muscle and nerve function, blood sugar levels, and blood pressure.

Benefits of Magnesium for Heart Health

- **Regulating Blood Pressure:** Magnesium helps relax blood vessels and improves blood flow, which can lower blood pressure and reduce the risk of heart disease.

- **Preventing Arrhythmias:** Magnesium is essential for maintaining a regular heartbeat. It works closely with potassium to regulate heart rhythm and prevent arrhythmias.

- **Reducing Inflammation:** Magnesium has anti-inflammatory properties that help protect the heart and blood vessels from damage.

Best Sources of Magnesium

To boost your magnesium intake, add these foods to your diet:

- **Dark Leafy Greens:** Spinach, kale, and Swiss chard are all excellent sources of magnesium.

- **Nuts and Seeds:** Almonds, pumpkin seeds, and sunflower seeds provide a healthy dose of magnesium, along with healthy fats.

- **Whole Grains:** Brown rice, quinoa, and whole-wheat bread are rich in magnesium and other important nutrients.

- **Legumes:** Beans, lentils, and chickpeas are not only high in fiber but also a great source of magnesium.

By incorporating potassium- and magnesium-rich foods into your diet, you can support your heart health and reduce your risk of cardiovascular disease.

How Food Choices Impact Heart Health

When it comes to protecting and nurturing your heart, the food you eat plays a crucial role. Every meal is an opportunity to make choices that either support your cardiovascular system or place it under strain. Understanding how specific foods and nutrients impact your heart is key to making informed decisions that promote long-term heart health. In this section, we'll explore the relationship between your diet and heart health, focusing on important aspects such as sodium, sugar, inflammation, the glycemic index, and the fascinating connection between gut health and cardiovascular well-being.

The Role of Sodium in Blood Pressure Regulation

Why Sodium Matters

Sodium, a mineral found in salt, is essential for many bodily functions, including maintaining fluid balance, transmitting nerve impulses, and aiding muscle contractions. However, consuming too much sodium can have detrimental effects on your heart, particularly by increasing your blood pressure.

How Sodium Affects Blood Pressure

Blood pressure is the force of blood pushing against the walls of your arteries as your heart pumps it around your body. When you consume excess sodium, your body retains more water to help flush out the sodium. This additional water increases the volume of blood, putting extra pressure on your blood vessels. Over time, this added strain can lead to high blood pressure (hypertension), a major risk factor for heart disease and stroke.

Sources of Excess Sodium

While sodium is naturally present in many foods, the majority of excess sodium in our diets comes from processed and packaged foods, including:

- **Processed Meats:** Ham, bacon, sausages, and deli meats are often loaded with sodium as a preservative and flavor enhancer.

- **Canned Soups and Vegetables:** Many canned goods contain high levels of sodium, used to extend shelf life and enhance taste.

- **Snack Foods:** Chips, pretzels, and salted nuts are common sources of excess sodium.

- **Restaurant and Fast Food:** Meals eaten out, particularly fast food, tend to be high in sodium due to the use of salt in cooking and preserving.

How to Manage Sodium Intake

Managing your sodium intake is one of the most effective ways to control blood pressure and protect your heart. Here are some practical steps to reduce sodium in your diet:

1. **Read Food Labels:** Check nutrition labels for sodium content and choose products labeled "low sodium" or "no added salt."

2. **Cook at Home:** Preparing meals at home allows you to control the amount of salt used. Experiment with herbs, spices, and citrus to flavor your food without relying on salt.

3. **Limit Processed Foods:** Reduce your consumption of processed and pre-packaged foods, which are often high in hidden sodium.

4. **Choose Fresh Ingredients:** Fresh fruits, vegetables, and lean proteins naturally contain less sodium than their processed counterparts.

5. **Rinse Canned Foods:** If you use canned beans or vegetables, rinse them under water to remove some of the sodium.

By making these adjustments, you can significantly reduce your sodium intake, helping to lower your blood pressure and decrease your risk of heart disease.

Sugar and Its Link to Heart Disease

The Sweet Truth About Sugar

Sugar is a common ingredient in many foods, but consuming too much added sugar can have serious consequences for your heart health. Unlike the naturally occurring sugars found in fruits and dairy, added sugars provide no nutritional benefits and contribute to various health issues, including weight gain, type 2 diabetes, and heart disease.

How Sugar Affects Your Heart

Excessive sugar intake impacts heart health in several ways:

- **Weight Gain and Obesity:** High sugar consumption, particularly from sugary drinks and snacks, can lead to weight gain. Excess body fat, especially around the abdomen, is associated with an increased risk of heart disease.

- **Increased Risk of Type 2 Diabetes:** Diets high in sugar can lead to insulin resistance, a precursor to type 2 diabetes. Having diabetes doubles your risk of developing heart disease.

- **Elevated Triglycerides:** Consuming large amounts of sugar can raise triglyceride levels in the blood, contributing to the hardening of the arteries (atherosclerosis), which increases the risk of heart attack and stroke.

- **Inflammation:** High sugar intake has been linked to chronic inflammation, which plays a key role in the development of heart disease.

Hidden Sources of Sugar

Sugar is often hidden in foods that might not even taste sweet, making it easy to consume more than you realize. Common sources of added sugars include:

- **Sugary Drinks:** Sodas, energy drinks, and sweetened teas are some of the biggest contributors to added sugar intake.

- **Baked Goods:** Cakes, cookies, pastries, and muffins often contain large amounts of sugar.

- **Condiments:** Ketchup, barbecue sauce, and salad dressings can be surprisingly high in sugar.

- **Breakfast Cereals:** Many cereals marketed as healthy options are actually loaded with added sugars.

Reducing Sugar in Your Diet

To protect your heart, it's important to be mindful of your sugar intake. Here are some strategies to help reduce the amount of sugar in your diet:

1. **Choose Water:** Opt for water, unsweetened tea, or sparkling water instead of sugary drinks.

2. **Read Labels:** Check ingredient lists for added sugars, which may appear under different names like high-fructose corn syrup, sucrose, or cane sugar.

3. **Limit Sweets:** Reserve desserts and sugary treats for special occasions, and enjoy them in moderation.

4. **Opt for Whole Foods:** Whole fruits, vegetables, and grains are naturally low in sugar and high in nutrients, making them better choices for heart health.

5. **Cook at Home:** When you prepare meals and snacks at home, you have control over the ingredients, allowing you to reduce or eliminate added sugars.

By cutting back on added sugars, you can lower your risk of heart disease and improve your overall health.

The Impact of Inflammation from Poor Dietary Choices

Understanding Inflammation

Inflammation is a natural response by your body's immune system to injury or infection. While acute inflammation is a protective mechanism, chronic inflammation can be harmful and is linked to several chronic diseases, including heart disease. Poor dietary choices are a significant contributor to chronic inflammation.

How Diet Influences Inflammation

Certain foods can trigger or worsen inflammation in the body, contributing to the development of atherosclerosis (the buildup of plaque in the arteries), which is a major risk factor for heart disease. Here's how diet influences inflammation:

- **Processed Foods:** Diets high in processed foods, which are often rich in trans fats, refined sugars, and refined carbohydrates, can promote inflammation. These foods can lead to the production of pro-inflammatory molecules in the body.

- **High Saturated and Trans Fat Intake:** Saturated fats found in red meat and full-fat dairy, along with trans fats found in many processed snacks and baked goods, are linked to higher levels of inflammation.

- **Low Intake of Anti-Inflammatory Foods:** Conversely, a lack of fruits, vegetables, whole grains, and omega-3-rich foods can reduce the body's ability to fight inflammation.

Anti-Inflammatory Foods for Heart Health

Incorporating anti-inflammatory foods into your diet can help reduce inflammation and protect your heart. Some of the best anti-inflammatory foods include:

- **Fruits and Vegetables:** Rich in antioxidants and phytonutrients, fruits and vegetables help combat oxidative stress and reduce inflammation. Berries, leafy greens, and tomatoes are particularly potent.

- **Omega-3 Fatty Acids:** As mentioned earlier, omega-3 fatty acids found in fatty fish, flaxseeds, and walnuts have strong anti-inflammatory properties.

- **Whole Grains:** Whole grains like oats, quinoa, and brown rice are high in fiber and can help reduce inflammation by stabilizing blood sugar levels.

- **Nuts and Seeds:** Almonds, walnuts, and chia seeds provide healthy fats and antioxidants that help lower inflammation.

- **Olive Oil:** Extra virgin olive oil is rich in monounsaturated fats and polyphenols, both of which have anti-inflammatory effects.

By focusing on a diet rich in anti-inflammatory foods, you can help reduce chronic inflammation, lower your risk of heart disease, and promote overall health.

Understanding the Glycemic Index

What Is the Glycemic Index?

The glycemic index (GI) is a ranking system that measures how quickly a carbohydrate-containing food raises blood glucose levels. Foods with a high GI are rapidly digested and absorbed, leading to a quick spike in blood sugar levels. In contrast, low-GI foods are digested and absorbed more slowly, resulting in a gradual rise in blood sugar levels.

Why the Glycemic Index Matters for Heart Health

Consistently consuming high-GI foods can lead to large fluctuations in blood sugar levels, which may contribute to insulin resistance, weight gain, and an increased risk of type 2 diabetes—all of which are risk factors for heart disease. By choosing low-GI foods, you can help stabilize blood sugar levels, reduce the risk of developing diabetes, and protect your heart.

Low-GI Foods for Heart Health

Here are some examples of low-GI foods that can be beneficial for heart health:

- **Whole Grains:** Foods like barley, quinoa, and whole oats have a low GI and provide sustained energy without causing rapid blood sugar spikes.

- **Legumes:** Lentils, chickpeas, and black beans are low-GI foods that are also high in fiber, making them excellent choices for heart health.

- **Non-Starchy Vegetables:** Vegetables such as broccoli, spinach, and bell peppers have a low GI and are packed with vitamins, minerals, and antioxidants.

- **Fruits:** Apples, pears, and berries are low-GI fruits that provide fiber and antioxidants while helping to maintain stable blood sugar levels.

- **Nuts:** Almonds, walnuts, and peanuts are low-GI foods that provide healthy fats and protein, making them heart-healthy snacks.

Balancing Your Glycemic Load

While the glycemic index is a useful tool, it's also important to consider the glycemic load (GL), which takes into account both the GI and the portion size of a food. To balance your glycemic load:

- **Combine High and Low-GI Foods:** Pair high-GI foods with low-GI foods to slow down the absorption of sugar and prevent spikes in blood sugar levels.

- **Watch Portion Sizes:** Even low-GI foods can contribute to blood sugar spikes if consumed in large quantities, so be mindful of portion sizes.

Understanding the glycemic index and making low-GI choices can help you manage blood sugar levels and support overall heart health.

The Connection Between Gut Health and Heart Health

The Gut-Heart Axis

Recent research has uncovered a fascinating connection between gut health and heart health, often referred to as the gut-heart axis. The gut is home to trillions of bacteria, known as the gut microbiome, which play a crucial role in digestion, immunity, and overall health. Emerging evidence suggests that the health of your gut microbiome can also influence your heart health.

How Gut Health Affects the Heart

The gut microbiome interacts with the cardiovascular system in several ways:

- **Production of Metabolites:** Certain gut bacteria produce metabolites, such as trimethylamine N-oxide (TMAO), which has been linked to an increased risk of atherosclerosis. A diet high in red meat and other animal products can lead to higher production of TMAO, potentially increasing the risk of heart disease.

- **Inflammation:** An imbalance in gut bacteria, known as dysbiosis, can lead to chronic inflammation, which is a known risk factor for heart disease. Maintaining a healthy gut microbiome can help reduce inflammation and protect your heart.

- **Blood Pressure Regulation:** Some studies suggest that gut bacteria may influence blood pressure regulation. A healthy gut microbiome may help maintain normal blood pressure levels, reducing the risk of hypertension and heart disease.

Supporting Gut Health for a Healthy Heart

To support a healthy gut microbiome and, in turn, a healthy heart, consider the following dietary strategies:

- **Eat a Diverse Diet:** A varied diet rich in different types of fiber, fruits, vegetables, and whole grains supports a diverse and healthy gut microbiome.

- **Include Probiotics:** Probiotic-rich foods like yogurt, kefir, sauerkraut, and kimchi introduce beneficial bacteria into your gut, supporting overall gut health.

- **Increase Fiber Intake:** Fiber is a prebiotic that feeds beneficial gut bacteria. Foods like beans, legumes, fruits, and whole grains are excellent sources of fiber.

- **Limit Red Meat:** Reducing your intake of red meat can help lower the production of TMAO, potentially reducing your risk of heart disease.

- **Avoid Excessive Antibiotic Use:** While antibiotics are sometimes necessary, overuse can disrupt the balance of your gut microbiome. Use antibiotics only when prescribed and follow your doctor's guidance.

By nurturing your gut health, you can take an important step toward protecting your heart and promoting overall well-being.

Debunking Diet Myths

Navigating the world of nutrition can be confusing, especially when it comes to heart health. With so much information—often conflicting—it's easy to feel overwhelmed. Many diet myths persist, leading to confusion and sometimes poor dietary choices. In this section, we'll address some of the most common myths about heart health, providing you with clear, science-backed information to help you make informed decisions. Let's explore the truth behind the cholesterol debate, the role of red meat in your diet, how moderation plays a role in enjoying your favorite treats, the differences between whole and refined grains, and the controversial role of dairy in heart health.

The Cholesterol Debate: Dietary vs. Blood Cholesterol

For years, cholesterol has been at the center of discussions about heart health. But understanding the relationship between the cholesterol you eat (dietary cholesterol) and the cholesterol in your blood (blood cholesterol) is key to making heart-healthy dietary choices.

Dietary Cholesterol vs. Blood Cholesterol

Dietary cholesterol is found in animal-based foods such as eggs, shellfish, meat, and dairy. Blood cholesterol, on the other hand, circulates in your bloodstream and includes two main types: low-density lipoprotein (LDL) and high-density lipoprotein (HDL). LDL is often referred to as "bad" cholesterol because it can build up in the walls of your arteries, leading to atherosclerosis—a major risk factor for heart disease. HDL, known as "good" cholesterol, helps remove LDL from your bloodstream.

The Myth: Eating Cholesterol-Rich Foods Raises Your Blood Cholesterol Levels

For decades, people were advised to avoid foods high in cholesterol, such as eggs and shellfish, out of fear that they would raise blood cholesterol levels and increase the risk of heart disease. However, research over the past few years has shown that for most people, dietary cholesterol has a minimal impact on blood cholesterol levels. The real culprits behind high LDL cholesterol levels are trans fats, saturated fats, and refined sugars—not dietary cholesterol.

The Reality: Focus on Overall Dietary Patterns

Rather than fixating on the cholesterol content of individual foods, it's more important to focus on your overall dietary pattern. Emphasizing a diet rich in fruits, vegetables, whole grains, lean proteins, and healthy fats is key to maintaining healthy cholesterol levels. If you enjoy eggs, for example, there's no need to eliminate them from your diet. Instead, be mindful of the foods you pair them with—like bacon or sausage, which are high in saturated fats.

Practical Tips:

- **Moderation is Key:** If you're at risk for heart disease, it's still wise to consume cholesterol-rich foods in moderation. Focus on portion control and balance within your diet.

- **Choose Healthy Fats:** Replace saturated and trans fats with unsaturated fats from sources like olive oil, nuts, seeds, and fatty fish.

- **Limit Processed Foods:** These often contain hidden trans fats and refined sugars, which can negatively impact your blood cholesterol levels.

The Truth About Red Meat and Heart Health

Red meat has long been a topic of debate in the context of heart health. While it's a good source of protein, iron, and other nutrients, it's also associated with risks when consumed in large quantities or when processed.

The Myth: All Red Meat Is Bad for Your Heart

The idea that all red meat is detrimental to heart health is a common belief, but it's an oversimplification. The type of red meat, how it's prepared, and how much you consume are all factors that influence its impact on your heart.

The Reality: Processed vs. Unprocessed Red Meat

Processed red meats—like bacon, sausages, and deli meats—are the most harmful to heart health. They're often high in sodium, preservatives, and unhealthy fats, all of which contribute to high blood pressure and increased risk of heart disease. Unprocessed red meat, like beef, pork, and lamb, can be part of a heart-healthy diet when consumed in moderation and prepared healthily.

Lean cuts of unprocessed red meat can provide essential nutrients such as protein, zinc, and B vitamins. However, it's important to choose lean cuts, limit portion sizes, and avoid charring or frying the meat, as these cooking methods can produce harmful compounds.

Practical Tips:

- **Choose Lean Cuts:** Opt for leaner cuts of red meat, such as sirloin, tenderloin, or round, which have less fat.

- **Limit Frequency:** Limit your intake of red meat to a few times a week, focusing more on plant-based proteins and lean poultry or fish.

- **Healthy Cooking Methods:** Grill, bake, or broil red meat instead of frying or charring it to reduce the formation of harmful compounds.

- **Balance Your Plate:** Pair red meat with plenty of vegetables, whole grains, and healthy fats to create a balanced, heart-healthy meal.

Can You Have Your Cake? Understanding Moderation

For many people, the idea of a heart-healthy diet conjures up images of restrictive eating and giving up favorite treats. But the reality is that you can enjoy the foods you love, including desserts, as long as you practice moderation.

The Myth: You Must Completely Avoid Sweets and Treats

A common misconception is that a heart-healthy diet means cutting out all sweets, treats, and indulgent foods. This all-or-nothing mindset can make healthy eating feel daunting and unsustainable.

The Reality: Moderation Is Key

The key to a sustainable heart-healthy diet is moderation. Rather than banning certain foods, it's about managing portion sizes and frequency. Enjoying a small piece of cake, a few squares of dark chocolate, or a serving of your favorite ice cream can be part of a balanced diet when done in moderation.

By allowing yourself the occasional treat, you can avoid feelings of deprivation that often lead to binge eating or giving up on your healthy eating plan altogether. The goal is to find a balance that works for you, allowing room for both nutrient-dense foods and the occasional indulgence.

Practical Tips:

- **Plan Treats Wisely:** Instead of impulsively reaching for sweets, plan when and how you'll enjoy them. This can help you savor the experience and control portions.

- **Mindful Eating:** Pay attention to your hunger and fullness cues. Enjoy each bite of your treat, eating slowly and without distractions.

- **Healthier Alternatives:** When possible, opt for healthier versions of your favorite treats, such as fruit-based desserts, whole-grain baked goods, or dark chocolate.

Whole Grains vs. Refined Grains: What's the Difference?

Grains are a staple in many diets, but not all grains are created equal. Understanding the difference between whole grains and refined grains can help you make better choices for your heart health.

The Myth: All Grains Are the Same

Some people believe that all grains are nutritionally similar, whether they're whole or refined. However, the refining process significantly alters the nutritional value of grains.

The Reality: Whole Grains Offer Superior Nutritional Benefits

Whole grains contain all three parts of the grain kernel: the bran, germ, and endosperm. This means they retain more fiber, vitamins, minerals, and phytonutrients than refined grains, which have had the bran and germ removed.

Refined grains, such as white bread, white rice, and many cereals, are stripped of these nutrient-rich components, leaving only the starchy endosperm. This results in a loss of fiber and essential nutrients, making refined grains less beneficial for heart health.

Whole grains, on the other hand, have been shown to reduce the risk of heart disease by improving cholesterol levels, reducing blood pressure, and aiding in weight management.

Practical Tips:

- **Choose Whole Grains:** Opt for whole grains like brown rice, quinoa, oats, whole-wheat bread, and barley. Look for products labeled "100% whole grain" or "whole wheat."

- **Read Labels:** Check the ingredient list to ensure that whole grains are the first ingredient listed.

- **Incorporate Variety:** Include a variety of whole grains in your diet to benefit from their different nutrient profiles.

- **Gradual Transition:** If you're used to refined grains, start by gradually replacing them with whole grains to ease the transition.

The Role of Dairy in Heart Health: Friend or Foe?

Dairy products have been both praised and vilified in discussions about heart health. While some believe dairy is essential for strong bones and overall health, others argue that its saturated fat content can be detrimental to the heart.

The Myth: Dairy Is Always Bad for Your Heart

The belief that all dairy products are harmful to heart health stems primarily from their saturated fat content, which can raise LDL cholesterol levels. However, the impact of dairy on heart health is more nuanced.

The Reality: The Type and Amount of Dairy Matter

Not all dairy products are created equal, and the effects of dairy on heart health can vary depending on the type and amount consumed. Full-fat dairy products, such as whole milk, butter, and cheese, contain higher levels of saturated fat, which can raise LDL cholesterol levels. However, research also shows that dairy products provide important nutrients like calcium, vitamin D, and potassium, which are beneficial for overall health.

Low-fat and fat-free dairy options can provide these nutrients without the added saturated fat, making them a better choice for heart health. Additionally, fermented dairy products like yogurt and kefir contain probiotics, which support gut health and may have a positive impact on cardiovascular health.

Practical Tips:

- **Choose Low-Fat or Fat-Free Options:** Opt for low-fat or fat-free versions of milk, yogurt, and cheese to reduce your intake of saturated fat while still benefiting from the nutrients dairy provides.

- **Limit Butter and Cream:** These high-fat dairy products can contribute to high LDL cholesterol levels. Use them sparingly or consider plant-based alternatives like olive oil or avocado.

- **Enjoy Fermented Dairy:** Incorporate fermented dairy products like yogurt and kefir into your diet to support gut health and potentially benefit your heart.

- **Balance Your Diet:** If you include full-fat dairy in your diet, do so in moderation and balance it with plenty of fruits, vegetables, whole grains, and lean proteins.

Understanding the complexities of dairy's role in heart health allows you to make informed choices that support your overall well-being. By focusing on moderation and choosing the right types of dairy, you can enjoy its benefits while minimizing potential risks.

Building a Balanced Heart-Healthy Diet

Crafting a heart-healthy diet is not about adhering to strict rules or following a one-size-fits-all plan. Instead, it's about making informed, thoughtful choices that nourish your body while supporting your cardiovascular health. In this section, we'll explore the essential components of a balanced heart-healthy diet, including the importance of whole foods, smart protein choices, the benefits of colorful vegetables and fruits, selecting the right carbohydrates, and the crucial role of hydration.

The Foundation: Whole Foods vs. Processed Foods

Whole Foods: The Cornerstone of Heart Health

Whole foods are foods that are as close to their natural state as possible, with minimal processing and no added sugars, fats, or preservatives. These include fruits, vegetables, whole grains, nuts, seeds, and lean proteins. Whole foods are nutrient-dense, meaning they provide a wealth of vitamins, minerals, antioxidants, and fiber that are essential for maintaining heart health.

When you eat whole foods, you're giving your body the best possible fuel to support cardiovascular function. Whole grains, for instance, are rich in fiber, which helps lower cholesterol levels and improve digestion. Fruits and vegetables are packed with antioxidants that combat oxidative stress, a key contributor to heart disease.

Processed Foods: Understanding the Risks

Processed foods, on the other hand, are often stripped of their natural nutrients and loaded with unhealthy additives like salt, sugar, and unhealthy fats. These foods include items like sugary cereals, chips, packaged snacks, and processed meats. Consuming too many processed foods can lead to weight gain, high blood pressure, elevated cholesterol levels, and ultimately, an increased risk of heart disease.

Processed foods are often convenient and affordable, which makes them appealing, but they should be consumed sparingly. Their high levels of sodium and trans fats can cause significant harm to your heart over time.

Practical Tips:

- **Focus on Fresh:** When grocery shopping, spend more time in the fresh produce, meat, and dairy sections, where whole foods are typically found.

- **Read Labels:** When choosing packaged foods, read the ingredient list carefully. Look for items with short ingredient lists and avoid those with added sugars, sodium, or artificial ingredients.

- **Cook at Home:** Preparing meals at home allows you to control what goes into your food. Use fresh, whole ingredients as much as possible.

Protein Choices: Plant-Based and Lean Animal Proteins

The Importance of Protein in a Heart-Healthy Diet

Protein is an essential macronutrient that plays a critical role in building and repairing tissues, producing enzymes and hormones, and supporting immune function. When it comes to heart health, the type of protein you choose can make a significant difference.

Plant-Based Proteins: A Heart-Healthy Choice

Plant-based proteins, such as beans, lentils, tofu, tempeh, nuts, seeds, and whole grains, are excellent choices for heart health. These foods are naturally low in saturated fat and cholesterol, and they provide fiber, vitamins, minerals, and antioxidants that support cardiovascular health.

Legumes, for example, are high in soluble fiber, which helps lower LDL cholesterol levels. Nuts and seeds are rich in healthy fats, such as omega-3 fatty acids, which reduce inflammation and support heart function.

Lean Animal Proteins: Opting for Healthier Choices

While plant-based proteins offer numerous benefits, lean animal proteins can also be part of a heart-healthy diet when chosen and prepared wisely. Lean cuts of poultry, such as chicken and turkey, as well as fish, particularly fatty fish like salmon and mackerel, are excellent sources of high-quality protein and essential nutrients like omega-3 fatty acids.

Fatty fish, in particular, are known for their heart-protective properties. The omega-3s found in fish help lower triglyceride levels, reduce blood pressure, and decrease the risk of arrhythmias.

Practical Tips:

- **Incorporate More Plant-Based Proteins:** Try to include plant-based protein sources in your meals several times a week. For example, enjoy a lentil soup, a chickpea salad, or a tofu stir-fry.

- **Choose Lean Cuts:** When eating meat, opt for lean cuts such as skinless poultry or lean beef cuts like sirloin or tenderloin. Trim any visible fat before cooking.

- **Prioritize Fish:** Aim to eat fatty fish at least twice a week. If fresh fish isn't available, canned or frozen options can be convenient and nutritious.

The Importance of Colorful Vegetables and Fruits

Why Color Matters

Eating a variety of colorful vegetables and fruits is one of the simplest and most effective ways to protect your heart. The vibrant colors in these foods are a result of phytonutrients, natural compounds that have powerful health benefits. Each color group provides different phytonutrients, vitamins, and minerals, contributing to a well-rounded, nutrient-rich diet.

Red and Purple: Antioxidants and Heart Health

Red and purple fruits and vegetables, such as tomatoes, berries, red grapes, and beets, are rich in anthocyanins and lycopene. These antioxidants help reduce inflammation, improve blood vessel function, and lower blood pressure. They also protect against the oxidative stress that can lead to heart disease.

Green: Crucial for Cardiovascular Function

Green vegetables, like spinach, kale, broccoli, and Brussels sprouts, are packed with vitamins K, C, and E, along with folate and potassium. These nutrients help maintain healthy blood pressure, support blood clotting, and reduce the risk of artery damage. Leafy greens, in particular, are also high in nitrates, which help relax blood vessels and improve blood flow.

Orange and Yellow: Supporting Heart Muscle Health

Orange and yellow fruits and vegetables, such as carrots, sweet potatoes, oranges, and bell peppers, are high in beta-carotene, vitamin C, and potassium. These nutrients are essential for maintaining a healthy heart muscle, supporting immune function, and promoting good vision and skin health.

Practical Tips:

- **Aim for Variety:** Strive to include a variety of colorful fruits and vegetables in your diet each day. The more colors you include, the broader the range of nutrients you'll consume.

- **Fill Half Your Plate:** As a simple guideline, fill half your plate with vegetables and fruits at each meal. This will help ensure you're getting plenty of heart-healthy nutrients.

- **Snack Smart:** Keep fresh fruits and cut vegetables readily available for snacking. This can help you reach your daily intake goals while curbing unhealthy snack cravings.

Carbohydrates: Choosing the Right Ones

The Role of Carbohydrates in Heart Health

Carbohydrates are a primary source of energy for your body, but not all carbs are created equal. The type of carbohydrates you consume can significantly impact your heart health.

Whole Grains: The Best Carbohydrate Choice

Whole grains are an excellent source of complex carbohydrates, fiber, and essential nutrients like B vitamins, iron, and magnesium. Unlike refined grains, which have been stripped of their nutrient-rich bran and germ, whole grains retain all parts of the grain kernel, making them more nutritious.

Eating whole grains has been shown to lower the risk of heart disease by reducing cholesterol levels, improving blood pressure, and aiding in weight management. Examples of whole grains include brown rice, quinoa, oats, barley, and whole wheat.

Refined Carbohydrates: The Less Healthy Option

Refined carbohydrates, such as white bread, white rice, pastries, and many processed snacks, have had their bran and germ removed during processing. This leaves them with fewer nutrients and less fiber, leading to quicker digestion and a rapid spike in blood sugar levels. Frequent consumption of refined carbs can contribute to weight gain, insulin resistance, and an increased risk of heart disease.

Practical Tips:

- **Choose Whole Grains:** Whenever possible, opt for whole grains instead of refined grains. For example, choose brown rice over white rice, and whole-grain bread over white bread.

- **Watch Your Portions:** Even with healthy carbohydrates, portion control is important. Aim for balanced meals that include a variety of food groups.

- **Be Cautious with Processed Foods:** Many processed foods contain hidden sugars and refined carbs. Read labels carefully and limit your intake of these products.

The Role of Hydration and Heart Health

Why Hydration Matters

Staying properly hydrated is crucial for overall health, including heart health. Water makes up about 60% of your body weight and is involved in many vital functions, including maintaining blood volume, regulating body temperature, and transporting nutrients.

How Hydration Affects the Heart

Adequate hydration helps the heart pump blood more easily through the blood vessels and improves the efficiency of circulation. When you're dehydrated, your blood volume decreases, making your heart work harder to pump blood throughout your body. Over time, this added strain can contribute to heart problems, particularly if you have underlying cardiovascular issues.

Signs of Dehydration

Dehydration can be mild, moderate, or severe, depending on how much of your body's fluid is lost or not replaced. Common signs of dehydration include:

- Thirst
- Dry mouth
- Dark-colored urine

- Fatigue or dizziness
- Confusion or difficulty concentrating

Practical Tips:

- **Drink Water Regularly:** Aim to drink at least eight 8-ounce glasses of water per day, but more if you are active, in a hot climate, or have a larger body size.

- **Limit Sugary and Caffeinated Beverages:** While water is the best choice for hydration, herbal teas and water-infused with fruits are also good options. Limit sugary drinks and caffeine, which can lead to dehydration.

- **Listen to Your Body:** Pay attention to your thirst cues and drink water throughout the day, rather than waiting until you feel thirsty.

By focusing on proper hydration, you can support your heart health and overall well-being.

Chapter 3: Practical Guide to Starting a Heart-Healthy Diet

Embarking on a heart-healthy diet is a rewarding journey that begins right in your own kitchen. By creating an environment that supports your goals, stocking up on essential ingredients, and equipping yourself with the right tools, you can make healthy eating an effortless and enjoyable part of your daily life. In this chapter, we'll explore practical steps to help you set up a heart-healthy kitchen, choose the best ingredients, and develop shopping habits that align with your health objectives.

Creating a Heart-Healthy Kitchen

Your kitchen is the heart of your home and the foundation of your heart-healthy lifestyle. A well-organized, thoughtfully stocked kitchen makes it easier to prepare nutritious meals, avoid unhealthy temptations, and stick to your dietary goals.

1. Declutter and Clean Out:

Start by decluttering your kitchen. Go through your pantry, fridge, and freezer to remove items that don't support your heart-healthy goals. Get rid of foods that are high in unhealthy fats, added sugars, and sodium, such as:

- Processed snacks (chips, cookies, crackers)
- Sugary cereals and granola bars
- Soda, sugary drinks, and flavored coffee creamers
- Processed meats (bacon, sausages, deli meats)
- High-fat dairy products (whole milk, cream, full-fat cheese)

By removing these items, you're reducing the chances of reaching for unhealthy options when hunger strikes.

2. Organize Your Space:

Once you've cleared out the unhealthy foods, organize your kitchen in a way that makes healthy eating easier. Group similar items together, and place healthy options at eye level where they're easy to see and reach. For example:

- Store whole grains (brown rice, quinoa, oats) in clear containers so you can quickly find what you need.

- Keep fruits and vegetables in the front of your fridge or on the counter to encourage you to eat them.

- Place nuts, seeds, and dried fruits in easily accessible spots for quick, healthy snacks.

3. Plan for Success:

Designate a space in your kitchen for meal planning and prepping. This could be a section of your countertop or a specific shelf in your pantry where you keep meal prep containers, cutting boards, and recipe books. Having a dedicated area for meal planning will help you stay organized and motivated.

Essential Pantry Staples for Heart Health

Stocking your pantry with heart-healthy staples ensures that you always have the ingredients needed to prepare nutritious meals. Here are some essential items to include:

Whole Grains:

Whole grains are rich in fiber, vitamins, and minerals, and they help regulate blood sugar levels and lower cholesterol.

- **Oats:** Perfect for a heart-healthy breakfast or baking.

- **Brown Rice:** A versatile side dish or base for stir-fries and salads.

- **Quinoa:** A protein-packed grain that works well in salads, soups, and as a side dish.

- **Whole Wheat Pasta:** A healthier alternative to regular pasta, providing more fiber and nutrients.

Legumes:

Legumes are an excellent source of plant-based protein, fiber, and essential nutrients.

- **Lentils:** Quick-cooking and ideal for soups, stews, and salads.

- **Chickpeas:** Great for hummus, salads, and roasting for a crunchy snack.

- **Black Beans:** Perfect for tacos, chili, and soups.

- **Kidney Beans:** A hearty addition to soups, stews, and casseroles.

Nuts and Seeds:

Nuts and seeds provide healthy fats, protein, and essential nutrients like magnesium and potassium.

- **Almonds:** Enjoy as a snack or add to oatmeal and salads.

- **Walnuts:** Rich in omega-3 fatty acids, perfect for adding to yogurt, salads, or baking.

- **Chia Seeds:** A versatile superfood that can be added to smoothies, oatmeal, and yogurt.

- **Flaxseeds:** Ground flaxseeds can be sprinkled on cereal, salads, and baked goods for added fiber and omega-3s.

Healthy Oils:

Healthy fats are essential for heart health, and the right oils can enhance the flavor and nutrition of your meals.

- **Extra Virgin Olive Oil:** Ideal for salad dressings, sautéing, and drizzling over vegetables.

- **Avocado Oil:** A high-heat cooking oil that's great for roasting and grilling.

- **Canola Oil:** Another good option for high-heat cooking and baking.

Spices and Herbs:

Spices and herbs add flavor without the need for extra salt, and many have anti-inflammatory properties.

- **Garlic and Onion Powder:** Enhance the flavor of dishes while providing heart-health benefits.
- **Turmeric:** Known for its anti-inflammatory properties, turmeric is great in curries, soups, and smoothies.
- **Cinnamon:** A warm spice that can be used in both sweet and savory dishes.
- **Basil, Oregano, and Thyme:** Fresh or dried, these herbs add depth to soups, sauces, and salads.

Must-Have Kitchen Tools for Easy Meal Prep

Having the right tools in your kitchen makes meal prep easier, faster, and more enjoyable. Here are some must-have kitchen tools to consider:

1. Sharp Knives:

A good set of sharp knives is essential for efficient meal prep. Invest in a quality chef's knife, paring knife, and serrated knife. Kooping your knives sharp will make chopping vegetables and slicing meats much easier.

2. Cutting Boards:

Having a few durable cutting boards on hand helps prevent cross-contamination between raw meats and vegetables. Choose cutting boards that are easy to clean and large enough for comfortable chopping.

3. Non-Stick Pans and Cast-Iron Skillets:

Non-stick pans are great for cooking with minimal oil, while cast-iron skillets are versatile for sautéing, roasting, and baking. Both types of pans should be part of your kitchen arsenal.

4. Food Processor:

A food processor is a versatile tool that can chop vegetables, make hummus, blend sauces, and even knead dough. It's a time-saver for many meal prep tasks.

5. Blender:

A high-quality blender is essential for making smoothies, soups, sauces, and even heart-healthy desserts. Consider investing in a blender with multiple settings for different textures.

6. Slow Cooker or Instant Pot:

These appliances are invaluable for busy individuals. A slow cooker allows you to set and forget your meals, while an Instant Pot offers the option for quick, pressure-cooked meals.

7. Measuring Cups and Spoons:

Accurate measuring tools are necessary for following recipes and managing portion sizes, which is important for maintaining a heart-healthy diet.

8. Storage Containers:

A good set of airtight storage containers helps keep your pantry organized and your food fresh. They're also useful for storing prepped meals and leftovers.

Tips for Reading and Understanding Food Labels

Understanding food labels is crucial for making heart-healthy choices, especially when shopping for packaged foods. Here's a guide to help you navigate food labels with confidence:

1. Serving Size:

Always check the serving size first. All the nutritional information on the label is based on this serving size, so it's important to compare it with the amount you actually eat.

2. Calories:

While calories are important, focus more on the quality of the calories than the quantity. Choose nutrient-dense foods that provide vitamins, minerals, and fiber rather than empty calories from added sugars and unhealthy fats.

3. Fats:

Look for foods that are low in saturated and trans fats. Choose products with healthy fats, such as unsaturated fats, which are beneficial for heart health.

- **Saturated Fat:** Aim for foods with less than 10% of your daily value (DV) of saturated fat per serving.
- **Trans Fat:** Avoid foods with trans fats, as they increase LDL cholesterol and lower HDL cholesterol.

4. Sodium:

High sodium intake is linked to high blood pressure, so it's important to limit your intake. Look for foods with less than 140 milligrams of sodium per serving, and be cautious of foods labeled as "reduced sodium," as they may still contain significant amounts.

5. Fiber:

Fiber is essential for heart health, as it helps lower cholesterol and maintain healthy blood sugar levels. Aim for foods that provide at least 3 grams of fiber per serving.

6. Sugars:

Check for added sugars, which can contribute to weight gain and increased risk of heart disease. Look for foods with little to no added sugars, and be aware of the many names sugar can go by, such as high-fructose corn syrup, cane sugar, and dextrose.

7. Ingredients List:

The ingredients list is key to understanding what's really in your food. Ingredients are listed in order of quantity, from highest to lowest. Avoid foods with long ingredient lists, especially those with unfamiliar or artificial ingredients.

Smart Shopping Strategies: What to Buy Organic

Organic foods are grown without synthetic pesticides, herbicides, and fertilizers, which many people prefer for health and environmental reasons. However, organic products can be more expensive, so it's important to know when it's worth the investment.

1. Prioritize the "Dirty Dozen":

The Environmental Working Group (EWG) releases an annual list called the "Dirty Dozen," which includes fruits and vegetables with the highest pesticide residues. If you're going to buy organic, prioritize these items:

- Strawberries
- Spinach
- Kale
- Nectarines
- Apples
- Grapes
- Cherries
- Peaches
- Pears
- Tomatoes
- Celery
- Potatoes

2. The "Clean Fifteen":

The EWG also publishes the "Clean Fifteen," which are fruits and vegetables with the lowest pesticide residues. These items are generally safer to buy non-organic:

- Avocados
- Sweet corn
- Pineapple
- Onions
- Papayas

- Frozen sweet peas
- Eggplant
- Asparagus
- Broccoli
- Cabbage

- Kiwi
- Cauliflower
- Mushrooms
- Honeydew melon
- Cantaloupe

3. Consider Organic for Animal Products:

Organic meat, dairy, and eggs are produced without antibiotics and hormones, and the animals are typically raised in better conditions. If budget allows, consider buying organic animal products.

4. Prioritize What Matters Most to You:

If buying all organic isn't feasible, prioritize the items that matter most to you based on your values, health goals, and budget. Remember, eating more fruits and vegetables—whether organic or not—is always beneficial for heart health.

Budget-Friendly Tips for Eating Heart-Healthy

Eating a heart-healthy diet doesn't have to be expensive. With some smart strategies, you can nourish your heart without breaking the bank.

1. Plan Your Meals:

Planning your meals in advance helps you make a shopping list based on what you need, reducing impulse purchases and food waste. Choose recipes that use similar ingredients to make the most of what you buy.

2. Buy in Bulk:

Buying staples like grains, beans, nuts, and seeds in bulk can save money and reduce packaging waste. Just be sure to store them properly to maintain freshness.

3. Cook at Home:

Eating out can be expensive and often leads to less healthy choices. Cooking at home allows you to control what goes into your food and is generally more cost-effective.

4. Shop Seasonal Produce:

Seasonal fruits and vegetables are often less expensive and fresher than out-of-season produce. Visit local farmers' markets or look for sales on in-season items.

5. Use Frozen and Canned Options:

Frozen and canned fruits and vegetables can be just as nutritious as fresh and are often more affordable. Look for options without added sugars, salt, or sauces.

6. Grow Your Own:

If you have space, consider starting a small garden to grow your own herbs, vegetables, and fruits. Even a few pots on a windowsill can provide fresh, heart-healthy ingredients at a minimal cost.

By following these practical tips, you can create a heart-healthy kitchen that supports your goals while staying within your budget. Remember, the choices you make in your kitchen can have a profound impact on your heart health, so take the time to set yourself up for success.

Crafting Your Meal Plan

Embarking on a heart-healthy diet is a powerful step toward improving your overall well-being. However, making these changes sustainable requires careful planning and consideration. Crafting a meal plan that fits your lifestyle, preferences, and nutritional needs can help you stay on track, reduce stress around food choices, and ensure that you're nourishing your heart every day. In this section, we'll explore how to build a weekly heart-healthy meal plan, understand portion control, adapt meals for different needs, and make meal prep easier and more efficient. We'll also discuss how to incorporate snacks and desserts into your plan mindfully.

How to Build a Weekly Heart-Healthy Meal Plan

Creating a weekly meal plan may seem daunting at first, but with a clear approach, it can become an enjoyable routine that supports your heart health and overall well-being.

1. Set Your Goals:

Start by setting clear goals for your meal plan. Are you looking to reduce cholesterol, manage blood pressure, lose weight, or simply eat more balanced meals? Your goals will guide your food choices and help you focus on what's most important for your heart health.

2. Choose Your Core Ingredients:

Select a variety of whole, nutrient-dense foods that will form the foundation of your meals. Aim to include:

- **Vegetables:** Leafy greens, cruciferous vegetables, root vegetables, and colorful peppers.

- **Fruits:** Berries, apples, oranges, and seasonal fruits.

- **Whole Grains:** Brown rice, quinoa, oats, whole wheat pasta, and barley.

- **Proteins:** Lean meats, fatty fish (like salmon and mackerel), legumes, tofu, and nuts.

- **Healthy Fats:** Olive oil, avocados, nuts, and seeds.

3. Plan Balanced Meals:

For each meal, aim to include a balance of macronutrients—protein, healthy fats, and complex carbohydrates—along with plenty of fiber-rich vegetables.

- **Breakfast:** Consider options like oatmeal with nuts and berries, whole-grain toast with avocado and eggs, or a smoothie with spinach, banana, and flaxseeds.

- **Lunch:** Focus on balanced meals like a quinoa salad with grilled chicken and mixed vegetables, or a wrap made with whole-grain tortillas, hummus, and fresh veggies.

- **Dinner:** Build hearty yet heart-healthy dinners such as baked salmon with roasted sweet potatoes and steamed broccoli, or a stir-fry with tofu, brown rice, and colorful vegetables.

4. Include Snacks and Desserts:

Don't forget to plan for snacks and occasional desserts. Choose heart-healthy options like fresh fruit, a handful of nuts, or yogurt with a drizzle of honey. For desserts, consider treats made with whole ingredients, like a small portion of dark chocolate or a homemade fruit parfait.

5. Make a Shopping List:

Based on your meal plan, create a detailed shopping list. Organize it by sections of the grocery store (produce, grains, proteins, etc.) to make your shopping trip more efficient.

6. Stay Flexible:

While it's great to have a plan, it's also important to stay flexible. Life happens, and sometimes you'll need to adjust your plan. Having a few backup options—like a frozen vegetable stir-fry mix or canned beans—can help you stay on track even when your week doesn't go as planned.

Portion Control: Understanding Serving Sizes

Understanding and managing portion sizes is crucial for maintaining a heart-healthy diet. Even healthy foods can contribute to weight gain and elevated cholesterol levels if consumed in large quantities. Here's how to approach portion control effectively:

1. Know the Difference Between a Portion and a Serving:

- **Portion:** The amount of food you choose to eat at one time, which can vary greatly depending on hunger, mood, or occasion.
- **Serving:** A standardized amount used to measure food (e.g., 1 slice of bread, 1/2 cup of cooked pasta). Nutrition labels provide information based on a single serving.

2. Use Visual Cues to Estimate Portions:

- **Protein:** A serving of meat, fish, or poultry is about the size of a deck of cards or the palm of your hand.
- **Grains:** A serving of cooked grains, like rice or pasta, is about the size of a tennis ball or 1/2 cup.
- **Fruits and Vegetables:** A serving of fruit is roughly the size of a baseball, while a serving of vegetables is about the size of your fist.
- **Fats:** A serving of fat, such as butter or oil, is about the size of a poker chip or one tablespoon.

3. Plate Method:

To make portion control easier, use the plate method:

- Fill half your plate with non-starchy vegetables (e.g., leafy greens, broccoli, carrots).
- Reserve one-quarter of your plate for lean protein (e.g., chicken, fish, beans).
- Use the remaining quarter for whole grains or starchy vegetables (e.g., brown rice, sweet potatoes).

4. Pay Attention to Hunger and Fullness Cues:

Listen to your body's signals. Eat slowly, and stop when you feel satisfied, not stuffed. This can help you avoid overeating and better manage your portions.

Adapting Meals for Family and Individual Needs

A heart-healthy diet doesn't mean you have to prepare separate meals for every family member. With a few simple strategies, you can adapt your meals to meet everyone's needs while keeping them heart-healthy.

1. Modify Portions:

While the base meal can remain the same, adjust portion sizes to meet individual energy needs. For example, children or more active family members might need larger portions of grains or proteins, while adults focused on weight management might opt for more vegetables.

2. Offer Customizable Options:

Create meals that allow for customization. For example, a taco bar with whole-grain tortillas, lean protein, beans, vegetables, and healthy toppings lets everyone build their own plate to suit their tastes and nutritional needs.

3. Incorporate Family Favorites:

Find ways to incorporate family favorites into a heart-healthy diet. If your family loves pasta, for instance, try using whole-grain pasta and adding plenty of vegetables and lean protein to the sauce. This approach allows you to enjoy familiar dishes while making them healthier.

4. Involve the Family:

Get your family involved in meal planning and preparation. This not only helps them feel more connected to the meals but also provides an opportunity to educate them about the importance of heart-healthy eating.

5. Be Mindful of Special Diets:

If someone in your family has dietary restrictions, such as gluten intolerance or diabetes, be sure to adapt recipes accordingly. There are plenty of heart-healthy options that cater to various dietary needs.

Meal Prep and Batch Cooking for Busy Schedules

Busy schedules can make it challenging to stick to a heart-healthy diet, but meal prep and batch cooking can help you stay on track even when time is limited.

1. Plan Ahead:

Set aside some time each week to plan your meals, create a shopping list, and prep ingredients. This might include chopping vegetables, marinating proteins, or cooking grains in advance. Having these components ready to go will make it easier to assemble meals during the week.

2. Batch Cooking:

Batch cooking involves preparing large quantities of food that can be stored and used throughout the week. For example, you could cook a big pot of soup, stew, or chili and portion it into containers for quick lunches or dinners.

3. Make Freezer-Friendly Meals:

Consider preparing meals that freeze well, such as casseroles, soups, and stews. On busy nights, you can simply defrost and reheat a healthy, homemade meal. Label your freezer containers with the contents and date to ensure you use them within a few months.

4. Utilize Leftovers:

Make the most of leftovers by repurposing them into new meals. For example, leftover roasted vegetables can be added to salads, sandwiches, or grain bowls. Cooked chicken can be used in soups, wraps, or stir-fries.

5. Invest in Quality Containers:

Invest in a set of airtight containers in various sizes to store prepped ingredients and cooked meals. This will keep your food fresh and make it easy to grab what you need.

Incorporating Snacks and Desserts Mindfully

Snacks and desserts can certainly be part of a heart-healthy diet when chosen and enjoyed mindfully. The key is to focus on quality, portion size, and balance.

1. Choose Nutrient-Dense Snacks:

Opt for snacks that provide nutritional value, rather than empty calories. Here are some heart-healthy snack ideas:

- **Nuts and Seeds:** A small handful of almonds, walnuts, or sunflower seeds.
- **Fresh Fruit:** Sliced apples with peanut butter, a bowl of berries, or a banana.
- **Vegetables with Hummus:** Carrot sticks, cucumber slices, or bell pepper strips paired with hummus.
- **Greek Yogurt:** Plain Greek yogurt topped with fresh fruit and a drizzle of honey or a sprinkle of chia seeds.

2. Practice Portion Control with Snacks:

Even healthy snacks can contribute to weight gain if eaten in large quantities. Measure out single servings instead of eating directly from the package to help manage portions.

3. Enjoy Desserts in Moderation:

Desserts don't have to be off-limits. The key is moderation and choosing desserts that offer some nutritional benefits. Consider these heart-healthy dessert options:

- **Dark Chocolate:** Enjoy a small square of dark chocolate (70% cocoa or higher) to satisfy your sweet tooth while benefiting from its antioxidant properties.
- **Baked Fruit:** Try baked apples or pears with a sprinkle of cinnamon and a dollop of Greek yogurt.
- **Chia Pudding:** Make a simple chia pudding with almond milk, chia seeds, and a touch of vanilla extract. Top with fresh berries for added flavor and nutrients.

4. Mindful Eating:

When enjoying snacks or desserts, practice mindful eating. Take the time to savor each bite, focusing on the flavors and textures. This can help you feel more satisfied with smaller portions.

By crafting a well-thought-out meal plan, understanding portion sizes, adapting meals to meet individual needs, and incorporating smart meal prep strategies, you can create a sustainable heart-healthy diet that fits your lifestyle. With mindful snacking and the occasional treat, you can enjoy a balanced diet that supports your heart health while allowing for flexibility and enjoyment.

Chapter 4: Navigating Dining Out and Social Eating

Eating out and attending social gatherings can be challenging when you're committed to a heart-healthy diet. However, with some thoughtful strategies and a bit of preparation, you can enjoy these experiences without compromising your health goals. In this chapter, we'll explore how to make heart-healthy choices when dining out, decode menu language to avoid hidden pitfalls, manage portions effectively, select the best options across different cuisines, communicate your dietary needs, and navigate social situations like parties, events, and travel.

Making Heart-Healthy Choices Away from Home

Dining out doesn't mean you have to abandon your heart-healthy habits. By being mindful of your choices and prepared with some key strategies, you can enjoy a meal out while staying on track with your health goals.

1. Do Your Research:

Before heading out to a restaurant, take a few minutes to look up the menu online. Many restaurants now provide nutritional information on their websites, which can help you make informed decisions. Look for dishes that feature whole grains, lean proteins, and plenty of vegetables. Avoid items that are fried, creamy, or labeled as "rich," as these are often high in unhealthy fats and calories.

2. Focus on Balance:

When choosing your meal, aim for balance. A good rule of thumb is to fill half your plate with vegetables, one-quarter with lean protein, and one-quarter with whole grains or a healthy carbohydrate. For example, if you're ordering a main dish, you might choose grilled fish with a side of steamed vegetables and a small portion of quinoa or brown rice.

3. Start with a Salad or Soup:

Starting your meal with a salad (dressed with olive oil and vinegar or a light vinaigrette) or a broth-based soup can help fill you up and prevent overeating during the main course. Just be cautious with dressings, croutons, and creamy soups, which can add unnecessary calories and unhealthy fats.

4. Be Mindful of Beverages:

Beverages can be a hidden source of added sugars and empty calories. Opt for water, sparkling water with a slice of lemon or lime, unsweetened iced tea, or a small glass of red wine if you choose to drink alcohol. Avoid sugary drinks like soda, sweetened tea, and cocktails made with syrups or mixers.

5. Ask for Modifications:

Don't be afraid to ask for modifications to make your meal healthier. Most restaurants are happy to accommodate requests like grilling instead of frying, steaming vegetables instead of sautéing in butter, or serving sauces and dressings on the side. You can also request smaller portions or share dishes to avoid overeating.

Decoding Menu Language: What to Look For and Avoid

Understanding menu language can help you make better choices when dining out. Some terms indicate healthier options, while others may signal that a dish is high in calories, fats, or sodium.

1. Healthier Terms to Look For:

- **Grilled:** Indicates that the food is cooked on a grill, which typically uses less fat than frying or sautéing.
- **Baked:** Baking is a dry cooking method that doesn't require added fats, making it a healthier option.
- **Steamed:** Steaming preserves nutrients and doesn't require oil or butter, making it a heart-healthy cooking method.
- **Poached:** Poaching involves cooking food in a liquid, often water or broth, without added fats.
- **Broiled:** Broiling is similar to grilling and typically involves cooking food under direct heat without added fats.
- **Fresh:** Fresh ingredients, particularly fruits and vegetables, are often lower in sodium and free of unhealthy preservatives.

2. Terms to Approach with Caution:

- **Crispy/Crunchy:** These terms often indicate that the food is fried, breaded, or cooked with added fats, making it higher in calories and unhealthy fats.
- **Creamy:** Creamy dishes usually contain heavy cream, butter, or cheese, contributing to high levels of saturated fats and calories.
- **Rich:** Describes dishes that are typically high in fats and calories, often due to the use of butter, cream, or cheese.
- **Smothered:** This usually means the dish is covered in a rich sauce or cheese, adding extra calories and fat.
- **Loaded/Stuffed:** These dishes are often packed with high-calorie ingredients like cheese, sour cream, and bacon.

Strategies for Managing Portions at Restaurants

Restaurant portions are often much larger than what we would typically serve ourselves at home, which can lead to overeating. Here are some strategies to help you manage portions when dining out:

1. Share a Dish:

Consider sharing an entrée with a dining companion. Many restaurant dishes are large enough to satisfy two people, especially when paired with a side salad or appetizer. This not only helps with portion control but can also save you money.

2. Ask for a Half-portion:

Some restaurants offer half-portion sizes or allow you to order from the appetizer menu as your main course. If half-portions aren't available, consider asking the server to box up half of your meal before it's served. This way, you're not tempted to eat the entire portion, and you'll have leftovers for another meal.

3. Avoid the "Clean Plate" Mentality:

It's okay not to finish everything on your plate. Eat slowly, savor your food, and stop when you feel satisfied, not stuffed. If you're dining with others, engage in conversation between bites to help pace yourself.

4. Order Smart Sides:

Choose healthier side dishes like steamed vegetables, a side salad, or a baked sweet potato instead of fries, onion rings, or mashed potatoes with gravy. These choices can significantly reduce the calorie and fat content of your meal.

5. Skip the Bread Basket:

If you know the bread basket will be a temptation, ask your server to remove it or skip it altogether. If you do indulge in bread, limit yourself to one small piece, and avoid adding butter or oil.

Tips for Selecting Heart-Healthy Options Across Cuisines

Different cuisines offer a wide variety of dishes, some more heart-healthy than others. Here's how to make smart choices at various types of restaurants:

1. Italian Cuisine:

- **Opt for:** Dishes with tomato-based sauces (like marinara) instead of creamy Alfredo or carbonara sauces. Choose grilled fish or chicken, and look for whole-wheat pasta options if available.

- **Avoid:** Fried appetizers (like calamari), heavy cream-based dishes, and excessive cheese. Limit the use of olive oil, as it can add up quickly.

2. Mexican Cuisine:

- **Opt for:** Grilled chicken or fish tacos, fajitas with plenty of vegetables, and black beans or pinto beans instead of refried beans. Request whole-grain tortillas or corn tortillas over flour tortillas.

- **Avoid:** Deep-fried items (like chimichangas), dishes smothered in cheese or sour cream, and high-fat meats like chorizo. Ask for guacamole on the side, as it's healthy but calorie-dense.

3. Asian Cuisine:

- **Opt for:** Steamed or lightly stir-fried dishes with lots of vegetables, brown rice or whole grains, and lean proteins like tofu, chicken, or shrimp. Choose dishes with soy sauce, ginger, garlic, or miso for flavor instead of heavy sauces.

- **Avoid:** Fried items (like tempura), dishes in thick, sugary sauces (like sweet and sour), and large amounts of white rice. Ask for sauces on the side to control the amount you use.

4. American Cuisine:

- **Opt for:** Grilled or baked chicken or fish, salads with lean proteins and a vinaigrette dressing, and side dishes like steamed vegetables or a baked potato.

- **Avoid:** Fried foods (like fries, chicken wings, and onion rings), burgers with high-fat toppings, and creamy coleslaws or potato salads. Skip the sugary beverages and opt for water or unsweetened tea.

Communicating Dietary Needs and Preferences

When dining out, it's important to communicate your dietary needs clearly to ensure your meal is prepared in a way that aligns with your heart-healthy goals.

1. Be Specific with Your Requests:

Don't be afraid to ask for what you need. Politely request modifications like grilling instead of frying, no added salt, dressing on the side, or substituting vegetables for fries. Most restaurants are happy to accommodate dietary preferences if you communicate them clearly.

2. Ask Questions:

If you're unsure about how a dish is prepared, ask your server for details. Inquire about cooking methods, ingredients, and portion sizes. This information can help you make more informed choices.

3. Be Aware of Hidden Ingredients:

Sometimes, even seemingly healthy dishes can contain hidden ingredients like butter, cream, or added sugars. Don't hesitate to ask if a dish contains any of these ingredients and request modifications if necessary.

4. Speak Up About Allergies:

If you have food allergies or intolerances, make sure to inform your server. Many restaurants have procedures in place to accommodate allergies, and it's better to be safe than sorry.

Handling Social Situations: Parties, Events, and Travel

Social gatherings, parties, and travel can present unique challenges to maintaining a heart-healthy diet. With a little planning, you can navigate these situations without compromising your health goals.

1. Parties and Events:

- **Eat Before You Go:** If you're unsure about the food options at an event, consider eating a healthy snack or light meal beforehand. This way, you won't arrive overly hungry and can make better choices.

- **Bring a Healthy Dish:** If it's a potluck or casual gathering, offer to bring a heart-healthy dish to share. This ensures there's at least one option you can enjoy without guilt.

- **Focus on Socializing:** Remember that these events are about connecting with others, not just the food. Spend more time mingling and less time hovering around the buffet table.

- **Watch Your Portions:** Use a smaller plate, fill it with healthier options first (like vegetables or lean proteins), and avoid going back for seconds.

2. Traveling:

- **Plan Ahead:** Research restaurants and food options at your destination ahead of time. Pack healthy snacks like nuts, fruit, or whole-grain crackers for the journey.

- **Stay Hydrated:** Travel can often lead to dehydration, which can make you feel hungrier. Carry a water bottle with you and sip throughout the day.

- **Choose Smart at Buffets:** Buffets can be tempting, but focus on filling your plate with vegetables, lean proteins, and whole grains. Avoid dishes that are fried, creamy, or heavily sauced.

- **Stay Active:** Incorporate physical activity into your travel plans. Whether it's walking around a new city, hiking, or swimming, staying active helps offset some of the indulgences that may come with travel.

By applying these strategies, you can confidently make heart-healthy choices when dining out, attending social events, or traveling. Remember that each decision you make is a step toward maintaining a heart-healthy lifestyle, even when you're away from home.

Chapter 5: Heart-Healthy Recipes: Understanding Ingredients

Building a heart-healthy diet starts with selecting the right ingredients. Every choice you make in the kitchen can have a profound impact on your cardiovascular health. In this chapter, we'll dive into the specifics of choosing the best ingredients for your heart, including whole grains, healthy fats, lean proteins, fruits and vegetables, and the often overlooked but powerful spices and herbs. Understanding these ingredients will empower you to create delicious, nutritious meals that support your heart health.

Selecting Ingredients for Heart Health

The foundation of any heart-healthy diet lies in the quality of the ingredients you use. By choosing nutrient-dense, whole foods, you can ensure that your meals are not only satisfying but also beneficial for your cardiovascular system.

1. Prioritize Whole Foods:

Whole foods are those that are minimally processed and closest to their natural state. These foods are rich in vitamins, minerals, fiber, and other essential nutrients that support heart health. They also lack the added sugars, unhealthy fats, and excessive sodium often found in processed foods.

- **Examples of Whole Foods:** Fresh fruits and vegetables, whole grains, legumes, nuts, seeds, lean meats, fish, and dairy products.

2. Read Labels Carefully:

When shopping for ingredients, particularly packaged ones, take the time to read the labels. Look for foods with short ingredient lists, no added sugars, low sodium, and healthy fats. Avoid products with trans fats, artificial ingredients, or high levels of saturated fat.

3. Shop Seasonally and Locally:

Seasonal fruits and vegetables are often fresher and more nutrient-dense than those that have been shipped long distances. Shopping at local farmers' markets can help you find seasonal produce that is ripe and full of flavor, ensuring you get the most health benefits.

Whole Grains: Best Choices for the Heart

Whole grains are a critical component of a heart-healthy diet. Unlike refined grains, whole grains retain all parts of the grain kernel—the bran, germ, and endosperm—providing more fiber, vitamins, minerals, and antioxidants.

1. Why Whole Grains Matter:

The fiber in whole grains helps reduce cholesterol levels, control blood sugar, and promote satiety, all of which are important for heart health. Whole grains also contain essential nutrients like B vitamins, iron, magnesium, and selenium, which contribute to overall cardiovascular health.

2. Top Whole Grains for Heart Health:

- **Oats:** Rich in soluble fiber, particularly beta-glucan, oats help lower LDL cholesterol and are a versatile ingredient in breakfast dishes, baking, and even savory meals.

- **Quinoa:** A complete protein, quinoa is also high in fiber and contains all nine essential amino acids. It's an excellent base for salads, bowls, and side dishes.

- **Brown Rice:** With more fiber and nutrients than white rice, brown rice is a staple whole grain that pairs well with almost any meal.

- **Barley:** High in soluble fiber, barley is known for its cholesterol-lowering effects. It can be used in soups, stews, and as a substitute for rice in many dishes.

- **Whole Wheat:** Whole wheat, found in products like whole-wheat bread, pasta, and flour, offers more fiber and nutrients than its refined counterparts. Look for 100% whole wheat on labels to ensure you're getting the full benefits.

3. Cooking Tips:

- **Soak Grains:** Soaking grains like brown rice or barley before cooking can reduce cooking time and make them easier to digest.

- **Batch Cook:** Cook a large batch of grains at the beginning of the week to use in various meals, making it easier to incorporate them into your diet.

Healthy Fats: Oils, Nuts, and Seeds

Fats are often misunderstood, but they are an essential part of a heart-healthy diet. The key is to focus on healthy fats—those that support heart health rather than compromise it.

1. Understanding Healthy Fats:

Healthy fats, particularly unsaturated fats, help reduce inflammation, lower LDL cholesterol levels, and provide essential fatty acids that the body cannot produce on its own. There are two main types of healthy fats: monounsaturated and polyunsaturated fats.

- **Monounsaturated Fats:** Found in olive oil, avocados, and certain nuts, these fats help maintain healthy cholesterol levels and provide antioxidant benefits.

- **Polyunsaturated Fats:** Found in fatty fish, walnuts, flaxseeds, and sunflower oil, these fats include omega-3 and omega-6 fatty acids, which are crucial for heart health.

2. Best Oils for Cooking and Dressings:

- **Extra Virgin Olive Oil:** A cornerstone of the Mediterranean diet, olive oil is rich in monounsaturated fats and antioxidants. Use it for salad dressings, drizzling over cooked vegetables, or light sautéing.

- **Avocado Oil:** With a higher smoke point than olive oil, avocado oil is excellent for high-heat cooking like grilling or roasting.

- **Flaxseed Oil:** High in omega-3 fatty acids, flaxseed oil is best used in dressings or drizzled over cold dishes, as it's sensitive to heat.

3. Incorporating Nuts and Seeds:

Nuts and seeds are nutrient-dense, providing healthy fats, protein, fiber, and essential minerals. Regular consumption of nuts and seeds has been linked to lower cholesterol levels and a reduced risk of heart disease.

- **Almonds:** A good source of vitamin E and magnesium, almonds make a great snack or topping for salads and yogurt.

- **Walnuts:** Rich in omega-3 fatty acids, walnuts are excellent for brain and heart health. Add them to oatmeal, salads, or baked goods.

- **Chia Seeds:** These tiny seeds are packed with fiber, omega-3s, and antioxidants. They can be sprinkled on cereals, added to smoothies, or used to make chia pudding.

- **Flaxseeds:** Ground flaxseeds are a great addition to smoothies, baked goods, or sprinkled on top of yogurt for a boost of fiber and omega-3s.

Lean Proteins: Meat, Fish, and Plant-Based Options

Protein is essential for building and repairing tissues, producing enzymes and hormones, and supporting overall health. When choosing proteins for a heart-healthy diet, focus on lean options that provide necessary nutrients without excessive saturated fats.

1. Lean Meats:

- **Poultry:** Skinless chicken and turkey are lower in saturated fat than red meat. They can be baked, grilled, or roasted with herbs and spices for a flavorful, heart-healthy meal.

- **Lean Cuts of Beef and Pork:** When choosing red meat, opt for lean cuts like sirloin, tenderloin, or pork loin. Trim any visible fat before cooking, and use methods like grilling, broiling, or roasting to reduce fat content.

2. Fish:

Fatty fish, such as salmon, mackerel, sardines, and trout, are rich in omega-3 fatty acids, which are known for their heart-protective benefits. Aim to include fish in your diet at least twice a week.

- **Salmon:** Packed with omega-3s, salmon is versatile and can be baked, grilled, or poached.

- **Mackerel:** A nutrient-dense fish, mackerel provides high levels of omega-3s and vitamin D. It's excellent grilled or smoked.

- **Sardines:** Often overlooked, sardines are a cost-effective source of omega-3s and calcium. They can be added to salads, pasta dishes, or eaten on whole-grain toast.

3. Plant-Based Proteins:

Plant-based proteins are excellent for heart health, as they are typically low in saturated fat and high in fiber, vitamins, and minerals.

- **Legumes:** Beans, lentils, and peas are rich in protein and fiber, making them a hearty addition to soups, stews, salads, and grain bowls.

- **Tofu and Tempeh:** These soy-based proteins are versatile and can be marinated, grilled, or added to stir-fries. They are also good sources of calcium and iron.

- **Quinoa:** A complete protein, quinoa is a fantastic plant-based option that can be used in salads, as a side dish, or in place of rice.

Heart-Boosting Fruits and Vegetables

Fruits and vegetables are packed with vitamins, minerals, fiber, and antioxidants, all of which contribute to heart health. The more colorful your plate, the more nutrients you're likely to get.

1. Berries:

Berries, such as strawberries, blueberries, raspberries, and blackberries, are particularly high in antioxidants like anthocyanins, which have been shown to reduce blood pressure and improve blood vessel function.

- **Blueberries:** Rich in fiber, vitamin C, and antioxidants, blueberries are great in smoothies, salads, or on their own as a snack.
- **Strawberries:** These berries are high in vitamin C and manganese. They can be added to yogurt, oatmeal, or enjoyed fresh.

2. Leafy Greens:

Leafy greens like spinach, kale, and Swiss chard are nutrient powerhouses. They are high in vitamins A, C, K, and folate, and provide essential minerals like calcium and magnesium.

- **Spinach:** An excellent source of iron and magnesium, spinach can be used in salads, smoothies, or sautéed as a side dish.
- **Kale:** This leafy green is rich in fiber and antioxidants. It's perfect for salads, smoothies, or making kale chips.

3. Cruciferous Vegetables:

Cruciferous vegetables, including broccoli, cauliflower, Brussels sprouts, and cabbage, contain compounds that help detoxify the body and reduce the risk of heart disease.

- **Broccoli:** High in fiber, vitamin C, and potassium, broccoli can be steamed, roasted, or added to stir-fries.
- **Brussels Sprouts:** These mini cabbages are packed with vitamins K and C. They're delicious roasted with a drizzle of olive oil and a sprinkle of herbs.

4. Citrus Fruits:

Citrus fruits like oranges, grapefruits, lemons, and limes are high in vitamin C, fiber, and flavonoids, which have been shown to reduce cholesterol and improve heart health.

- **Oranges:** A great source of vitamin C and fiber, oranges can be eaten fresh or juiced.
- **Grapefruit:** Known for its tart flavor, grapefruit is rich in antioxidants and can be enjoyed fresh or in salads.

Spices and Herbs: Flavor and Health Benefits

Spices and herbs are not only essential for adding flavor to your dishes, but they also come with a host of health benefits. Many spices and herbs have anti-inflammatory, antioxidant, and cholesterol-lowering properties, making them valuable additions to a heart-healthy diet.

1. Turmeric:

Turmeric contains curcumin, a powerful anti-inflammatory compound that can help reduce the risk of heart disease. It's often used in curry dishes, soups, and teas.

- **How to Use:** Add turmeric to soups, stews, or smoothies. Pair it with black pepper to enhance absorption.

2. Garlic:

Garlic is well-known for its heart-healthy properties, including lowering blood pressure and cholesterol levels. It can be used in a wide variety of dishes.

- **How to Use:** Mince garlic and add it to sautés, marinades, dressings, and soups. Roasted garlic also makes a delicious spread for whole-grain bread.

3. Ginger:

Ginger has anti-inflammatory and antioxidant effects, making it beneficial for heart health. It's also known to help with digestion.

- **How to Use:** Grate fresh ginger into stir-fries, soups, smoothies, or teas. Dried ginger can be used in baking or spice blends.

4. Cinnamon:

Cinnamon can help regulate blood sugar levels and has been shown to reduce cholesterol levels. It's a versatile spice that can be used in both sweet and savory dishes.

- **How to Use:** Sprinkle cinnamon on oatmeal, yogurt, or fruit. It's also great in baked goods or added to spice rubs for meats.

5. Parsley:

Parsley is rich in vitamins A, C, and K, and it's known for its diuretic properties, which can help manage blood pressure.

- **How to Use:** Add fresh parsley to salads, soups, and sauces. It's also a great garnish for almost any dish.

By understanding and incorporating these ingredients into your diet, you can create meals that are not only delicious but also support your heart health. Remember, the choices you make in your kitchen have a profound impact on your overall well-being, so embrace these heart-healthy ingredients and enjoy the benefits they bring to your life.

Cooking Techniques for Optimal Health

Cooking is more than just preparing food—it's a powerful way to enhance or diminish the nutritional value of what you eat. The way you cook your meals can significantly impact the retention of nutrients, the flavor, and ultimately, your heart health. In this section, we'll explore cooking techniques that help retain the nutrients in your food, methods to create delicious dishes without relying on added sugars and salt, and strategies for reducing processed ingredients in your meals. Let's delve into how you can make every meal as heart-healthy as possible.

Methods to Retain Nutrients During Cooking

Cooking can either preserve or deplete the nutrients in your food, depending on the methods you use. Certain nutrients, like water-soluble vitamins (Vitamin C and B vitamins), can be lost during cooking if not handled properly. Here's how to maximize nutrient retention while cooking:

1. Steaming:

Steaming is one of the best methods to retain nutrients, especially for vegetables. Since the food doesn't come into direct contact with water, water-soluble vitamins are preserved. Steaming also helps maintain the color, flavor, and texture of vegetables.

- **How to Steam:** Use a steamer basket over a pot of boiling water. Place the vegetables in the basket, cover, and steam until they are tender but still crisp.

2. Microwaving:

Surprisingly, microwaving can be an excellent way to preserve nutrients, as it cooks food quickly with minimal water. This method is particularly effective for cooking vegetables.

- **How to Microwave Vegetables:** Place chopped vegetables in a microwave-safe dish with a small amount of water. Cover and microwave for a few minutes until tender. Be careful not to overcook, as this can lead to nutrient loss.

3. Stir-Frying:

Stir-frying is a quick-cooking method that uses high heat and a small amount of oil. This technique helps seal in nutrients while maintaining the texture and flavor of the food. The short cooking time also minimizes nutrient loss.

- **How to Stir-Fry:** Use a wok or a large skillet over medium-high heat. Add a small amount of healthy oil, such as olive or avocado oil, and cook the ingredients quickly, stirring constantly.

4. Roasting:

Roasting enhances the flavor of vegetables and proteins while retaining nutrients. However, it's important to avoid over-roasting, as high temperatures for extended periods can degrade some nutrients.

- **How to Roast:** Preheat your oven to 400°F (200°C). Toss vegetables or lean proteins in a small amount of healthy oil and your favorite herbs and spices. Spread them evenly on a baking sheet and roast until tender and slightly browned.

5. Grilling:

Grilling is a popular method that can retain nutrients and add a delicious, smoky flavor to your food. However, it's important to avoid charring, which can produce harmful compounds.

- **How to Grill:** Preheat the grill to medium-high. Marinate your protein or vegetables in a heart-healthy marinade (such as one made with olive oil, lemon juice, and herbs) to enhance flavor and reduce the formation of harmful compounds. Grill until the food is cooked through but not overly charred.

Grilling, Steaming, and Sautéing: Healthy Cooking Techniques

Healthy cooking techniques not only help retain nutrients but also allow you to enjoy flavorful, satisfying meals without adding unnecessary fats, sugars, or sodium. Let's explore some of the most heart-healthy cooking techniques:

1. Grilling:

Grilling is a heart-healthy way to cook lean proteins and vegetables without adding extra fats. The high heat helps sear the food, locking in juices and flavors.

- **Grilling Tips:** To avoid charring, cook food over medium heat and turn it frequently. Use marinades with citrus or vinegar bases to add flavor without adding fat or sodium. Grilled vegetables like bell peppers, zucchini, and asparagus make excellent side dishes.

2. Steaming:

Steaming is one of the healthiest ways to cook vegetables, fish, and even grains like couscous or quinoa. It requires no added fat and helps food retain its natural flavors and nutrients.

- **Steaming Tips:** To add more flavor to steamed dishes, try seasoning the water with herbs, garlic, or ginger. You can also drizzle a little lemon juice or olive oil over steamed vegetables before serving.

3. Sautéing:

Sautéing uses a small amount of oil and high heat to cook food quickly, making it a great method for maintaining the nutrients and flavors of your ingredients.

- **Sautéing Tips:** Use heart-healthy oils like olive or avocado oil, and keep the heat at medium-high. Cook your ingredients in batches to avoid overcrowding the pan, which can lead to steaming rather than sautéing.

Minimizing the Use of Added Sugars and Salt

Excessive consumption of added sugars and salt is linked to numerous health issues, including high blood pressure, obesity, and heart disease. Reducing these ingredients in your cooking can significantly improve your heart health without sacrificing flavor.

1. Reducing Added Sugars:

Added sugars are often hidden in processed foods and can easily find their way into home-cooked meals, especially in sauces, dressings, and baked goods. Here's how to cut back:

- **Use Natural Sweeteners:** Replace refined sugars with natural sweeteners like honey, maple syrup, or mashed fruit. These alternatives have a lower glycemic index and provide some nutritional benefits, but they should still be used in moderation.

- **Flavor with Spices:** Instead of adding sugar, enhance the natural sweetness of foods with spices like cinnamon, nutmeg, or vanilla extract.

- **Limit Sweetened Beverages:** Reduce your intake of sugary drinks by opting for water, herbal teas, or infused water with slices of fruit or herbs.

2. Reducing Sodium:

Excess sodium can lead to high blood pressure and increase the risk of heart disease. While salt is a common way to enhance flavor, there are plenty of other methods to season your food.

- **Use Herbs and Spices:** Fresh and dried herbs, such as basil, oregano, rosemary, and thyme, add robust flavors without the need for salt. Spices like cumin, paprika, and turmeric can also add depth to your dishes.

- **Citrus and Vinegar:** Acidic ingredients like lemon juice, lime juice, and vinegar can brighten flavors and reduce the need for added salt.

- **Choose Low-Sodium Options:** When buying canned goods or packaged foods, look for low-sodium or no-salt-added versions. You can also rinse canned beans and vegetables to remove some of the sodium.

Creating Flavors Without Unhealthy Additives

Creating delicious, flavorful meals without relying on unhealthy additives like excessive salt, sugar, or unhealthy fats is easier than you might think. Here are some strategies to enhance flavor naturally:

1. Layering Flavors:

Building layers of flavor throughout the cooking process can result in a more complex and satisfying dish.

- **Sauté Aromatics:** Start by sautéing onions, garlic, and herbs in a small amount of heart-healthy oil to create a flavorful base for soups, stews, and sauces.

- **Use Broths and Stocks:** Cooking with low-sodium broths or stocks adds depth and richness to grains, soups, and sauces without needing extra salt.

- **Add Acidity:** Balancing your dish with a touch of acid, such as lemon juice, vinegar, or a splash of wine, can elevate the flavors and reduce the need for salt or sugar.

2. Experiment with Herbs and Spices:

Herbs and spices are powerful tools for creating bold, interesting flavors without unhealthy additives.

- **Herb Mixes:** Create your own herb blends, such as Italian seasoning or a Mexican spice mix, to add flavor without added salt.
- **Spice Rubs:** Rub spices like smoked paprika, cumin, and coriander onto meats or vegetables before grilling or roasting to add flavor without extra fat or salt.

3. Incorporating Umami:

Umami, the savory fifth taste, can be achieved naturally in your cooking and enhances the overall flavor profile of a dish.
- **Use Mushrooms:** Mushrooms, particularly shiitake and porcini, are rich in umami and can be added to soups, stews, and sauces for a deeper flavor.
- **Add Soy Sauce or Miso:** Low-sodium soy sauce or a small amount of miso paste can add umami without overwhelming the dish with salt.
- **Tomato Paste:** Adding a spoonful of tomato paste to sauces, soups, or stews can boost umami and create a rich, savory flavor.

Tips for Reducing Processed Ingredients in Meals

Processed ingredients often contain unhealthy additives like trans fats, added sugars, and sodium, which can negatively impact heart health. Here are some tips for reducing processed ingredients in your meals:

1. Cook from Scratch:

Cooking meals from scratch allows you to control exactly what goes into your food, reducing the need for processed ingredients.
- **Start Simple:** Begin by making simple meals with whole ingredients, such as grilled chicken with roasted vegetables or a hearty vegetable soup.
- **Batch Cook:** Prepare larger batches of home-cooked meals that can be frozen for later use, making it easier to avoid the convenience of processed foods on busy nights.

2. Substitute Whole Ingredients:

Swap out processed ingredients for whole, unprocessed ones whenever possible.
- **Whole Grains for Refined Grains:** Use whole grains like brown rice, quinoa, or whole-wheat pasta instead of their refined counterparts.
- **Homemade Sauces:** Make your own sauces and dressings using whole ingredients like fresh tomatoes, herbs, and olive oil, rather than relying on store-bought versions.
- **Fresh or Frozen Vegetables:** Choose fresh or frozen vegetables over canned ones to avoid added sodium and preservatives.

3. Read Labels Carefully:

When you do use packaged ingredients, read labels carefully to choose the healthiest options available.
- **Look for Short Ingredient Lists:** Choose products with minimal ingredients, and avoid those with added sugars, unhealthy fats, or high sodium.
- **Avoid Artificial Additives:** Steer clear of products containing artificial colors, flavors, or preservatives.

By mastering these cooking techniques and making thoughtful ingredient choices, you can create meals that are not only delicious but also supportive of your heart health. Remember, small changes in the way you cook and select ingredients can have a significant impact on your overall well-being. Embrace these techniques and enjoy the journey of cooking for a healthier heart.

Chapter 6: Managing Cravings and Emotional Eating

Understanding and managing cravings and emotional eating is an essential part of maintaining a heart-healthy diet. Cravings can strike at any time, often leading to unhealthy eating habits that sabotage your best intentions. By understanding the science behind cravings, recognizing how emotions influence your eating habits, and identifying triggers, you can take control of your diet and make choices that support your heart health. In this chapter, we'll explore these topics in depth and provide practical strategies to help you manage cravings and emotional eating effectively.

Understanding Cravings

Cravings are intense, often overwhelming desires to eat specific foods. They are different from hunger in that they aren't necessarily driven by the body's need for energy or nutrients but rather by psychological and emotional factors. Cravings can be triggered by a variety of cues, including stress, emotions, environmental factors, or even certain nutritional deficiencies.

1. The Difference Between Hunger and Cravings:

Hunger is a physiological response to the body's need for energy and nutrients. It develops gradually and can be satisfied by eating a variety of foods. Cravings, on the other hand, are more specific and often involve a desire for certain types of food, typically those high in sugar, fat, or salt. Understanding this distinction is crucial in managing cravings because it allows you to address the root cause rather than simply responding to a temporary desire.

2. Common Triggers for Cravings:

- **Emotional Triggers:** Stress, anxiety, sadness, and even boredom can lead to cravings as the body seeks comfort or distraction through food.

- **Environmental Triggers:** The sight or smell of food, social situations, or even watching food advertisements can trigger cravings.

- **Nutritional Triggers:** Sometimes, cravings can be linked to nutritional deficiencies. For example, a craving for chocolate might indicate a need for magnesium, while a desire for salty foods could be linked to dehydration or electrolyte imbalance.

The Science Behind Cravings and How They Develop

Cravings are complex and involve both physiological and psychological processes. Understanding the science behind cravings can help you develop strategies to manage them more effectively.

1. The Brain's Reward System:

Cravings are closely tied to the brain's reward system, particularly the release of dopamine, a neurotransmitter that plays a key role in pleasure and motivation. When you eat a food that you crave, your brain releases dopamine, which creates a feeling of pleasure and reinforces the desire to eat that food again. This reward cycle can become particularly strong with foods that are high in sugar, fat, and salt, which are often engineered to be highly palatable and addictive.

2. Hormonal Influences:

Hormones also play a significant role in the development of cravings. For example, ghrelin, known as the "hunger hormone," stimulates appetite and can increase cravings, especially when you're stressed or sleep-deprived. Conversely, leptin, a hormone that signals satiety, can help curb cravings when functioning properly. However, in cases of leptin resistance, often seen in obesity, the brain doesn't receive the signal to stop eating, leading to increased cravings and overeating.

3. Blood Sugar Levels:

Fluctuations in blood sugar levels can trigger cravings, particularly for sugary or high-carbohydrate foods. When you consume refined carbs or sugary foods, your blood sugar spikes, leading to a surge of energy. However, this spike is often followed by a rapid drop in blood sugar, which can trigger feelings of hunger and cravings for more sugary foods, creating a vicious cycle.

The Role of Emotions in Eating Habits

Emotions are powerful drivers of eating behavior. Emotional eating occurs when you use food to cope with feelings rather than to satisfy hunger. This can lead to overeating, poor food choices, and ultimately, a negative impact on your heart health.

1. Why We Turn to Food for Comfort:

Food can provide a temporary sense of relief or pleasure during times of stress, sadness, or anxiety. This is often because eating certain foods triggers the release of feel-good neurotransmitters like serotonin and dopamine, which can momentarily improve your mood. However, this relief is usually short-lived, and the underlying emotions remain unaddressed, often leading to a cycle of emotional eating.

2. The Impact of Emotional Eating on Heart Health:

Emotional eating often involves consuming high-calorie, nutrient-poor foods like sweets, chips, and fast food, which can contribute to weight gain, elevated blood pressure, and increased cholesterol levels—all risk factors for heart disease. Moreover, emotional eating can lead to feelings of guilt and shame, further exacerbating stress and emotional turmoil, which in turn can trigger more emotional eating.

3. Strategies to Break the Cycle:

- **Identify Emotional Triggers:** Keep a journal to track your eating habits and emotions. Note when and what you eat, and how you're feeling at the time. This can help you identify patterns and triggers for emotional eating.

- **Find Alternative Coping Mechanisms:** Develop healthier ways to cope with emotions, such as exercising, meditating, practicing deep breathing, or engaging in a hobby you enjoy.

- **Practice Mindful Eating:** Mindful eating involves paying full attention to the experience of eating, from the taste and texture of the food to your body's hunger and fullness signals. This practice can help you become more aware of emotional eating triggers and make more intentional food choices.

Nutritional Deficiencies and Their Link to Cravings

Cravings can sometimes be linked to specific nutritional deficiencies. When your body lacks certain nutrients, it may signal a craving for foods that contain those nutrients, or, more commonly, for foods that provide quick energy, such as those high in sugar and fat.

1. Common Nutritional Deficiencies and Associated Cravings:

- **Magnesium:** A deficiency in magnesium can lead to cravings for chocolate, as cocoa is a good source of this mineral. Magnesium is essential for muscle function, nerve function, and energy production.

- **Iron:** Low iron levels can cause cravings for red meat or even non-food items like ice (a condition known as pica). Iron is crucial for oxygen transport in the blood.

- **Zinc:** A zinc deficiency can lead to a reduced sense of taste and smell, which might increase cravings for salty or sugary foods in an attempt to enhance flavor.

- **Omega-3 Fatty Acids:** A lack of omega-3s may lead to cravings for fatty foods. Omega-3s are important for brain function and reducing inflammation.

2. Addressing Nutritional Deficiencies:

If you suspect that your cravings are linked to a nutritional deficiency, it's important to address this with a balanced diet or supplements as needed. Incorporate a variety of nutrient-rich foods into your diet, such as:

- **Magnesium:** Nuts, seeds, leafy greens, and whole grains.

- **Iron:** Lean meats, beans, lentils, and fortified cereals.

- **Zinc:** Shellfish, beans, nuts, and dairy products.

- **Omega-3s:** Fatty fish (like salmon and mackerel), flaxseeds, and walnuts.

Consider speaking with a healthcare provider or nutritionist to assess your nutrient levels and develop a plan to address any deficiencies.

Identifying Triggers for Unhealthy Eating

Recognizing and understanding your triggers is a crucial step in managing cravings and emotional eating. Triggers can be internal (emotions, thoughts) or external (environments, social situations), and they often lead to impulsive eating behaviors.

1. Common Triggers for Unhealthy Eating:

- **Stress:** Stress is one of the most common triggers for unhealthy eating. When stressed, the body releases cortisol, which can increase appetite and cravings for high-calorie comfort foods.

- **Fatigue:** Lack of sleep or physical exhaustion can lead to poor food choices, as your body seeks quick energy through sugary or high-carb foods.

- **Social Situations:** Social gatherings often involve food, and the pressure to indulge in unhealthy options can be strong, especially in celebratory or communal settings.

- **Boredom:** Eating out of boredom is common, as food can provide a distraction or a sense of purpose when you're not mentally or physically engaged.

2. Strategies for Managing Triggers:

- **Create a Plan:** Have a plan in place for dealing with triggers. For example, if you know that stress leads you to crave sweets, plan to go for a walk or practice deep breathing instead of reaching for a snack.

- **Environment Control:** Manage your environment by keeping unhealthy foods out of your home or workspace. Surround yourself with healthy snacks and meal options to make better choices easier.

- **Delay Gratification:** When a craving strikes, try delaying your response. Wait 10-15 minutes and use that time to distract yourself with another activity. Often, the craving will pass on its own.

How Stress Affects Food Choices

Stress has a profound impact on food choices and can be a major obstacle in maintaining a heart-healthy diet. When you're stressed, your body's natural response can drive you toward unhealthy eating patterns.

1. The Stress Response:

When you experience stress, your body releases stress hormones like cortisol and adrenaline. While these hormones are essential for dealing with immediate threats, chronic stress can lead to prolonged elevated cortisol levels, which are associated with increased appetite and cravings for high-calorie, high-fat foods.

2. Stress-Eating Cycle:

Stress eating often becomes a cycle where stress triggers cravings, leading to overeating, which then causes feelings of guilt or discomfort, further increasing stress levels. This cycle can be particularly detrimental to heart health, as it often leads to the consumption of foods high in sugar, salt, and unhealthy fats.

3. Breaking the Stress-Eating Cycle:

- **Stress Management Techniques:** Incorporate stress management practices into your daily routine, such as regular physical activity, meditation, yoga, or deep breathing exercises. These activities help lower cortisol levels and reduce the urge to eat in response to stress.

- **Mindful Eating:** Pay attention to your eating habits and recognize when you're eating due to stress rather than hunger. Mindful eating encourages you to savor each bite, recognize true hunger cues, and make conscious food choices.

- **Healthy Comfort Foods:** If you find that you still need comfort foods during stressful times, opt for healthier alternatives. For example, instead of reaching for ice cream, try a bowl of Greek yogurt with fresh berries, or swap chips for air-popped popcorn with a sprinkle of herbs.

Understanding the connection between stress and eating habits allows you to make more intentional choices that support your heart health. By recognizing triggers, addressing emotional and physiological factors, and implementing healthy coping strategies, you can manage cravings and emotional eating effectively, paving the way for a more balanced and heart-healthy diet.

Practical Strategies to Control Cravings

Cravings are a natural part of life, but they can sometimes lead to unhealthy eating habits that undermine your heart health goals. The good news is that there are practical strategies you can use to control cravings and make healthier choices without feeling deprived. By understanding how to manage cravings effectively, you can stay on track with your heart-healthy diet and still enjoy the foods you love.

1. Identify and Understand Your Cravings:

The first step in controlling cravings is to identify when and why they occur. Keep a food diary to track your cravings, noting the time of day, the type of food you crave, and any emotions or situations that might be influencing your desires. Understanding the root cause of your cravings—whether it's stress, boredom, or a specific nutrient deficiency—can help you address them more effectively.

2. Stay Hydrated:

Sometimes what feels like a craving is actually thirst. Dehydration can often be mistaken for hunger or a desire for a specific food. Make sure you're drinking enough water throughout the day to stay hydrated and help keep cravings at bay. Aim for at least 8 glasses of water daily, and consider starting your day with a glass of water to set the tone for proper hydration.

3. Manage Stress Levels:

Stress is a significant trigger for cravings, particularly for comfort foods high in sugar, fat, or salt. Incorporating stress-management techniques like deep breathing exercises, yoga, or regular physical activity can help reduce stress-related cravings. Even taking a few minutes to meditate or practice mindfulness can make a big difference in how you respond to stress and the food choices you make as a result.

4. Get Enough Sleep:

Lack of sleep can disrupt your hormones, leading to increased hunger and stronger cravings, particularly for high-calorie, high-carbohydrate foods. Prioritize getting 7-9 hours of quality sleep each night to help regulate your appetite and reduce the likelihood of craving unhealthy foods.

Smart Swaps for Common Cravings

When cravings strike, it's important to have healthy alternatives at your fingertips. Making smart swaps can satisfy your cravings without derailing your heart-healthy diet.

1. Craving Sweets? Opt for Naturally Sweet Foods:

Instead of reaching for candy or baked goods, satisfy your sweet tooth with naturally sweet options that also provide nutritional benefits.

- **Swap Candy with Fresh Fruit:** Berries, apples, and oranges offer natural sweetness along with fiber and antioxidants. If you crave something more indulgent, try dipping strawberries in a small amount of dark chocolate.

- **Replace Ice Cream with Greek Yogurt:** Greek yogurt with a drizzle of honey and a handful of fresh berries or nuts can provide the creaminess and sweetness you're craving while adding protein and probiotics to your diet.

- **Substitute Sugary Snacks with Dates or Dried Fruit:** A couple of dates or a small handful of dried apricots can provide the sweetness you crave along with fiber, which helps keep you full.

2. Craving Salty Foods? Choose Healthier Alternatives:

Salty snacks like chips and pretzels are often high in sodium and unhealthy fats. Instead, look for options that satisfy your salt craving without compromising your heart health.

- **Swap Chips with Air-Popped Popcorn:** Air-popped popcorn seasoned with a sprinkle of nutritional yeast or a pinch of sea salt can satisfy your craving for something salty and crunchy without the extra fat and calories.

- **Replace Pretzels with Nuts:** Opt for unsalted nuts like almonds or pistachios. They provide healthy fats, protein, and fiber, making them a more nutritious choice.

- **Substitute Processed Snacks with Veggies and Hummus:** Fresh vegetables like cucumber slices, cherry tomatoes, and bell pepper strips dipped in hummus can provide the crunch and flavor you crave with the added benefit of vitamins and minerals.

3. Craving Rich or Fatty Foods? Opt for Healthy Fats:

Cravings for rich, fatty foods often stem from a desire for the satisfying texture and flavor that fats provide. Choose healthier fat sources that support heart health.

- **Swap Fried Foods with Baked or Grilled Options:** Instead of fried chicken or fish, try baking or grilling your protein with heart-healthy olive oil and herbs. This method reduces the fat content while still delivering a satisfying taste and texture.

- **Replace Butter with Avocado:** Spread mashed avocado on whole-grain toast instead of butter. Avocado provides healthy monounsaturated fats, fiber, and a range of vitamins and minerals.

- **Substitute Creamy Sauces with Greek Yogurt or Tahini:** Use Greek yogurt as a base for creamy dressings or sauces instead of sour cream or mayonnaise. Alternatively, tahini (sesame seed paste) can be used to create rich, flavorful sauces with heart-healthy fats.

Techniques to Practice Mindful Eating

Mindful eating is a powerful tool that helps you become more aware of your eating habits, making it easier to control cravings and make healthier choices. By paying attention to what, when, and how you eat, you can enjoy your food more fully and avoid overeating.

1. Slow Down and Savor Each Bite:

One of the simplest ways to practice mindful eating is to slow down. Take small bites, chew your food thoroughly, and focus on the flavors, textures, and aromas of each bite. Eating slowly allows your body to register fullness, reducing the likelihood of overeating.

2. Eliminate Distractions:

Try to eat without distractions like television, smartphones, or computers. When you're distracted, it's easy to eat mindlessly, leading to overeating. Instead, focus solely on your meal, which will help you tune into your body's hunger and fullness cues.

3. Listen to Your Body:

Before eating, take a moment to assess your hunger level. Are you truly hungry, or are you eating out of boredom, stress, or habit? Eat when you're physically hungry and stop when you're satisfied, not full. This approach helps you avoid eating based on external cues rather than your body's needs.

4. Practice Gratitude for Your Food:

Take a moment before your meal to appreciate the food in front of you—its origins, the effort it took to prepare, and the nourishment it provides. This practice of gratitude can enhance your eating experience and foster a healthier relationship with food.

The Role of Regular Meals in Reducing Cravings

Regular meals play a crucial role in managing cravings and maintaining stable energy levels throughout the day. Skipping meals or going too long between meals can lead to intense hunger and stronger cravings, making it harder to make healthy choices.

1. Eat Balanced Meals:

Each meal should include a balance of macronutrients—protein, healthy fats, and complex carbohydrates. This balance helps keep you full and satisfied, reducing the likelihood of cravings later on.

- **Breakfast:** Start your day with a meal that includes protein (like eggs or Greek yogurt), healthy fats (like avocado or nuts), and whole grains (like oats or whole-grain toast). This combination will keep your blood sugar stable and reduce mid-morning cravings.

- **Lunch and Dinner:** Aim for meals that include lean proteins, plenty of vegetables, whole grains, and a source of healthy fat. For example, a quinoa salad with grilled chicken, mixed vegetables, and a drizzle of olive oil offers a satisfying and balanced meal.

2. Don't Skip Meals:

Skipping meals can lead to low blood sugar, which often triggers cravings for quick energy sources like sugary snacks or refined carbs. Eating regular meals helps keep your blood sugar stable, reducing the urge to reach for unhealthy options.

3. Incorporate Healthy Snacks:

Healthy snacks between meals can help curb hunger and prevent overeating during main meals. Choose snacks that are high in fiber and protein, such as a handful of nuts, a piece of fruit with nut butter, or whole-grain crackers with hummus.

Incorporating Healthy Treats to Stay Satisfied

A heart-healthy diet doesn't mean you have to give up all treats. Incorporating healthy treats in moderation can help you stay satisfied and prevent feelings of deprivation, which can lead to binge eating.

1. Enjoy Treats in Moderation:

Allow yourself to enjoy your favorite treats occasionally, but in smaller portions. For example, if you love chocolate, savor a small piece of dark chocolate rather than eating an entire bar. This approach helps you indulge without overindulging.

2. Make Healthier Versions of Your Favorites:

There are plenty of ways to create healthier versions of your favorite treats using whole, nutrient-dense ingredients.

- **Bake with Whole Grains:** Use whole-grain flours like whole wheat or oat flour in your baked goods. You can also reduce the amount of sugar and use natural sweeteners like honey or maple syrup.

- **Use Healthy Fats:** Replace butter or margarine with healthier fats like olive oil, avocado, or coconut oil in recipes. These fats provide more nutrients and are better for your heart.

- **Add Fruits and Vegetables:** Incorporate fruits and vegetables into your treats. For example, add grated zucchini or carrots to muffins, or make a fruit-based sorbet instead of ice cream.

3. Practice Portion Control:

When enjoying a treat, serve yourself a small portion and savor it slowly. This mindful approach allows you to fully enjoy your treat without feeling the need to overindulge.

Building a Support System for Success

Having a strong support system can make a significant difference in your ability to manage cravings and stick to your heart-healthy diet. Surround yourself with people who encourage your healthy choices and provide motivation when you need it.

1. Share Your Goals with Loved Ones:

Let your family and friends know about your heart-health goals and the steps you're taking to achieve them. When those around you understand your intentions, they're more likely to support your efforts and help you stay accountable.

2. Find a Health Buddy:

Partnering with someone who shares similar health goals can provide mutual motivation and accountability. Whether it's a friend, family member, or coworker, having someone to share your journey with can make it easier to stay on track.

3. Seek Professional Guidance:

If you're struggling with managing cravings or emotional eating, consider seeking the guidance of a nutritionist, dietitian, or therapist. These professionals can provide personalized strategies and support to help you overcome challenges and maintain a healthy relationship with food.

4. Join a Community:

Online forums, social media groups, or local support groups focused on heart health or healthy eating can be valuable resources. Connecting with others who are on a similar journey can provide inspiration, ideas, and encouragement.

By implementing these practical strategies to control cravings, making smart food swaps, practicing mindful eating, and building a support system, you can create a sustainable heart-healthy lifestyle that allows you to enjoy food while prioritizing your well-being. Remember, it's not about perfection—it's about making consistent, positive choices that support your health and happiness.

Chapter 7: Exercise and Its Role in Heart Health

Physical activity is one of the most powerful tools you have to support and enhance your heart health. Regular exercise doesn't just help you feel better in the short term—it also plays a crucial role in preventing and managing cardiovascular disease, improving overall cardiovascular function, managing cholesterol and blood pressure levels, and even aiding in weight control and stress reduction. In this chapter, we'll explore the importance of physical activity for heart health and provide practical guidance on how to incorporate exercise into your daily routine.

The Importance of Physical Activity

The benefits of regular physical activity extend far beyond just burning calories. Exercise is vital for maintaining a healthy heart and preventing cardiovascular disease. The heart is a muscle, and like any other muscle in the body, it becomes stronger and more efficient with regular use. Physical activity improves the heart's ability to pump blood, reduces the risk of heart disease, and enhances overall cardiovascular function.

1. Reducing the Risk of Cardiovascular Disease:

Regular exercise helps to lower the risk of developing cardiovascular disease by improving various risk factors such as high blood pressure, high cholesterol, and obesity. It also improves circulation, helping to prevent the buildup of plaque in the arteries, which can lead to heart attacks and strokes.

2. Enhancing Cardiovascular Function:

Exercise improves the efficiency of the heart, allowing it to pump more blood with each beat. This not only improves the delivery of oxygen and nutrients to tissues throughout the body but also enhances your overall stamina and endurance.

3. Supporting Mental Health:

Exercise has significant mental health benefits as well. It can reduce symptoms of depression and anxiety, improve mood, and boost overall well-being. Since mental health is closely linked to heart health, these benefits further reinforce the importance of regular physical activity.

How Exercise Improves Cardiovascular Function

Your cardiovascular system is made up of the heart, blood vessels, and blood. It's responsible for delivering oxygen and nutrients to every cell in your body while also removing waste products like carbon dioxide. Exercise plays a critical role in keeping this system functioning at its best.

1. Strengthening the Heart Muscle:

When you engage in aerobic exercise, your heart works harder to pump blood throughout your body. Over time, this strengthens the heart muscle, allowing it to pump blood more efficiently and with less effort. A stronger heart means that your resting heart rate is lower, which reduces the overall workload on the heart and decreases the risk of cardiovascular disease.

2. Improving Circulation:

Exercise promotes the growth of new blood vessels, improving circulation and ensuring that your tissues receive adequate oxygen and nutrients. This process, known as angiogenesis, is particularly important for preventing the narrowing of arteries that can lead to heart disease.

3. Enhancing Oxygen Utilization:

During exercise, your muscles require more oxygen to produce energy. Regular physical activity improves your body's ability to extract and utilize oxygen from the blood, increasing your endurance and reducing fatigue during physical exertion.

4. Reducing Inflammation:

Chronic inflammation is a known risk factor for heart disease. Regular exercise helps reduce inflammation by lowering levels of inflammatory markers in the blood, such as C-reactive protein (CRP). This anti-inflammatory effect contributes to a healthier cardiovascular system.

The Relationship Between Exercise and Blood Pressure

High blood pressure, or hypertension, is a major risk factor for heart disease and stroke. Exercise is one of the most effective lifestyle interventions for lowering blood pressure and keeping it within a healthy range.

1. Lowering Blood Pressure Naturally:

Exercise helps lower blood pressure by improving the efficiency of the heart and blood vessels. When you engage in regular physical activity, your heart doesn't have to work as hard to pump blood, which reduces the pressure on the artery walls.

- **Aerobic Exercise:** Activities like walking, jogging, swimming, and cycling are particularly effective at lowering blood pressure. Aim for at least 150 minutes of moderate-intensity aerobic exercise each week.

- **Resistance Training:** Strength training can also help lower blood pressure by improving overall cardiovascular health and reducing body fat. Include resistance exercises like weightlifting, bodyweight exercises, or resistance band workouts two to three times per week.

2. Improving Blood Vessel Function:

Exercise enhances the flexibility of your blood vessels, allowing them to expand more easily when blood flow increases. This improved vascular function helps maintain healthy blood pressure levels and reduces the risk of hypertension.

3. Managing Blood Pressure Over the Long Term:

The blood pressure-lowering effects of exercise are not just immediate—they also contribute to long-term improvements in blood pressure control. Regular physical activity can prevent the onset of hypertension and help manage it in individuals who already have high blood pressure.

Exercise for Cholesterol Management

Cholesterol plays a significant role in heart health, and exercise is a powerful tool for managing cholesterol levels. It helps improve your lipid profile by increasing levels of high-density lipoprotein (HDL), the "good" cholesterol, and reducing levels of low-density lipoprotein (LDL), the "bad" cholesterol.

1. Increasing HDL Cholesterol:

HDL cholesterol helps remove LDL cholesterol from the bloodstream, transporting it to the liver where it can be processed and eliminated from the body. Regular aerobic exercise is particularly effective at raising HDL levels, which provides greater protection against heart disease.

- **Effective Exercises:** Activities like brisk walking, running, cycling, swimming, and dancing are all excellent for increasing HDL cholesterol. Aim for at least 30 minutes of aerobic exercise most days of the week.

2. Reducing LDL Cholesterol:

Exercise also helps lower LDL cholesterol by promoting weight loss, reducing body fat, and improving the overall health of your cardiovascular system. Lower LDL levels reduce the risk of plaque buildup in the arteries, a leading cause of heart attacks and strokes.

3. Lowering Triglycerides:

Triglycerides are a type of fat found in the blood, and high levels are associated with an increased risk of heart disease. Regular physical activity helps lower triglyceride levels, further reducing your risk.

4. Combining Exercise with a Healthy Diet:

While exercise is crucial for managing cholesterol, combining it with a heart-healthy diet amplifies the benefits. Focus on consuming plenty of fruits, vegetables, whole grains, lean proteins, and healthy fats to support your cholesterol management efforts.

Weight Control Through Physical Activity

Maintaining a healthy weight is essential for heart health, and regular exercise plays a key role in weight management. By balancing the calories you consume with the calories you burn, exercise helps prevent weight gain and supports weight loss, if needed.

1. Burning Calories:

Physical activity increases the number of calories you burn, which helps create a calorie deficit if you're aiming to lose weight. Both aerobic exercise and resistance training contribute to calorie expenditure, making them important components of a weight management plan.

- **Aerobic Exercise:** High-intensity activities like running, swimming, and cycling burn a significant number of calories. Even lower-intensity activities, like walking or gardening, contribute to your overall calorie burn when done consistently.

- **Strength Training:** Building muscle through strength training increases your resting metabolic rate, meaning you burn more calories even when you're not exercising.

2. Preventing Weight Gain:

Regular exercise helps prevent weight gain by maintaining muscle mass, improving metabolism, and regulating appetite. Even if you're not trying to lose weight, staying active is important for preventing the gradual weight gain that can occur with age.

3. Supporting Sustainable Weight Loss:

For those looking to lose weight, combining regular exercise with a balanced diet is the most effective approach. Aim for a mix of aerobic exercise, which helps burn calories, and strength training, which helps build and maintain muscle mass.

4. Enhancing Body Composition:

Beyond weight loss, exercise improves body composition by increasing muscle mass and reducing body fat. A healthier body composition reduces the risk of heart disease and other chronic conditions, even if the number on the scale doesn't change dramatically.

Reducing Stress with Regular Exercise

Stress is a major contributor to heart disease, and exercise is one of the most effective ways to manage and reduce stress. Physical activity helps alleviate stress by releasing endorphins, improving mood, and providing a natural outlet for tension and anxiety.

1. The Stress-Relieving Power of Exercise:

When you exercise, your body releases endorphins—often referred to as "feel-good" hormones—that naturally elevate your mood and reduce feelings of stress. Regular physical activity also promotes better sleep, which is crucial for stress management and overall health.

2. Aerobic Exercise for Stress Reduction:

Aerobic exercise is particularly effective at reducing stress because it increases the production of endorphins and improves cardiovascular health simultaneously. Activities like walking, jogging, swimming, and cycling are all excellent choices.

3. Mind-Body Exercises:

Mind-body exercises like yoga, tai chi, and Pilates combine physical movement with breathing exercises and meditation, making them especially beneficial for stress relief. These practices not only improve physical fitness but also help calm the mind and reduce anxiety.

4. Social Interaction and Exercise:

Engaging in group exercise classes or participating in team sports can also provide social interaction, which is an important factor in managing stress. Connecting with others through exercise can enhance your sense of community and support, further reducing stress levels.

5. Making Exercise a Habit:

To maximize the stress-relieving benefits of exercise, consistency is key. Aim to incorporate physical activity into your daily routine, even if it's just a short walk or a few minutes of stretching. The cumulative effect of regular exercise will help you manage stress more effectively and protect your heart health.

By understanding the vital role that exercise plays in heart health, you can take proactive steps to incorporate physical activity into your daily life. Whether you're just starting out or looking to enhance your existing routine, the key is to find activities that you enjoy and can sustain over the long term. Regular exercise, combined with a heart-healthy diet, is one of the most powerful ways to protect your cardiovascular health and improve your overall quality of life.

Developing an Exercise Routine

Starting and maintaining a regular exercise routine is one of the most impactful steps you can take toward improving your heart health. Exercise is a cornerstone of a healthy lifestyle, and when combined with a heart-healthy diet, it can dramatically reduce your risk of cardiovascular disease. In this section, we'll explore the different types of exercise that are beneficial for your heart, how to begin if you're new to exercise, and strategies for creating a balanced weekly exercise plan that fits into your busy life. We'll also discuss how to stay motivated to keep moving, even when challenges arise.

Types of Exercise: Aerobic, Strength, and Flexibility

To create a well-rounded exercise routine that supports heart health, it's essential to incorporate a variety of exercise types. Each type of exercise offers unique benefits that contribute to overall cardiovascular fitness and well-being.

1. Aerobic Exercise:

Aerobic exercise, also known as cardiovascular or endurance exercise, is any activity that increases your heart rate and breathing for an extended period. This type of exercise is particularly effective for improving heart health because it strengthens the heart muscle, enhances circulation, and increases your body's ability to use oxygen.

- **Examples:** Walking, jogging, cycling, swimming, dancing, and aerobic classes.
- **Benefits:** Regular aerobic exercise helps lower blood pressure, reduce LDL (bad) cholesterol, increase HDL (good) cholesterol, and improve overall cardiovascular function.

2. Strength Training:

Strength training, or resistance training, involves exercises that work your muscles against a force, such as weights, resistance bands, or your own body weight. While strength training is often associated with building muscle, it also offers significant heart health benefits.

- **Examples:** Weightlifting, bodyweight exercises (such as push-ups, squats, and lunges), resistance band exercises, and using weight machines.
- **Benefits:** Strength training helps maintain and build muscle mass, which is important for metabolism and weight management. It also contributes to better glucose metabolism, reduces the risk of osteoporosis, and can lower blood pressure.

3. Flexibility and Balance Exercises:

Flexibility and balance exercises are often overlooked but are crucial components of a heart-healthy exercise routine. These exercises improve your range of motion, reduce the risk of injury, and enhance overall physical function, especially as you age.

- **Examples:** Stretching exercises, yoga, tai chi, and Pilates.
- **Benefits:** Flexibility exercises help prevent stiffness and maintain joint health, while balance exercises reduce the risk of falls and improve coordination.

How to Start if You're New to Exercise

If you're new to exercise or haven't been active in a while, it's important to start slowly and gradually build up your fitness level. Here's how to get started safely and effectively:

1. Start with Small, Manageable Goals:

Begin with realistic and achievable goals that match your current fitness level. For example, if you're starting from a sedentary lifestyle, aim to incorporate 10-15 minutes of walking into your daily routine. As you become more comfortable, gradually increase the duration and intensity of your workouts.

2. Focus on Consistency Over Intensity:

When starting out, consistency is more important than intensity. Focus on making exercise a regular part of your routine, even if it's just a short walk or a few minutes of stretching each day. Over time, you can increase the intensity and variety of your workouts as your fitness improves.

3. Listen to Your Body:

Pay attention to how your body feels during and after exercise. It's normal to experience some muscle soreness when you're starting a new routine, but if you feel pain, dizziness, or shortness of breath, stop and rest. Consult with your healthcare provider before beginning any new exercise program, especially if you have a pre-existing health condition.

4. Incorporate Warm-Up and Cool-Down:

Always start your workouts with a warm-up to prepare your body for exercise and reduce the risk of injury. A warm-up might include 5-10 minutes of light aerobic activity, such as walking or cycling, followed by dynamic stretching. After your workout, cool down with gentle stretching to help your muscles recover and prevent stiffness.

5. Seek Support:

If you're unsure where to start or feel overwhelmed, consider working with a personal trainer or joining a beginner-friendly exercise class. A professional can help you develop a safe and effective exercise plan tailored to your needs and goals.

Creating a Balanced Weekly Exercise Plan

To achieve optimal heart health, it's important to create a balanced exercise plan that includes aerobic, strength, and flexibility exercises. A well-rounded plan ensures that you're working all aspects of your fitness and reduces the risk of overuse injuries.

1. Plan for Aerobic Exercise:

Aim for at least 150 minutes of moderate-intensity aerobic exercise per week, or 75 minutes of vigorous-intensity exercise. This can be broken down into sessions of 30 minutes, five times per week, or shorter sessions if that fits your schedule better.

- **Moderate-Intensity Examples:** Brisk walking, cycling on flat terrain, or swimming at a leisurely pace.
- **Vigorous-Intensity Examples:** Running, cycling on hilly terrain, or swimming laps at a fast pace.

2. Incorporate Strength Training:

Include strength training exercises at least two days per week. Focus on working all major muscle groups, including the legs, hips, back, abdomen, chest, shoulders, and arms. Each session should include 2-3 sets of 8-12 repetitions for each exercise.

- **Sample Strength Routine:** On two non-consecutive days, perform exercises like squats, lunges, push-ups, dumbbell rows, and planks. Use weights that are challenging but allow you to maintain good form.

3. Add Flexibility and Balance Exercises:

Incorporate flexibility and balance exercises into your routine at least two to three times per week. These exercises can be included as part of your warm-up, cool-down, or on days when you're not doing aerobic or strength training.

- **Sample Routine:** After your workout, spend 10-15 minutes stretching all major muscle groups. You can also practice yoga or tai chi for a more comprehensive approach to flexibility and balance.

4. Mix It Up:

Variety is key to preventing boredom and overuse injuries. Mix up your routine by trying different types of exercise, such as swimming one day, walking another, and taking a yoga class on another. This not only keeps things interesting but also ensures that you're working different muscles and aspects of your fitness.

Incorporating Exercise into a Busy Lifestyle

Finding time for exercise can be challenging, especially with a busy schedule. However, with a bit of creativity and planning, you can incorporate physical activity into your daily routine, no matter how hectic it may be.

1. Break It Up:

You don't need to exercise for long periods to reap the benefits. If you're short on time, break your workouts into shorter sessions throughout the day. For example, three 10-minute walks can be just as effective as one 30-minute session.

2. Make It Part of Your Daily Routine:

Incorporate physical activity into your existing routine. Walk or bike to work if possible, take the stairs instead of the elevator, or do a quick workout while watching TV. Even small changes like standing or pacing while on phone calls can add up over time.

3. Schedule It Like an Appointment:

Treat exercise as an important appointment that you can't miss. Schedule your workouts in your calendar, just like any other meeting or commitment. By prioritizing exercise, you're more likely to follow through.

4. Combine Exercise with Social Time:

Combine physical activity with socializing by inviting friends or family to join you for a walk, a hike, or a fitness class. Exercising with others can make the experience more enjoyable and provide additional motivation to stay active.

5. Use Technology to Your Advantage:

There are many apps and online resources available that can help you stay active, even on the busiest days. Fitness apps can provide guided workouts, track your progress, and offer reminders to stay on track with your exercise goals.

Staying Motivated to Keep Moving

Staying motivated to exercise regularly can be challenging, especially when life gets busy or when you're faced with obstacles like fatigue, stress, or lack of time. However, there are strategies you can use to maintain your motivation and make exercise a consistent part of your life.

1. Set Clear, Achievable Goals:

Set specific, measurable, achievable, relevant, and time-bound (SMART) goals for your exercise routine. For example, instead of saying, "I want to exercise more," set a goal like, "I will walk for 30 minutes, five days a week." Clear goals give you something to work toward and help you track your progress.

2. Celebrate Small Wins:

Celebrate your achievements, no matter how small. Whether it's completing your first 5K, lifting a heavier weight, or simply sticking to your exercise routine for a month, take the time to acknowledge and celebrate your progress. These small wins can boost your confidence and keep you motivated.

3. Keep It Fun:

Exercise doesn't have to be a chore. Find activities you enjoy and look forward to, whether it's dancing, hiking, swimming, or playing a sport. When you enjoy what you're doing, you're more likely to stick with it.

4. Mix Up Your Routine:

If you start to feel bored or unmotivated, try mixing up your routine. Experiment with new activities, change the location of your workouts, or set new challenges for yourself. Variety keeps things fresh and prevents burnout.

5. Stay Accountable:

Share your exercise goals with a friend, family member, or online community. Having someone to check in with can provide accountability and encouragement. You can also keep a workout journal to track your progress and reflect on your achievements.

6. Focus on the Positive Benefits:

Remind yourself of the benefits of regular exercise, not just for your heart health but for your overall well-being. Regular physical activity can improve your mood, boost your energy levels, reduce stress, and enhance your quality of life. Keeping these positive outcomes in mind can help you stay motivated, even on challenging days.

By developing a balanced exercise routine that fits your lifestyle, you can take significant strides toward improving your heart health and overall well-being. Whether you're just starting out or looking to refine your existing routine, the key is to find what works for you and stay consistent. Remember, every bit of movement counts, and the journey to better heart health is built on small, sustainable steps.

Chapter 8: Long-Term Strategies for Sustaining a Heart-Healthy Diet

Adopting a heart-healthy diet is a powerful step towards improving your cardiovascular health, but sustaining these changes over the long term is where the real transformation happens. Building and maintaining heart-healthy habits requires dedication, consistency, and a clear understanding of your goals and motivations. In this chapter, we'll explore strategies for creating sustainable habits, setting realistic goals, understanding the stages of behavior change, reinforcing positive habits daily, overcoming setbacks, and leveraging social support to stay on track.

Building Sustainable Habits

Building habits that support your heart health is crucial for long-term success. Habits are the routines and behaviors that you perform automatically, and they play a significant role in your overall lifestyle. To make heart-healthy eating a natural part of your life, you need to establish habits that are both sustainable and aligned with your goals.

1. Start Small:

One of the most effective ways to build sustainable habits is to start small. When you set goals that are too ambitious or try to change too much at once, it can be overwhelming and lead to burnout. Instead, focus on making one small change at a time. For example, if you're trying to eat more vegetables, start by adding an extra serving of vegetables to one meal each day. Once that becomes a habit, you can build on it by incorporating vegetables into more meals.

2. Make It Easy:

Habits are more likely to stick if they are easy to implement. Simplify your environment to make heart-healthy choices the default option. For instance, keep healthy snacks like fruits and nuts easily accessible, and store less healthy options out of sight. Prepping meals in advance or having healthy recipes on hand can also make it easier to stick to your diet.

3. Focus on Consistency:

Consistency is key when it comes to building habits. It's better to make a small change and stick with it consistently than to make a drastic change that you can't maintain. Whether it's choosing whole grains over refined grains or swapping sugary beverages for water, focus on making these changes consistently to build lasting habits.

4. Reward Yourself:

Positive reinforcement can help reinforce new habits. When you successfully make a heart-healthy choice, acknowledge your effort and reward yourself in a way that doesn't involve food. This could be something as simple as taking a few minutes to relax, enjoying a favorite hobby, or treating yourself to a new book or movie.

Setting Realistic and Achievable Goals

Setting goals is an essential part of creating a heart-healthy lifestyle, but it's important that your goals are realistic and achievable. Setting overly ambitious goals can lead to frustration and disappointment, while setting achievable goals can boost your confidence and keep you motivated.

1. SMART Goals:

Use the SMART criteria to set your goals:

- **Specific:** Be clear about what you want to achieve. For example, instead of saying, "I want to eat healthier," set a specific goal like, "I will eat at least five servings of fruits and vegetables each day."

- **Measurable:** Your goal should be quantifiable so that you can track your progress. For instance, "I will exercise for 30 minutes, five times a week" is a measurable goal.

- **Achievable:** Ensure that your goal is realistic given your current lifestyle, resources, and commitments. If you're new to exercise, starting with a goal of daily 10-minute walks may be more achievable than aiming for an hour-long workout.

- **Relevant:** Your goal should align with your overall objectives and values. If heart health is a priority for you, focus on goals that directly contribute to that outcome, such as reducing sodium intake or increasing physical activity.

- **Time-bound:** Set a deadline for your goal to create a sense of urgency. For example, "I will reduce my intake of processed foods by 50% within the next three months."

2. Break Down Larger Goals:

Large goals can feel overwhelming, so break them down into smaller, more manageable steps. For example, if your goal is to lose 20 pounds, break it down into a monthly goal of losing 2-3 pounds. Celebrate each small victory along the way to stay motivated.

3. Be Flexible:

Life is unpredictable, and there will be times when you need to adjust your goals. If you find that a goal is no longer achievable or relevant, don't be afraid to modify it. The key is to stay focused on your overall objective and remain adaptable.

Understanding the Stages of Behavior Change

Behavior change is a process that occurs in stages. Understanding these stages can help you navigate the challenges of adopting and maintaining heart-healthy habits.

1. The Stages of Change Model:

The Stages of Change model, also known as the Transtheoretical Model, outlines five stages that individuals typically go through when changing a behavior:

- **Precontemplation:** At this stage, you may not yet recognize the need to change. You might not be aware of the risks associated with your current habits or may feel resistant to making changes.

- **Contemplation:** In this stage, you start to recognize the benefits of change and consider taking action. You may weigh the pros and cons of changing your behavior but haven't yet committed to taking steps.

67

- **Preparation:** You're ready to take action and may start planning how you'll make the change. This could involve setting goals, gathering resources, or seeking support.

- **Action:** At this stage, you're actively working on changing your behavior. You've started implementing new habits and are working to sustain them.

- **Maintenance:** In this stage, you've successfully adopted the new behavior and are focused on maintaining it over the long term. You're also working to prevent relapse into old habits.

2. Navigating the Stages:

Recognize that behavior change is not always linear. You may move back and forth between stages, and that's okay. The key is to be patient with yourself and understand that change takes time.

- **Precontemplation to Contemplation:** Educate yourself about the benefits of heart-healthy habits and the risks of not making changes. Seek out resources, such as books, articles, or support groups, that can help you build awareness.

- **Contemplation to Preparation:** Set specific, actionable goals and create a plan for how you'll achieve them. Consider what obstacles might arise and how you'll address them.

- **Preparation to Action:** Start small and build momentum. Take the first step toward your goal, whether it's trying a new heart-healthy recipe or going for a short walk.

- **Action to Maintenance:** Focus on consistency and reinforce your new habits daily. Celebrate your progress and continue setting new goals to keep yourself motivated.

Reinforcing Positive Habits Daily

Once you've established heart-healthy habits, it's important to reinforce them daily to ensure they become a permanent part of your lifestyle.

1. Create a Routine:

Habits are more likely to stick when they're part of a daily routine. For example, if you want to exercise regularly, schedule your workouts at the same time each day. Whether it's morning walks, meal prepping on Sundays, or having a healthy breakfast every day, consistency helps solidify these habits.

2. Use Reminders:

Reminders can help keep you on track, especially in the early stages of habit formation. Set alarms on your phone, place sticky notes in visible areas, or use a habit-tracking app to remind yourself of your goals and actions.

3. Positive Self-Talk:

Your mindset plays a significant role in sustaining positive habits. Practice positive self-talk by encouraging yourself and acknowledging your efforts. Replace negative thoughts like "I can't do this" with affirmations like "I am capable of making healthy choices."

4. Reflect on Progress:

Take time each day to reflect on your progress. Consider keeping a journal where you can note what went well, what challenges you faced, and how you overcame them. This reflection not only reinforces your habits but also helps you learn from your experiences.

Overcoming Setbacks and Staying on Track

Setbacks are a natural part of any journey, including the pursuit of a heart-healthy lifestyle. What's important is how you respond to these setbacks and stay committed to your goals.

1. Acknowledge Setbacks Without Judgment:

Everyone faces setbacks, whether it's skipping a workout, indulging in unhealthy foods, or experiencing a lapse in motivation. Acknowledge these moments without judgment and avoid the trap of all-or-nothing thinking. Instead of seeing a setback as a failure, view it as an opportunity to learn and grow.

2. Identify Triggers:

Setbacks often occur in response to specific triggers, such as stress, social situations, or emotional challenges. Identifying these triggers can help you develop strategies to manage them more effectively. For example, if stress leads you to overeat, consider incorporating stress-reduction techniques like meditation, deep breathing, or physical activity into your routine.

3. Develop a Plan for Getting Back on Track:

When setbacks happen, having a plan in place can help you get back on track more quickly. This plan might include reaching out to a friend for support, revisiting your goals, or engaging in a specific activity that reinforces your commitment to heart health.

4. Practice Self-Compassion:

Be kind to yourself when setbacks occur. Remember that change is a process, and it's normal to encounter obstacles along the way. Treat yourself with the same compassion you would offer to a friend in a similar situation.

The Role of Social Support in Long-Term Success

Social support is a powerful factor in sustaining heart-healthy habits. Surrounding yourself with people who encourage and support your goals can make a significant difference in your ability to maintain a healthy lifestyle.

1. Share Your Goals with Others:

Let your friends, family, and colleagues know about your heart-health goals. Sharing your intentions with others not only increases your accountability but also helps them understand your choices and offer support.

2. Engage in Group Activities:

Participating in group activities, such as exercise classes, cooking workshops, or community health programs, can provide a sense of camaraderie and motivation. Being part of a group with similar goals can make the journey more enjoyable and less isolating.

3. Seek Out a Supportive Community:

If you don't have a strong support network in your immediate environment, consider seeking out online communities, support groups, or social media groups focused on heart health. These communities can provide valuable advice, encouragement, and a sense of belonging.

4. Be a Source of Support for Others:

Supporting others in their heart-health journey can also reinforce your own commitment. Whether it's offering to go on a walk with a friend, sharing healthy recipes, or simply providing words of encouragement, being a source of support can strengthen your own resolve.

5. Involve Your Family:

Incorporate your family into your heart-healthy lifestyle. Prepare meals together, engage in physical activities as a family, and create an environment at home that supports everyone's health. When your loved ones are involved, it becomes easier to maintain your habits and achieve long-term success.

By building sustainable habits, setting realistic goals, understanding the stages of behavior change, reinforcing positive habits daily, overcoming setbacks, and leveraging social support, you can create a heart-healthy lifestyle that lasts a lifetime. Remember, the journey to better heart health is ongoing, and each step you take brings you closer to a healthier, happier life.

Maintaining Progress

Embarking on a heart-healthy diet is an important step, but maintaining your progress over the long term is where the real impact on your health is made. Staying on track requires commitment, ongoing effort, and a willingness to adapt as your needs change. In this section, we'll explore strategies to help you maintain your progress, including tracking your diet and exercise, the importance of regular health check-ups, adapting your diet over time, keeping your meals enjoyable and varied, and continuing to educate yourself on heart health.

Tracking Your Diet and Exercise

One of the most effective ways to maintain progress is by tracking your diet and exercise. Monitoring your habits helps you stay accountable, identify patterns, and make informed adjustments to your routine.

1. The Benefits of Tracking:

Tracking what you eat and how much you exercise provides valuable insights into your behaviors and progress. It can help you:

- **Stay Accountable:** Writing down your meals and activities makes you more conscious of your choices and less likely to deviate from your goals.

- **Identify Patterns:** Tracking allows you to see patterns in your eating and exercise habits, such as times when you're more likely to indulge or skip workouts. Recognizing these patterns helps you develop strategies to address them.

- **Celebrate Progress:** Seeing your progress over time can be highly motivating. Whether it's losing weight, lowering your blood pressure, or increasing your stamina, tracking allows you to celebrate your successes.

2. Tools for Tracking:

There are several tools you can use to track your diet and exercise:

- **Journals:** A simple notebook or a dedicated food and exercise journal can be an effective way to record your meals, workouts, and how you feel each day.

- **Apps:** Many apps, such as MyFitnessPal, Lose It!, or Fitbit, offer easy ways to log your food intake and physical activity. These apps often include features like calorie counting, nutrient tracking, and exercise logging.

- **Wearable Devices:** Fitness trackers like Fitbit, Garmin, or Apple Watch can monitor your physical activity, heart rate, and even sleep patterns. These devices often sync with apps to give you a comprehensive view of your health data.

3. What to Track:

When tracking your diet and exercise, consider including the following:

- **Food Intake:** Record what you eat, including portion sizes, to monitor your nutrient intake and ensure you're meeting your dietary goals.

- **Exercise:** Track the type, duration, and intensity of your workouts. This helps you ensure you're getting a balanced mix of aerobic, strength, and flexibility exercises.

- **Mood and Energy Levels:** Note how you feel before and after eating or exercising. This can help you identify how different foods and activities impact your mood, energy, and overall well-being.

- **Health Metrics:** Keep track of key health metrics like weight, blood pressure, cholesterol levels, and blood sugar. Regularly monitoring these metrics helps you see how your lifestyle changes are affecting your health.

The Importance of Regular Health Check-Ups

Regular health check-ups are a critical component of maintaining heart health. They provide an opportunity to monitor your progress, detect any potential issues early, and adjust your diet and lifestyle as needed.

1. Regular Monitoring:

Regular visits to your healthcare provider allow you to monitor important health indicators such as blood pressure, cholesterol levels, blood sugar, and weight. These metrics provide valuable information about your cardiovascular health and can highlight areas that may need attention.

- **Blood Pressure:** High blood pressure is a major risk factor for heart disease. Regular monitoring can help you and your doctor catch any increases early and make necessary adjustments to your lifestyle or medications.

- **Cholesterol Levels:** Monitoring your LDL (bad) cholesterol, HDL (good) cholesterol, and triglycerides helps assess your risk for atherosclerosis and other cardiovascular issues.

- **Blood Sugar:** If you have or are at risk for diabetes, regular blood sugar checks are essential for managing your condition and reducing the risk of heart disease.

2. Preventive Screenings:

In addition to routine check-ups, preventive screenings are important for early detection of heart disease and other related conditions. These screenings may include:

- **Electrocardiogram (ECG):** An ECG measures the electrical activity of your heart and can detect irregularities that may indicate heart problems.

- **Stress Test:** A stress test assesses how your heart performs under physical stress and can help diagnose coronary artery disease.

- **Lipid Panel:** A lipid panel measures your cholesterol and triglyceride levels, providing insight into your risk for heart disease.

3. Discussing Your Progress:

Use your check-ups as an opportunity to discuss your progress with your healthcare provider. Share any challenges you've faced and ask for advice on how to overcome them. Your provider can offer personalized recommendations based on your current health status and goals.

4. Staying Proactive:

Don't wait for symptoms to appear before seeing your doctor. Regular check-ups allow you to stay proactive about your health, catching potential issues early and addressing them before they become serious.

Adapting Your Diet as Your Needs Change

Your dietary needs can change over time due to factors such as aging, changes in activity level, weight loss or gain, and the development of new health conditions. It's important to regularly reassess your diet and make adjustments to ensure it continues to meet your nutritional needs and support your heart health.

1. Adjusting Caloric Intake:

As you age, your metabolism may slow down, which means you might require fewer calories than you did when you were younger. If your activity level decreases, you may also need to reduce your caloric intake to avoid weight gain. Conversely, if you become more active, you might need to increase your caloric intake to support your energy needs.

2. Modifying Macronutrient Ratios:

Your macronutrient needs (carbohydrates, proteins, and fats) may also change over time. For example:

- **Protein:** As you age, your body may require more protein to maintain muscle mass and support overall health. Incorporate lean sources of protein, such as fish, poultry, beans, and tofu, into your diet.

- **Fats:** Focus on getting healthy fats from sources like olive oil, avocados, nuts, and fatty fish. These fats are beneficial for heart health and can help manage cholesterol levels.

- **Carbohydrates:** Choose complex carbohydrates, such as whole grains, fruits, and vegetables, which provide sustained energy and fiber. If you're managing blood sugar levels, you may need to adjust your carbohydrate intake accordingly.

3. Adapting to Health Conditions:

If you develop a new health condition, such as diabetes, high blood pressure, or kidney disease, your dietary needs may change. Work with a healthcare provider or a registered dietitian to adjust your diet to manage your condition while continuing to support heart health.

4. Staying Flexible:

Your dietary needs are not static, so it's important to stay flexible and open to making changes as necessary. Regularly reassess your diet, and don't be afraid to try new foods or adjust your eating habits to better suit your current lifestyle and health goals.

Keeping the Diet Enjoyable and Varied

A heart-healthy diet should be enjoyable, not restrictive. Keeping your meals varied and flavorful is key to maintaining your diet over the long term.

1. Experiment with New Recipes:

Trying new recipes is a great way to keep your meals interesting and prevent boredom. Explore different cuisines and cooking methods to discover new flavors and textures. Look for heart-healthy recipes that incorporate a variety of fruits, vegetables, whole grains, and lean proteins.

2. Use Herbs and Spices:

Herbs and spices are powerful tools for adding flavor to your meals without relying on added salt, sugar, or unhealthy fats. Experiment with different combinations to enhance the taste of your dishes and keep your meals exciting.

3. Seasonal Eating:

Eating seasonally ensures that you're getting the freshest, most flavorful produce available. Seasonal fruits and vegetables are often more nutrient-dense and can inspire you to try new ingredients that you might not have considered before.

4. Mindful Indulgence:

Allow yourself to enjoy occasional treats in moderation. Whether it's a piece of dark chocolate, a slice of homemade cake, or a glass of wine, mindful indulgence can help you maintain a healthy relationship with food and prevent feelings of deprivation.

5. Social Dining:

Enjoying meals with family and friends is an important aspect of a healthy lifestyle. Social dining can make mealtime more enjoyable and provide opportunities to share heart-healthy recipes and cooking tips with others.

Continuing Education: Staying Informed on Heart Health

Staying informed about the latest research and recommendations in heart health is crucial for maintaining your progress and adapting your lifestyle as needed. Continuing education empowers you to make informed decisions and stay motivated on your journey to better heart health.

1. Stay Updated on Research:

Heart health research is continually evolving, with new studies shedding light on how diet, exercise, and other lifestyle factors impact cardiovascular health. Stay updated on the latest findings by reading reputable sources, such as scientific journals, health websites, or newsletters from heart health organizations.

2. Attend Workshops and Seminars:

Many communities offer workshops, seminars, and webinars on heart health, nutrition, and wellness. Attending these events can provide you with valuable knowledge, practical tips, and the opportunity to connect with others who share your health goals.

3. Consult with Experts:

Regular consultations with healthcare providers, registered dietitians, or nutritionists can help you stay informed and receive personalized advice. These experts can provide guidance on how to incorporate new research findings into your lifestyle and help you navigate any challenges you encounter.

4. Join a Community:

Consider joining a community or support group focused on heart health. These groups often share resources, offer encouragement, and provide a sense of camaraderie. Being part of a community can help you stay motivated and committed to your heart-healthy lifestyle.

5. Keep Learning:

Heart health is a lifelong journey, and there's always something new to learn. Whether it's discovering a new superfood, trying a different form of exercise, or exploring the impact of stress management on heart health, continue to educate yourself and apply what you learn to your daily life.

By tracking your diet and exercise, regularly checking in with your healthcare provider, adapting your diet as your needs change, keeping your meals enjoyable and varied, and staying informed about heart health, you can maintain your progress and continue to improve your cardiovascular health over the long term. Remember, the key to success is consistency, flexibility, and a commitment to lifelong learning and self-care.

Chapter 9: Advanced Heart-Healthy Topics

As you continue your journey toward a heart-healthy lifestyle, you may find yourself ready to explore more advanced topics that can help you tailor your diet and lifestyle to your specific needs. In this chapter, we'll delve into the concept of personalized nutrition, how genetics can influence your diet, ways to tailor your eating habits to your unique health profile, the role of supplements in heart health, emerging research on heart-healthy foods, and the use of technology tools to monitor your cardiovascular health. These insights will empower you to make more informed decisions and take your heart health to the next level.

Personalized Nutrition

Personalized nutrition is an emerging field that focuses on tailoring dietary recommendations to an individual's specific needs, preferences, and genetic makeup. Unlike one-size-fits-all dietary guidelines, personalized nutrition considers the unique characteristics that make each person different.

1. The Concept of Personalized Nutrition:

Personalized nutrition goes beyond general dietary advice by considering factors such as your genetics, lifestyle, health status, and personal preferences. This approach aims to optimize your diet for your specific health goals, whether it's managing cholesterol levels, controlling blood pressure, or reducing inflammation.

- **Example:** Two individuals with high cholesterol might receive different dietary recommendations based on their genetic predisposition, metabolic rate, and response to certain foods.

2. Benefits of Personalized Nutrition:

- **Improved Outcomes:** By tailoring your diet to your specific needs, personalized nutrition can lead to better health outcomes, such as more effective weight management, improved cholesterol levels, and better blood sugar control.

- **Sustainability:** Personalized recommendations are more likely to fit into your lifestyle and preferences, making them easier to follow and maintain over the long term.

- **Prevention:** Understanding your unique risk factors allows you to take preventive measures before health issues arise, helping you stay ahead of potential problems.

3. How to Access Personalized Nutrition:

To access personalized nutrition advice, you can work with a registered dietitian or nutritionist who specializes in this area. Some healthcare providers also offer genetic testing that can provide insights into how your body responds to certain nutrients. Additionally, several companies offer at-home genetic tests that provide personalized dietary recommendations based on your DNA.

How Genetics Influence Your Diet Needs

Genetics play a significant role in how your body processes nutrients and how you respond to different foods. Understanding your genetic predispositions can help you make more informed dietary choices.

1. Nutrigenomics:

Nutrigenomics is the study of how your genes interact with the foods you eat. It explores how certain genetic variations can affect your risk of developing chronic conditions, such as heart disease, and how your diet can influence the expression of thoco gonoε.

- **Example:** Some people have a genetic variant that affects how their body processes fats, making them more prone to high cholesterol when they consume a diet high in saturated fats. By understanding this, they can tailor their diet to include more unsaturated fats and reduce their risk of heart disease.

2. Common Genetic Variants:

There are several genetic variants that can influence your dietary needs and health outcomes:

- **APOE Gene:** Variants of the APOE gene can affect cholesterol levels and the risk of cardiovascular disease. Individuals with certain APOE variants may need to be more cautious about their fat intake.

- **FTO Gene:** The FTO gene is associated with obesity. People with certain variants of this gene may be more likely to gain weight and might benefit from a diet lower in refined carbohydrates.

- **MTHFR Gene:** Variants of the MTHFR gene can affect how the body processes folate, which is important for heart health. Individuals with these variants may need to ensure they get enough folate through diet or supplements.

3. Genetic Testing and Diet:

Genetic testing can provide insights into how your body processes nutrients and identify potential risks for certain conditions. While genetic testing is not a crystal ball, it can offer valuable information that, when combined with other factors like lifestyle and health history, can help you make more personalized dietary choices.

- **Considerations:** Before undergoing genetic testing, it's important to consult with a healthcare provider or genetic counselor to understand the implications of the results and how to interpret them.

Tailoring Your Diet to Your Specific Health Profile

As you age or as your health status changes, your dietary needs may evolve. Tailoring your diet to your specific health profile ensures that you're meeting your nutritional needs and supporting your heart health.

1. Age-Related Dietary Adjustments:

As you get older, your metabolism slows down, and your body's nutritional needs change. You may need fewer calories but more of certain nutrients, such as calcium, vitamin D, and protein, to maintain bone density, muscle mass, and overall health.

- **Focus on Nutrient Density:** Choose foods that provide more nutrients per calorie, such as fruits, vegetables, whole grains, lean proteins, and healthy fats. This helps you meet your nutritional needs without overeating.

- **Stay Hydrated:** Older adults are more prone to dehydration, so it's important to drink plenty of water and include hydrating foods like fruits and vegetables in your diet.

2. Managing Chronic Conditions:

If you have a chronic condition, such as diabetes, hypertension, or high cholesterol, your diet may need to be adjusted to help manage these conditions.

- **Diabetes:** Focus on controlling blood sugar levels by choosing low-glycemic foods, such as whole grains, non-starchy vegetables, and lean proteins. Monitor carbohydrate intake and pair carbs with protein and healthy fats to prevent spikes in blood sugar.

- **Hypertension:** A diet rich in potassium, magnesium, and calcium can help lower blood pressure. Incorporate foods like leafy greens, bananas, sweet potatoes, and low-fat dairy into your meals while reducing sodium intake.

- **High Cholesterol:** Choose foods that help lower LDL cholesterol, such as oats, nuts, fatty fish, and avocados. Reduce intake of saturated fats and trans fats.

3. Dietary Adjustments for Specific Goals:

Whether your goal is weight loss, muscle gain, or improving athletic performance, tailoring your diet to your specific goals can enhance your results.

- **Weight Loss:** Focus on creating a calorie deficit by reducing portion sizes, choosing lower-calorie foods, and increasing physical activity. Prioritize whole, unprocessed foods that keep you full and satisfied.

- **Muscle Gain:** Increase your protein intake to support muscle repair and growth. Incorporate strength training exercises into your routine and ensure you're consuming enough calories to fuel your workouts.

- **Athletic Performance:** Depending on your sport, you may need to adjust your macronutrient ratios. Endurance athletes may benefit from a higher carbohydrate intake, while strength athletes might prioritize protein.

The Role of Supplements in Heart Health

While a balanced diet is the foundation of good health, certain supplements can play a role in supporting heart health, especially if you have specific nutrient deficiencies or increased needs.

1. Omega-3 Fatty Acids:

Omega-3 fatty acids, found in fish oil supplements, have been shown to reduce inflammation, lower triglycerides, and support overall heart health. If you don't consume enough fatty fish (such as salmon, mackerel, or sardines), an omega-3 supplement may be beneficial.

- **Dosage:** A typical dose of omega-3s ranges from 1,000 to 3,000 mg per day, but it's best to consult with your healthcare provider for personalized recommendations.

2. Fiber Supplements:

If you struggle to get enough fiber from your diet, a fiber supplement can help lower cholesterol levels and improve digestion. Psyllium husk, in particular, has been shown to reduce LDL cholesterol.

- **Dosage:** Aim for 25-30 grams of fiber per day, including both dietary and supplemental sources.

3. Coenzyme Q10 (CoQ10):

CoQ10 is an antioxidant that plays a key role in energy production and may help improve heart function, particularly in individuals with heart failure or those taking statin medications, which can deplete CoQ10 levels.

- **Dosage:** A common dose of CoQ10 ranges from 100 to 200 mg per day.

4. Magnesium:

Magnesium supports heart health by helping to regulate blood pressure and maintain a steady heartbeat. Many people don't get enough magnesium through diet alone, making supplementation beneficial.

- **Dosage:** The recommended daily intake of magnesium is 310-420 mg, depending on age and sex.

5. Vitamin D:

Vitamin D is essential for bone health and immune function, and emerging research suggests it may also play a role in heart health. If you're deficient in vitamin D, a supplement can help.

- **Dosage:** The recommended daily intake of vitamin D varies, but many experts suggest 600-800 IU per day. Your healthcare provider can determine the right dose based on your blood levels.

Emerging Research on Heart-Healthy Foods

Scientific research is continually uncovering new insights into how certain foods can impact heart health. Staying informed about these developments can help you make more informed dietary choices.

1. Plant-Based Diets:

Research continues to support the benefits of plant-based diets for heart health. Diets rich in fruits, vegetables, whole grains, legumes, and nuts are associated with lower risks of heart disease, hypertension, and high cholesterol.

- **Focus on Whole Foods:** Whole, unprocessed plant foods are rich in fiber, antioxidants, and other nutrients that support heart health. Consider incorporating more plant-based meals into your diet, even if you don't follow a fully vegetarian or vegan diet.

2. Fermented Foods:

Emerging research suggests that fermented foods, such as yogurt, kefir, kimchi, and sauerkraut, may benefit heart health by supporting a healthy gut microbiome. A balanced gut microbiome can reduce inflammation and improve cholesterol levels.

- **Include Probiotics:** Probiotic-rich foods can enhance the health of your gut microbiome, which in turn supports cardiovascular health. Aim to include a variety of fermented foods in your diet.

3. Dark Chocolate:

Studies have shown that dark chocolate, particularly varieties with a high cocoa content (70% or more), can have heart-protective effects due to its high levels of flavonoids, which are antioxidants that improve blood flow and reduce inflammation.

- **Moderation is Key:** Enjoy dark chocolate in moderation, as it is still high in calories and can contribute to weight gain if consumed in excess.

4. Olive Oil:

Olive oil, especially extra virgin olive oil, is a staple of the Mediterranean diet and is rich in monounsaturated fats and antioxidants. Research shows that olive oil can reduce the risk of heart disease by lowering LDL cholesterol and reducing inflammation.

- **Use Daily:** Incorporate olive oil into your diet by using it as a salad dressing, drizzling it over cooked vegetables, or using it as a healthy cooking oil.

Technology Tools for Monitoring Your Heart Health

Advances in technology have made it easier than ever to monitor your heart health and make informed decisions about your diet and lifestyle.

1. Wearable Devices:

Wearable devices like fitness trackers and smartwatches can monitor various aspects of your health, including heart rate, physical activity, sleep patterns, and even electrocardiograms (ECGs). These devices provide real-time data that can help you stay on top of your heart health.

- **Popular Options:** Devices like the Apple Watch, Fitbit, and Garmin offer heart rate monitoring, activity tracking, and other health metrics. Some models also include ECG functionality, which can detect irregular heart rhythms.

2. Mobile Apps:

There are numerous apps available that can help you track your diet, exercise, and overall health. These apps can provide insights into your habits, offer personalized recommendations, and help you stay accountable.

- **Diet Tracking Apps:** MyFitnessPal, Lose It!, and Cronometer are popular apps that allow you to log your food intake, track your nutrients, and set dietary goals.

- **Fitness Apps:** Apps like Strava, Nike Training Club, and Fitbit Coach offer guided workouts, activity tracking, and motivational tools to keep you moving.

3. Telemedicine and Online Consultations:

Telemedicine has made it easier to consult with healthcare providers and specialists from the comfort of your home. This can be particularly useful for regular check-ups, discussing test results, and getting personalized advice on managing your heart health.

- **Scheduling Virtual Appointments:** Many healthcare providers now offer telemedicine services. You can schedule virtual appointments for consultations, follow-ups, and ongoing care.

4. Blood Pressure Monitors:

Home blood pressure monitors allow you to keep track of your blood pressure between doctor visits. Regular monitoring can help you detect any changes early and take action if necessary.

- **Choosing a Monitor:** Look for a clinically validated blood pressure monitor that fits your needs. Some models sync with mobile apps, allowing you to track and share your readings with your healthcare provider.

By exploring these advanced heart-healthy topics, you can deepen your understanding of how to optimize your diet and lifestyle for your unique needs. Personalized nutrition, genetic insights, tailored diets, strategic use of supplements, and emerging research all contribute to a more nuanced approach to heart health. Leveraging technology tools can further enhance your ability to monitor and manage your cardiovascular well-being, empowering you to take control of your heart health and continue progressing on your journey to a healthier life.

Future Trends in Heart Health

As our understanding of heart health continues to evolve, so do the strategies and approaches we use to protect and improve cardiovascular well-being. With advances in research, nutrition, and technology, several key trends are shaping the future of heart health. These trends include the growing popularity of plant-based diets, the emerging role of probiotics and gut health, new insights into the Mediterranean diet, the rise of functional foods, and the potential of personalized medicine. By staying informed about these trends, you can continue to make informed decisions that support your heart health.

The Growing Popularity of Plant-Based Diets

Plant-based diets are gaining widespread popularity, not just among vegetarians and vegans but also among those looking to reduce their consumption of animal products for health, environmental, and ethical reasons. Research consistently shows that plant-based diets are associated with a lower risk of heart disease, making them a powerful tool for promoting cardiovascular health.

1. What is a Plant-Based Diet?

A plant-based diet emphasizes whole, minimally processed plant foods, including fruits, vegetables, legumes, whole grains, nuts, and seeds. While some people choose to eliminate animal products entirely, others may follow a flexitarian approach, which includes occasional consumption of meat, dairy, and eggs.

- **Benefits for Heart Health:** Plant-based diets are naturally low in saturated fat and cholesterol and high in fiber, antioxidants, and phytonutrients, all of which contribute to heart health. Studies have shown that individuals who follow plant-based diets tend to have lower blood pressure, cholesterol levels, and body weight, reducing their overall risk of heart disease.

2. Transitioning to a Plant-Based Diet:

If you're considering incorporating more plant-based meals into your diet, it's important to do so in a way that ensures you're getting all the necessary nutrients.

- **Start Gradually:** Begin by adding more plant-based meals to your weekly routine. For example, you might start with "Meatless Mondays" and gradually increase the number of plant-based meals you eat each week.

- **Focus on Variety:** A well-rounded plant-based diet includes a variety of foods to ensure you're getting all the essential nutrients. Incorporate a range of fruits, vegetables, legumes, whole grains, nuts, and seeds into your meals.

- **Pay Attention to Protein:** While plant-based diets can provide ample protein, it's important to include protein-rich foods like beans, lentils, tofu, tempeh, and quinoa in your meals. Combining different plant proteins can help ensure you're getting all the essential amino acids.

3. Addressing Potential Nutrient Gaps:

While plant-based diets are generally nutrient-dense, there are a few nutrients that may require special attention:

- **Vitamin B12:** Vitamin B12 is primarily found in animal products, so those on a strict plant-based diet should consider fortified foods or supplements to meet their needs.

- **Iron:** Plant-based sources of iron are less easily absorbed by the body than animal sources. To enhance absorption, pair iron-rich plant foods like lentils and spinach with vitamin C-rich foods like citrus fruits or bell peppers.

- **Omega-3 Fatty Acids:** While fish is a common source of omega-3s, plant-based sources include flaxseeds, chia seeds, walnuts, and algae-based supplements.

The Role of Probiotics and Gut Health

The gut microbiome—the community of trillions of bacteria and other microorganisms living in your digestive tract—plays a crucial role in overall health, including heart health. Emerging research suggests that the balance of bacteria in your gut can influence inflammation, cholesterol levels, and even blood pressure, making probiotics and gut health an exciting area of focus in cardiovascular care.

1. Understanding the Gut-Heart Connection:

The gut microbiome interacts with the body in ways that can directly affect heart health. For example, certain gut bacteria produce compounds that help regulate cholesterol metabolism, while others may influence blood pressure and inflammation.

- **Inflammation:** Chronic inflammation is a known risk factor for heart disease. A healthy gut microbiome helps regulate the immune system and reduce inflammation, which can protect the heart.

- **Cholesterol:** Some gut bacteria can produce compounds that help lower LDL (bad) cholesterol and increase HDL (good) cholesterol. By promoting a healthy balance of gut bacteria, you may be able to positively influence your cholesterol levels.

2. Incorporating Probiotics into Your Diet:

Probiotics are live bacteria that can benefit your health when consumed in adequate amounts. They are found in fermented foods and supplements.

- **Food Sources:** Include probiotic-rich foods in your diet, such as yogurt, kefir, sauerkraut, kimchi, miso, and kombucha. These foods can help populate your gut with beneficial bacteria.

- **Prebiotics:** Prebiotics are non-digestible fibers that feed the beneficial bacteria in your gut. Foods like garlic, onions, bananas, asparagus, and whole grains are excellent sources of prebiotics.

3. The Future of Probiotics and Heart Health:

As research continues to explore the gut-heart connection, we may see more targeted probiotic strains and supplements designed specifically to support heart health. Personalized probiotics based on an individual's unique microbiome may also become more common, allowing for more tailored approaches to maintaining cardiovascular health.

New Insights into the Mediterranean Diet

The Mediterranean diet has long been celebrated for its heart-healthy benefits, and new research continues to shed light on why this eating pattern is so effective at reducing the risk of heart disease.

1. Key Components of the Mediterranean Diet:

The Mediterranean diet is rich in fruits, vegetables, whole grains, legumes, nuts, seeds, and olive oil, with moderate consumption of fish, poultry, and dairy, and limited intake of red meat and sweets. This diet also emphasizes the importance of enjoying meals with family and friends and leading an active lifestyle.

- **Healthy Fats:** Olive oil, a staple of the Mediterranean diet, is rich in monounsaturated fats and antioxidants, which help reduce inflammation and improve heart health.

- **Omega-3 Fatty Acids:** Fatty fish, such as salmon, mackerel, and sardines, provide omega-3 fatty acids, which are known for their protective effects on the heart.

2. The Longevity Factor:

Research has shown that the Mediterranean diet is associated not only with a lower risk of heart disease but also with increased longevity. The combination of nutrient-rich foods, healthy fats, and a focus on whole foods contributes to overall health and well-being.

- **Polyphenols:** The Mediterranean diet is rich in polyphenols, a type of antioxidant found in foods like olives, berries, red wine, and dark chocolate. Polyphenols have been shown to protect against oxidative stress and inflammation, both of which are linked to heart disease.

3. Adapting the Mediterranean Diet:

While the Mediterranean diet originates from the regions surrounding the Mediterranean Sea, its principles can be adapted to different cultures and cuisines. The key is to focus on whole, minimally processed foods, healthy fats, and a variety of fruits and vegetables.

- **Cultural Adaptations:** Whether you live in Asia, Africa, or the Americas, you can apply the principles of the Mediterranean diet to your local cuisine. For example, you might use avocado oil instead of olive oil or incorporate local fish and produce into your meals.

Functional Foods: What's on the Horizon?

Functional foods are foods that have been enhanced with additional nutrients or compounds that provide health benefits beyond basic nutrition. As interest in these foods grows, the market is seeing an influx of products designed to support heart health and overall well-being.

1. The Rise of Functional Foods:

Functional foods are becoming increasingly popular as consumers seek out foods that do more than just satisfy hunger. These foods are often fortified with vitamins, minerals, fiber, probiotics, or antioxidants and are marketed for their specific health benefits.

- **Examples of Functional Foods:** Common examples include fortified breakfast cereals, probiotic yogurts, omega-3 enriched eggs, and beverages infused with plant sterols or antioxidants.

2. Heart-Healthy Functional Foods:

Several functional foods are specifically designed to support heart health. These include:

- **Plant Sterols and Stanols:** These compounds, found naturally in small amounts in certain fruits, vegetables, nuts, and seeds, have been shown to lower cholesterol levels. Some margarine spreads, orange juices, and yogurt drinks are fortified with plant sterols and stanols.
- **Fiber-Enriched Foods:** Foods fortified with soluble fiber, such as certain cereals and snack bars, can help lower LDL cholesterol and improve heart health.

3. The Future of Functional Foods:

As research continues to uncover the health benefits of various nutrients and compounds, we can expect to see more innovative functional foods designed to target specific health concerns, including heart health. Personalized functional foods, tailored to an individual's genetic profile and health needs, may also become a reality in the near future.

The Potential of Personalized Medicine in Heart Health

Personalized medicine, also known as precision medicine, is an emerging approach that tailors medical treatment to the individual characteristics of each patient. This approach holds great promise for the future of heart health, as it allows for more targeted and effective interventions.

1. What is Personalized Medicine?

Personalized medicine takes into account an individual's genetic makeup, environment, and lifestyle to develop more precise and effective treatment plans. In the context of heart health, this could mean personalized dietary recommendations, exercise plans, and medication regimens based on a person's unique risk factors.

- **Genetic Testing:** Genetic testing can identify specific genetic variants that influence how your body responds to certain medications, foods, and lifestyle factors. This information can be used to tailor treatment plans that are more likely to be effective for you.

2. Personalized Nutrition and Heart Health:

As mentioned earlier, personalized nutrition is a key component of personalized medicine. By understanding how your genetics influence your response to different foods, you can make more informed choices that support your heart health.

- **Example:** If genetic testing reveals that you are at higher risk for high cholesterol due to a variant in the APOE gene, your healthcare provider may recommend a diet that is particularly low in saturated fats and high in fiber and omega-3 fatty acids.

3. The Future of Heart Health Management:

As personalized medicine continues to evolve, it has the potential to revolutionize the way we manage heart health. In the future, we may see:

- **Tailored Medication Plans:** Medications prescribed based on an individual's genetic makeup, reducing the risk of side effects and increasing effectiveness.

- **Preventive Care:** Proactive strategies to prevent heart disease based on genetic risk factors, including personalized lifestyle interventions and monitoring.

- **Integration of Technology:** The use of wearable devices, apps, and other technologies to collect real-time health data that informs personalized treatment plans.

4. The Role of Big Data and AI:

Big data and artificial intelligence (AI) are playing an increasingly important role in personalized medicine. By analyzing large datasets, AI can identify patterns and correlations that may not be apparent to humans, leading to more accurate predictions and treatment recommendations.

- **AI in Heart Health:** AI algorithms can analyze data from genetic tests, wearable devices, and electronic health records to provide personalized insights and recommendations for managing heart health.

By staying informed about these future trends in heart health, you can continue to adapt your lifestyle and make choices that support your long-term cardiovascular well-being. Whether it's embracing a plant-based diet, optimizing your gut health, exploring the benefits of functional foods, or taking advantage of the latest advances in personalized medicine, these emerging strategies offer new opportunities to protect and enhance your heart health.

Chapter 10: Special Considerations and FAQs

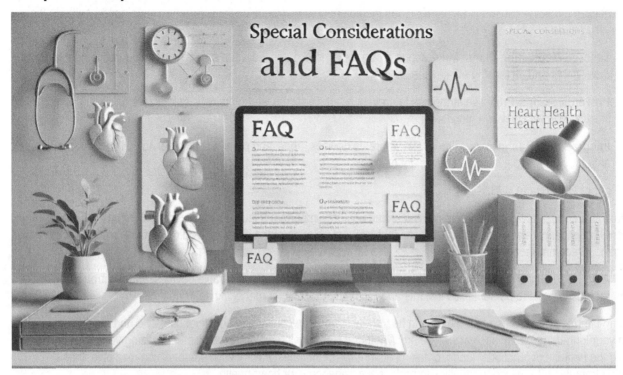

When it comes to heart-healthy eating, one size does not fit all. Our nutritional needs evolve throughout different stages of life, and other factors such as gender, health conditions, and life circumstances can significantly influence dietary requirements. This chapter addresses how to adapt a heart-healthy diet to various life stages and situations, including teens and young adults, women's heart health, aging adults, managing diabetes, and considerations for pregnant women and new mothers.

Adapting the Diet for Different Life Stages

Throughout your life, your body's nutritional needs change, and it's important to adapt your diet accordingly to maintain heart health. Whether you're a teenager, an adult, or a senior, each stage of life presents unique challenges and opportunities for maintaining a heart-healthy diet.

Heart-Healthy Eating for Teens and Young Adults

The teenage and young adult years are critical periods for establishing lifelong eating habits. During these years, the body undergoes significant growth and development, which increases nutritional needs. However, this is also a time when dietary choices can be influenced by peer pressure, fast food culture, and busy lifestyles, leading to habits that may negatively impact heart health.

1. Nutritional Needs for Growth and Development:

- **Calcium and Vitamin D:** These nutrients are essential for bone development during adolescence. Encourage the consumption of dairy products, fortified plant-based milk, and leafy greens to support bone health.

- **Iron:** Iron needs increase during adolescence, particularly for young women due to menstruation. Include iron-rich foods like lean meats, beans, lentils, and fortified cereals, paired with vitamin C-rich foods to enhance absorption.

- **Fiber:** Encourage the consumption of whole grains, fruits, and vegetables to support digestive health and help establish heart-healthy habits early on.

2. Addressing Common Challenges:

- **Fast Food and Processed Snacks:** Teens and young adults often gravitate toward fast food and processed snacks that are high in unhealthy fats, sugar, and sodium. Encourage healthier alternatives, such as homemade versions of favorite snacks, and educate them on reading nutrition labels.

- **Skipping Meals:** Busy schedules may lead to skipped meals, particularly breakfast, which can result in overeating later in the day. Emphasize the importance of regular meals and provide quick, easy-to-prepare options like smoothies, whole-grain toast with nut butter, or yogurt with fruit.

- **Sugar-Sweetened Beverages:** Excessive consumption of sugary drinks is common in this age group. Encourage water, herbal teas, or naturally flavored seltzers as healthier alternatives.

3. Building Lifelong Habits:

- **Involvement in Meal Planning:** Encourage teens and young adults to get involved in meal planning and preparation. This not only teaches valuable life skills but also increases the likelihood that they'll make healthier choices.

- **Education and Awareness:** Educate young people about the long-term benefits of a heart-healthy diet, including reduced risk of chronic diseases. Empower them to make informed choices that will benefit their health now and in the future.

Diet Adjustments for Women's Heart Health

Women's heart health is influenced by unique factors, including hormonal changes throughout life, pregnancy, and menopause. These factors can affect how women experience heart disease and their nutritional needs.

1. Understanding the Impact of Hormones:

- **Estrogen and Heart Health:** Estrogen has a protective effect on the heart, helping to maintain healthy cholesterol levels and blood vessel function. However, after menopause, estrogen levels decline, which can increase the risk of heart disease.

- **Menopause and Cholesterol:** Post-menopausal women often experience an increase in LDL (bad) cholesterol and a decrease in HDL (good) cholesterol. It's important to focus on a diet rich in fiber, healthy fats, and antioxidants to manage these changes.

2. Nutritional Considerations for Women:

- **Calcium and Vitamin D:** Women are at higher risk for osteoporosis, particularly after menopause. Ensure adequate intake of calcium and vitamin D to support bone health. Include dairy products, fortified plant-based milks, leafy greens, and fatty fish in the diet.

- **Folate:** Folate is essential for women of childbearing age to prevent birth defects, but it also plays a role in heart health by helping to regulate homocysteine levels, which are associated with cardiovascular risk. Include leafy greens, beans, citrus fruits, and fortified grains.

- **Omega-3 Fatty Acids:** These healthy fats support heart health by reducing inflammation and lowering triglyceride levels. Include sources like salmon, flaxseeds, chia seeds, and walnuts in your diet.

3. Special Considerations During Pregnancy:

- **Increased Nutrient Needs:** Pregnancy increases the need for certain nutrients, such as folate, iron, calcium, and protein. Focus on nutrient-dense foods that provide these essentials while avoiding excess sodium, added sugars, and unhealthy fats.

- **Managing Blood Pressure:** Some women experience elevated blood pressure during pregnancy (gestational hypertension). A diet low in sodium and rich in potassium, magnesium, and calcium can help manage blood pressure. Include foods like bananas, leafy greens, sweet potatoes, and yogurt.

Special Considerations for Aging Adults

As we age, our bodies undergo changes that can affect nutritional needs, metabolism, and overall health. Aging adults face unique challenges in maintaining a heart-healthy diet, but with the right strategies, it's possible to support heart health and overall well-being.

1. Nutritional Needs in Older Adults:

- **Protein:** Muscle mass tends to decrease with age, leading to a condition known as sarcopenia. To combat this, older adults should ensure adequate protein intake, including sources like lean meats, fish, eggs, beans, and dairy products.

- **Fiber:** Digestive health can decline with age, leading to constipation and other issues. A diet high in fiber from whole grains, fruits, vegetables, and legumes can help maintain regularity and support heart health.

- **Hydration:** Older adults are at higher risk of dehydration due to a reduced sense of thirst. Encourage regular water intake and include hydrating foods like fruits and vegetables.

2. Managing Age-Related Health Conditions:

- **Hypertension:** High blood pressure is common in older adults. A diet low in sodium and rich in potassium, magnesium, and calcium can help manage blood pressure. Consider the DASH (Dietary Approaches to Stop Hypertension) diet as a guide.

- **Cholesterol Management:** Aging can lead to increased cholesterol levels. Focus on reducing saturated and trans fats while incorporating more fiber and healthy fats from sources like nuts, seeds, and olive oil.

3. Adapting to Changes in Appetite and Taste:

- **Appetite Changes:** Aging can lead to a reduced appetite, which may result in inadequate nutrient intake. Focus on nutrient-dense foods and consider smaller, more frequent meals if large meals are unappealing.

- **Taste Changes:** Taste and smell often diminish with age, which can affect food enjoyment and intake. Experiment with herbs, spices, and other flavor enhancers to make meals more appealing without adding excess salt or sugar.

Adapting the Diet for Those with Diabetes

Diabetes management is closely linked to heart health, as people with diabetes are at a higher risk for cardiovascular disease. Adapting a heart-healthy diet to meet the needs of those with diabetes involves careful attention to carbohydrate intake, blood sugar control, and overall nutrition.

1. Balancing Carbohydrates:

- **Choose Complex Carbohydrates:** Opt for whole grains, legumes, and vegetables over refined grains and sugary foods. These complex carbohydrates provide steady energy and help manage blood sugar levels.

- **Portion Control:** Monitoring portion sizes of carbohydrate-rich foods is crucial for blood sugar management. Consider using tools like the plate method or carbohydrate counting to help regulate intake.

2. Incorporating Heart-Healthy Fats:

- **Focus on Unsaturated Fats:** Include sources of healthy fats like avocados, nuts, seeds, and olive oil, which support heart health and help improve cholesterol levels.

- **Limit Saturated and Trans Fats:** Avoid foods high in saturated and trans fats, such as fried foods, fatty cuts of meat, and processed snacks, as these can negatively impact both heart health and diabetes management.

3. Fiber and Blood Sugar Control:

- **Increase Fiber Intake:** Fiber helps slow the absorption of sugar and improve blood sugar control. Include high-fiber foods like oats, beans, fruits, and vegetables in your diet.

- **Monitor Glycemic Index:** Choose foods with a low glycemic index (GI) to minimize blood sugar spikes. Examples include most vegetables, whole grains, legumes, and some fruits.

4. Regular Monitoring and Adjustments:

- **Work with a Healthcare Provider:** It's important for individuals with diabetes to work closely with their healthcare provider or a registered dietitian to monitor blood sugar levels and make necessary dietary adjustments.

- **Stay Active:** Regular physical activity is key to managing diabetes and supporting heart health. Aim for a combination of aerobic exercise, strength training, and flexibility exercises.

Considerations for Pregnant Women and New Mothers

Pregnancy and the postpartum period bring unique nutritional challenges and needs. A heart-healthy diet during this time supports both the mother's health and the development of the baby.

1. Nutrient Needs During Pregnancy:

- **Folate:** Folate is essential for preventing neural tube defects in the developing baby. Include folate-rich foods like leafy greens, beans, and fortified grains.

- **Iron:** Pregnancy increases iron needs to support the increased blood volume and prevent anemia. Include iron-rich foods like lean meats, beans, and fortified cereals, and pair them with vitamin C-rich foods to enhance absorption.

- **Omega-3 Fatty Acids:** Omega-3s are important for the baby's brain development. Include sources like salmon, flaxseeds, and walnuts.

2. Managing Weight Gain:

- **Healthy Weight Gain:** Weight gain during pregnancy is normal and necessary, but it's important to manage it to avoid complications. Focus on nutrient-dense foods and avoid excessive intake of empty calories from sugary snacks and beverages.

- **Postpartum Weight Loss:** After childbirth, focus on gradual weight loss through a balanced diet and regular physical activity. Avoid crash diets, as they can deplete energy levels and negatively impact breastfeeding.

3. Supporting Breastfeeding:

- **Increased Caloric Needs:** Breastfeeding increases caloric needs, so it's important to consume enough calories to support milk production while maintaining a balanced diet.

- **Hydration:** Adequate hydration is essential for milk production. Drink plenty of water throughout the day and include hydrating foods in your diet.

- **Nutrient-Rich Foods:** Focus on nutrient-rich foods that support both your health and the quality of your breast milk. Include a variety of fruits, vegetables, whole grains, lean proteins, and healthy fats.

By adapting your diet to meet the specific needs of different life stages and health conditions, you can ensure that you're providing the best possible support for your heart health and overall well-being. Whether you're a teenager, an aging adult, a woman navigating pregnancy, or someone managing diabetes, these tailored approaches can help you maintain a heart-healthy lifestyle that fits your unique circumstances.

Frequently Asked Questions

Embarking on a heart-healthy diet often comes with questions and concerns. In this section, I've addressed some of the most common questions I've encountered in my practice, with the aim of providing you with clear, practical, and encouraging advice. Whether you're wondering about enjoying alcohol, managing social events, accommodating dietary restrictions, getting your family on board, or finding ongoing support, I'm here to guide you every step of the way.

Can I Enjoy Alcohol on a Heart-Healthy Diet?

Alcohol is a common part of many social and cultural traditions, and it's natural to wonder how it fits into a heart-healthy diet. The key with alcohol, as with many things in life, is moderation.

1. Understanding Moderation:

Moderate alcohol consumption is generally defined as up to one drink per day for women and up to two drinks per day for men. A "drink" is typically considered to be:

- 5 ounces of wine

- 12 ounces of beer

- 1.5 ounces of distilled spirits (such as whiskey, vodka, or gin)

Moderation is important because excessive alcohol consumption can lead to high blood pressure, heart failure, and an increased risk of stroke. It can also contribute to weight gain, which is a risk factor for heart disease.

2. Potential Benefits and Risks:

Some studies suggest that moderate alcohol consumption, particularly red wine, may have heart-protective benefits due to its content of antioxidants like resveratrol. However, these potential benefits must be weighed against the risks, and the consensus among health experts is that alcohol should not be consumed for the sole purpose of protecting the heart.

3. Making Smart Choices:

- **Choose Heart-Healthy Options:** If you choose to drink, consider red wine, which contains antioxidants that may benefit heart health. However, even with red wine, moderation is crucial.

- **Avoid High-Calorie Cocktails:** Many mixed drinks and cocktails are high in added sugars and calories. Opt for simpler options, such as a glass of wine, a light beer, or spirits mixed with soda water.

- **Stay Hydrated:** Alcohol can be dehydrating, so be sure to drink plenty of water, especially if you're consuming alcohol.

4. Consider Your Personal Health:

If you have certain health conditions, such as high blood pressure, liver disease, or a history of alcohol abuse, it may be best to avoid alcohol altogether. Always consult with your healthcare provider to determine what's right for you.

How Do I Manage Eating Out and Social Events?

Eating out and attending social events can be challenging when you're trying to stick to a heart-healthy diet, but it's entirely possible to enjoy these occasions while making mindful choices.

1. Planning Ahead:

Before heading out to a restaurant or social event, take a few minutes to plan ahead. Many restaurants have their menus available online, so you can review them in advance and decide on a healthy option. Look for dishes that are grilled, baked, or steamed rather than fried, and opt for meals that include plenty of vegetables.

- **Portion Control:** Restaurant portions are often larger than what you would serve at home. Consider splitting an entrée with someone, ordering a half-portion, or saving half of your meal to take home.

- **Ask for Modifications:** Don't hesitate to ask for modifications to make your meal healthier. For example, you can request that sauces and dressings be served on the side, or that your meal be prepared with less salt or oil.

2. Making Smart Choices at Buffets and Parties:

Social events often involve buffets or potlucks, where it's easy to overindulge. Here's how to navigate these situations:

- **Survey the Options:** Before filling your plate, take a look at all the options available. Choose the healthiest options first, such as salads, grilled proteins, and vegetable dishes.

- **Use a Smaller Plate:** If possible, choose a smaller plate, which can help you control portion sizes. Fill most of your plate with vegetables and lean proteins, and take smaller portions of higher-calorie dishes.

- **Practice Mindful Eating:** Pay attention to your hunger and fullness cues. Eat slowly and savor each bite, which can help prevent overeating.

3. Staying Mindful of Beverages:

Beverages can be a hidden source of calories and sugar at social events. Opt for water, sparkling water, or unsweetened tea. If you choose to have an alcoholic drink, do so in moderation and balance it with water.

4. Don't Stress About Occasional Indulgences:

Social events are meant to be enjoyed, so don't stress if you indulge a little. The key is to balance occasional indulgences with healthy eating the rest of the time.

What If I Have Dietary Restrictions or Allergies?

Dietary restrictions and food allergies can make following any diet challenging, but with careful planning, it's possible to maintain a heart-healthy diet that meets your needs.

1. Understanding Your Restrictions:

First, it's important to fully understand your dietary restrictions or allergies. Whether you're dealing with gluten intolerance, lactose intolerance, nut allergies, or another condition, knowing which foods to avoid and which alternatives are available is crucial.

2. Finding Heart-Healthy Alternatives:

- **Gluten-Free:** If you need to avoid gluten, there are plenty of heart-healthy gluten-free options available. Choose whole grains like quinoa, brown rice, and gluten-free oats, and look for gluten-free bread and pasta made from whole grains.

- **Dairy-Free:** For those who are lactose intolerant or avoid dairy for other reasons, choose calcium-fortified plant-based milks such as almond, soy, or oat milk. Incorporate other calcium-rich foods like leafy greens, tofu, and fortified orange juice.

- **Nut-Free:** If you're allergic to nuts, you can still get healthy fats from seeds (like flaxseeds, chia seeds, and sunflower seeds), avocados, and olive oil.

3. Navigating Social Situations:

When attending social events or eating out, it's important to communicate your dietary restrictions clearly. Don't hesitate to ask about ingredients or request modifications to ensure your meal is safe and healthy.

- **Bring Your Own Dish:** If you're attending a potluck or party, consider bringing a dish that meets your dietary needs. This ensures you'll have something safe to eat and can share your healthy dish with others.

- **Use Technology:** Many apps and online resources can help you find recipes and restaurants that cater to your dietary needs. These tools can make it easier to stick to your heart-healthy diet without feeling restricted.

How Can I Get My Family on Board?

Incorporating a heart-healthy diet into your family's routine can have benefits for everyone, but it can also be challenging if not everyone is on board. Here are some strategies to encourage your family to join you on your heart-healthy journey.

1. Lead by Example:

One of the most effective ways to encourage your family to adopt heart-healthy habits is by leading by example. When your family sees the positive changes in your health and well-being, they may be more motivated to make changes themselves.

- **Share Your Why:** Explain to your family why heart health is important to you and how making dietary changes can benefit everyone. Whether it's reducing the risk of heart disease, improving energy levels, or supporting overall health, sharing your reasons can help inspire others.

2. Make It a Family Effort:

Involve your family in the process of making dietary changes. This can help everyone feel included and invested in the outcome.

- **Meal Planning:** Sit down together to plan meals for the week, and encourage each family member to suggest heart-healthy dishes they'd like to try. This gives everyone a say in what's on the menu and increases the likelihood that they'll enjoy the meals.
- **Cooking Together:** Involve your family in cooking meals. Cooking together can be a fun and educational activity that helps everyone learn about healthy eating. Plus, it's a great way to spend quality time together.

3. Make Healthy Swaps Gradually:

Rather than overhauling your family's diet overnight, make gradual changes that are easier to accept. Start by introducing healthier versions of favorite dishes, such as whole-grain pasta instead of white pasta or baked chicken instead of fried.

- **Healthy Snacking:** Replace unhealthy snacks with heart-healthy options, such as fruits, vegetables, nuts, and seeds. Keep these options readily available so they're easy to grab when hunger strikes.

4. Be Patient and Supportive:

Change takes time, and it's important to be patient with your family as they adjust to new eating habits. Encourage and support them along the way, and celebrate small victories together.

- **Flexibility:** Recognize that everyone is on their own journey, and it's okay if some family members make changes at their own pace. Offer positive reinforcement and avoid being overly critical or forceful.

What Are the Best Resources for Ongoing Support?

Maintaining a heart-healthy diet is an ongoing journey, and having the right resources can make all the difference. Whether you're looking for information, motivation, or community support, there are plenty of resources available to help you stay on track.

1. Educational Resources:

Staying informed is key to making the best choices for your heart health. There are many reputable organizations and websites that offer reliable information on heart-healthy eating.

- **American Heart Association (AHA):** The AHA's website is a comprehensive resource for heart health information, including dietary guidelines, recipes, and tips for a heart-healthy lifestyle.

- **National Institutes of Health (NIH):** The NIH offers a wealth of information on heart health, including the DASH diet, which is designed to help lower blood pressure and improve heart health.
- **Books and Journals:** Consider reading books and scientific journals that focus on heart health and nutrition. Staying updated on the latest research can empower you to make informed decisions.

2. Support Groups and Online Communities:

Connecting with others who are on a similar journey can provide motivation, encouragement, and a sense of community.

- **Online Forums:** Websites like MyFitnessPal and Reddit have forums where you can discuss heart health, share tips, and get support from others who are working towards similar goals.
- **Social Media:** Follow heart health-focused accounts on platforms like Instagram, Facebook, and Twitter for daily inspiration, recipes, and advice.
- **Local Support Groups:** Check if there are local support groups or classes focused on heart health or nutrition. These can be great places to meet others, share experiences, and learn from experts.

3. Professional Support:

Working with healthcare professionals can provide personalized guidance and support tailored to your specific needs.

- **Registered Dietitians:** A registered dietitian can help you create a heart-healthy eating plan that's customized to your lifestyle, preferences, and health goals. They can also offer support and accountability as you make changes.
- **Healthcare Providers:** Regular check-ins with your healthcare provider are important for monitoring your heart health and making any necessary adjustments to your diet and lifestyle.

4. Apps and Tools:

There are many apps and tools available that can help you track your progress, set goals, and stay motivated.

- **Fitness Trackers:** Wearable fitness trackers like Fitbit, Garmin, or Apple Watch can monitor your physical activity, heart rate, and even sleep patterns, helping you stay on top of your heart health.
- **Nutrition Apps:** Apps like MyFitnessPal, Lose It!, and Cronometer allow you to track your food intake, monitor nutrients, and set dietary goals. These tools can be invaluable for staying on track with your heart-healthy diet.

Conclusion

Embarking on a heart-healthy journey is one of the most important steps you can take to protect your health and enhance your quality of life. Along the way, you may encounter challenges and questions, but remember that you are not alone. By staying informed, seeking support, and making gradual, sustainable changes, you can achieve and maintain a heart-healthy lifestyle that supports your long-term well-being.

This book has provided you with the tools, knowledge, and guidance to take control of your heart health through evidence-based, practical advice. Whether you're just starting out or looking to refine your approach, the strategies and tips shared here are designed to empower you to make positive changes that last a lifetime.

Your journey to heart health is ongoing, and it's a journey worth taking. With each step, you're making a powerful investment in your future—one that will pay off in the form of better health, more energy, and a longer, more fulfilling life. Keep moving forward, stay committed, and remember that every healthy choice you make brings you closer to a stronger, healthier heart.

Section 2: Heart-Healthy Recipes

Chapter 11: Energizing Breakfasts

Breakfast is the foundation of a successful day, setting the tone for your energy levels, mood, and overall well-being. Starting your day with a heart-healthy meal not only nourishes your body but also supports your cardiovascular health in the long run. In this chapter, I'm excited to share ten delicious, easy-to-make breakfast recipes that are designed to be both nutritious and satisfying. These recipes are packed with wholesome ingredients that promote heart health, giving you the confidence to make positive changes for your health each morning.

1. Oatmeal with Fresh Berries and Almonds

A classic, warm bowl of oatmeal packed with fiber and topped with fresh berries and crunchy almonds. This breakfast is perfect for a heart-healthy start to your day.

- **Servings:** 1
- **Preparation Time:** 5 minutes
- **Cooking Time:** 5 minutes

Ingredients:
1/2 cup (45 g) rolled oats
1 cup (240 ml) water or unsweetened almond milk
1/2 cup (75 g) mixed fresh berries (blueberries, strawberries, raspberries)
1 tbsp (15 g) sliced almonds
1/2 tsp (2.5 ml) ground cinnamon
1 tsp (5 ml) honey or maple syrup (optional)

Directions:
1. In a small saucepan, bring the water or almond milk to a boil.
2. Stir in the oats and reduce the heat to low. Cook for 3-5 minutes, stirring occasionally, until the oats are soft and creamy.
3. Remove from heat and stir in the ground cinnamon.
4. Pour the oatmeal into a bowl and top with fresh berries and sliced almonds.
5. Drizzle with honey or maple syrup if desired.

Nutritional Facts (per serving):
Calories: 250
Carbohydrates: 40 g
Protein: 6 g
Fats: 8 g
Sugars: 10 g
Salt: 10 mg

2. Greek Yogurt Parfait with Walnuts and Honey

This simple yet delicious parfait combines protein-rich Greek yogurt with heart-healthy walnuts and a touch of honey for sweetness. A perfect balance of flavors and textures.

- **Servings:** 1
- **Preparation Time:** 5 minutes
- **Cooking Time:** None

Ingredients:
1/2 cup (120 g) plain Greek yogurt
1/4 cup (30 g) walnuts, chopped
1/4 cup (75 g) mixed berries (blueberries, raspberries)
1 tsp (5 ml) honey
1/2 tsp (2.5 ml) ground cinnamon

Directions:
1. In a glass or bowl, layer half of the Greek yogurt.
2. Add a layer of mixed berries, followed by a sprinkle of chopped walnuts.
3. Repeat with the remaining yogurt and top with the rest of the berries and walnuts.

4. Drizzle with honey and sprinkle with cinnamon.

5. Serve immediately.

Nutritional Facts (per serving):
Calories: 220
Carbohydrates: 20 g
Protein: 12 g
Fats: 12 g
Sugars: 15 g
Salt: 60 mg

3. Spinach and Mushroom Breakfast Wrap

A hearty, veggie-packed wrap that's full of flavor and nutrients. This easy-to-make breakfast is perfect for those busy mornings when you need something quick yet satisfying.

- **Servings:** 1
- **Preparation Time:** 5 minutes
- **Cooking Time:** 5 minutes

Ingredients:
1 whole-grain tortilla
1 cup (30 g) fresh spinach leaves
1/2 cup (50 g) mushrooms, sliced
1 large egg
1 tbsp (15 ml) olive oil
1/4 tsp (1.25 ml) black pepper
A pinch of salt

Directions:
1. Heat the olive oil in a non-stick skillet over medium heat.
2. Add the mushrooms and cook for 3-4 minutes until softened.
3. Add the spinach and cook until wilted, about 1 minute.
4. In a small bowl, whisk the egg with a pinch of salt and pepper, then pour into the skillet with the veggies. Cook until the egg is set, stirring occasionally.
5. Warm the tortilla in the microwave or on a skillet, then place the egg and vegetable mixture in the center.
6. Wrap the tortilla tightly and serve immediately.

Nutritional Facts (per serving):
Calories: 280
Carbohydrates: 24 g
Protein: 10 g
Fats: 16 g
Sugars: 2 g
Salt: 200 mg

4. Apple Cinnamon Quinoa

This warm and comforting breakfast combines the protein power of quinoa with the sweet and tart flavor of apples and cinnamon. It's a great alternative to traditional oatmeal.

- **Servings:** 2
- **Preparation Time:** 5 minutes
- **Cooking Time:** 15 minutes

Ingredients:
1/2 cup (90 g) quinoa, rinsed
1 cup (240 ml) water or unsweetened almond milk
1 apple, diced
1/2 tsp (2.5 ml) ground cinnamon
1 tbsp (15 ml) honey or maple syrup (optional)
1 tbsp (15 ml) chopped walnuts or almonds

Directions:
1. In a medium saucepan, combine quinoa and water (or almond milk) and bring to a boil.
2. Reduce the heat to low, cover, and simmer for 12-15 minutes, or until the quinoa is cooked and the liquid is absorbed.
3. Stir in the diced apple, cinnamon, and honey or maple syrup (if using). Cook for another 2-3 minutes until the apple is slightly softened.
4. Serve warm, topped with chopped walnuts or almonds.

Nutritional Facts (per serving):
Calories: 220
Carbohydrates: 40 g
Protein: 6 g
Fats: 5 g
Sugars: 14 g
Salt: 10 mg

5. Avocado and Tomato Toast

A simple, quick, and nutritious breakfast option that's packed with healthy fats and fiber. Avocado and tomato on whole-grain toast is a heart-healthy way to start your day.

- **Servings:** 1
- **Preparation Time:** 5 minutes
- **Cooking Time:** None

Ingredients:
1 slice whole-grain bread
1/2 ripe avocado, mashed
1/2 small tomato, sliced
1/4 tsp (1.25 ml) black pepper

A pinch of salt
Fresh lemon juice (optional)

Directions:
1. Toast the whole-grain bread to your desired level of crispiness.
2. Spread the mashed avocado evenly on the toast.
3. Top with tomato slices and sprinkle with black pepper and a pinch of salt.
4. Squeeze a little fresh lemon juice over the top if desired.
5. Serve immediately.

Nutritional Facts (per serving):
Calories: 200
Carbohydrates: 20 g
Protein: 5 g
Fats: 12 g
Sugars: 2 g
Salt: 150 mg

6. Sweet Potato Breakfast Hash

A savory and filling breakfast dish that combines the natural sweetness of sweet potatoes with the heartiness of black beans and the freshness of bell peppers.
- **Servings:** 2
- **Preparation Time:** 10 minutes
- **Cooking Time:** 20 minutes

Ingredients:
1 medium sweet potato, peeled and diced
1/2 red bell pepper, diced
1/4 red onion, diced
1/2 cup (120 ml) black beans, drained and rinsed
1 tbsp (15 ml) olive oil
1/2 tsp (2.5 ml) cumin
1/2 tsp (2.5 ml) smoked paprika
Salt and pepper to taste

Directions:
1. Heat the olive oil in a large skillet over medium heat.
2. Add the diced sweet potato and cook for 10 minutes, stirring occasionally, until tender.
3. Add the red bell pepper, onion, cumin, smoked paprika, salt, and pepper. Cook for another 5 minutes until the vegetables are softened.
4. Stir in the black beans and cook for an additional 2 minutes to heat through.
5. Serve warm.

Nutritional Facts (per serving):
Calories: 250

Carbohydrates: 42 g
Protein: 6 g
Fats: 10 g
Sugars: 8 g
Salt: 150 mg

7. Cottage Cheese and Berry Bowl

A simple, protein-packed breakfast that's perfect for busy mornings. The cottage cheese provides a creamy base, while the berries add a sweet and tart contrast.
- **Servings:** 1
- **Preparation Time:** 5 minutes
- **Cooking Time:** None

Ingredients:
1/2 cup (120 g) low-fat cottage cheese
1/2 cup (75 g) mixed berries (blueberries, raspberries, strawberries)
1 tbsp (15 ml) sliced almonds or walnuts
1 tsp (5 ml) honey or maple syrup (optional)

Directions:
1. In a bowl, scoop the cottage cheese.
2. Top with mixed berries and sliced almonds or walnuts.
3. Drizzle with honey or maple syrup if desired.
4. Serve immediately.

Nutritional Facts (per serving):
Calories: 180
Carbohydrates: 20 g
Protein: 15 g
Fats: 7 g
Sugars: 12 g
Salt: 250 mg

8. Blueberry Almond Breakfast Smoothie

A refreshing and nutrient-rich smoothie that's perfect for a quick breakfast on the go. This smoothie is loaded with antioxidants, protein, and healthy fats to keep you energized throughout the morning.
- **Servings:** 1
- **Preparation Time:** 5 minutes
- **Cooking Time:** None

Ingredients:
1/2 cup (75 g) fresh or frozen blueberries
1/2 banana
1/2 cup (120 ml) low-fat Greek yogurt
1/2 cup (120 ml) unsweetened almond milk
1 tbsp (15 ml) almond butter
1 tsp (5 ml) honey or maple syrup (optional)

Directions:
1. Place all ingredients in a blender.
2. Blend until smooth and creamy.
3. Pour into a glass and enjoy immediately.

Nutritional Facts (per serving):
Calories: 250
Carbohydrates: 30 g
Protein: 10 g
Fats: 10 g
Sugars: 18 g
Salt: 100 mg

9. Veggie Omelette with Tomatoes and Spinach

A protein-packed omelette loaded with heart-healthy vegetables. This savory breakfast is quick to prepare and will keep you full and satisfied for hours.
- **Servings:** 1
- **Preparation Time:** 5 minutes
- **Cooking Time:** 7 minutes

Ingredients:
2 large eggs
1/2 cup (60 g) fresh spinach, chopped
1/4 cup (60 ml) diced tomatoes
1 tbsp (15 ml) feta cheese, crumbled
1/4 tsp (1.25 ml) black pepper
A pinch of salt
1 tsp (5 ml) olive oil

Directions:
1. In a bowl, whisk the eggs with a pinch of salt and pepper until well combined.
2. Heat the olive oil in a non-stick skillet over medium heat.
3. Add the spinach and tomatoes and sauté for 2-3 minutes until the spinach is wilted.
4. Pour the egg mixture over the vegetables and cook until the edges start to set, about 2 minutes.
5. Sprinkle the feta cheese over one half of the omelette.
6. Fold the omelette in half and cook for another 1-2 minutes, until the eggs are fully set.
7. Slide onto a plate and serve immediately.

Nutritional Facts (per serving):
Calories: 210
Carbohydrates: 3 g
Protein: 14 g
Fats: 16 g
Sugars: 1 g
Salt: 300 mg

10. Peanut Butter Banana Toast

A simple and delicious toast that combines the creamy richness of peanut butter with the natural sweetness of banana. It's a perfect breakfast to keep you energized throughout the morning.
- **Servings:** 1
- **Preparation Time:** 5 minutes
- **Cooking Time:** None

Ingredients:
1 slice whole-grain bread
1 tbsp (15 g) natural peanut butter
1/2 banana, sliced
1/4 tsp (1.25 ml) ground cinnamon

Directions:
1. Toast the whole-grain bread to your desired level of crispiness.
2. Spread the peanut butter evenly over the toast.
3. Top with banana slices and sprinkle with ground cinnamon.
4. Serve immediately.

Nutritional Facts (per serving):
Calories: 230
Carbohydrates: 28 g
Protein: 8 g
Fats: 10 g
Sugars: 10 g
Salt: 150 mg

11. Whole-Grain Banana Pancakes

These fluffy pancakes are made with whole-grain flour and ripe bananas, offering a sweet start to your day with plenty of fiber and nutrients.
- **Servings:** 2
- **Preparation Time:** 10 minutes
- **Cooking Time:** 15 minutes

Ingredients:
1 cup (120 g) whole-wheat flour
1 tbsp (15 ml) baking powder
1/2 tsp (2.5 ml) cinnamon
1/4 tsp (1.25 ml) salt
1 ripe banana, mashed
1 large egg
1 cup (240 ml) low-fat milk or almond milk
1 tbsp (15 ml) olive oil
1 tsp (5 ml) vanilla extract
1/2 cup (75 g) fresh or frozen blueberries (optional)

Directions:

1. In a large bowl, whisk together the whole-wheat flour, baking powder, cinnamon, and salt.
2. In another bowl, mash the banana and mix in the egg, milk, olive oil, and vanilla extract.
3. Pour the wet ingredients into the dry ingredients and stir until just combined. If using blueberries, fold them into the batter.
4. Heat a non-stick skillet over medium heat and lightly grease with a little olive oil.
5. Pour 1/4 cup (60 ml) of batter onto the skillet for each pancake. Cook until bubbles form on the surface, then flip and cook until golden brown on both sides.
6. Serve warm, with your choice of toppings like fresh fruit or a drizzle of maple syrup.

Nutritional Facts (per serving):
Calories: 320
Carbohydrates: 50 g
Protein: 8 g
Fats: 9 g
Sugars: 12 g
Salt: 300 mg

12. Avocado and Egg Breakfast Sandwich

A protein-packed breakfast sandwich with creamy avocado and a perfectly cooked egg, served on whole-grain bread for a satisfying and heart-healthy meal.

- **Servings:** 1
- **Preparation Time:** 5 minutes
- **Cooking Time:** 5 minutes

Ingredients:
2 slices whole-grain bread
1/2 ripe avocado, mashed
1 large egg
1 slice tomato
1/4 tsp (1.25 ml) black pepper
A pinch of salt
1 tsp (5 ml) olive oil

Directions:

1. Toast the whole-grain bread to your desired level of crispiness.
2. Heat the olive oil in a small non-stick skillet over medium heat. Crack the egg into the skillet and cook until the white is set but the yolk is still runny, or cook longer if you prefer a firmer yolk.
3. Spread the mashed avocado on one slice of the toasted bread.

4. Place the cooked egg on top of the avocado, followed by the tomato slice.
5. Sprinkle with black pepper and a pinch of salt.
6. Top with the second slice of bread and serve immediately.

Nutritional Facts (per serving):
Calories: 310
Carbohydrates: 30 g
Protein: 13 g
Fats: 17 g
Sugars: 2 g
Salt: 220 mg

13. Apple Walnut Oatmeal

This hearty oatmeal is flavored with apples and walnuts, providing a sweet and nutty start to your morning, rich in fiber and healthy fats.

- **Servings:** 1
- **Preparation Time:** 5 minutes
- **Cooking Time:** 10 minutes

Ingredients:
1/2 cup (45 g) rolled oats
1 cup (240 ml) water or unsweetened almond milk
1/2 apple, diced
1 tbsp (15 g) chopped walnuts
1/2 tsp (2.5 ml) ground cinnamon
1 tsp (5 ml) honey or maple syrup (optional)

Directions:

1. In a small saucepan, bring the water or almond milk to a boil.
2. Stir in the oats and reduce the heat to low. Cook for 5-7 minutes, stirring occasionally.
3. Add the diced apple and cinnamon and cook for another 2-3 minutes until the apple softens.
4. Pour the oatmeal into a bowl and top with chopped walnuts.
5. Drizzle with honey or maple syrup if desired.

Nutritional Facts (per serving):
Calories: 260
Carbohydrates: 40 g
Protein: 6 g
Fats: 8 g
Sugars: 15 g
Salt: 10 mg

14. Veggie-Packed Frittata

A versatile and nutritious frittata filled with vegetables and eggs, making it an excellent choice for a protein-rich breakfast that can be prepared ahead of time.

- **Servings:** 4
- **Preparation Time:** 10 minutes
- **Cooking Time:** 25 minutes

Ingredients:
6 large eggs
1/2 cup (120 ml) low-fat milk
1 cup (150 g) diced vegetables (bell peppers, onions, spinach, tomatoes)
1/4 cup (30 g) feta cheese, crumbled
1/4 tsp (1.25 ml) black pepper
A pinch of salt
1 tbsp (15 ml) olive oil

Directions:
1. Preheat your oven to 375°F (190°C).
2. In a large bowl, whisk together the eggs, milk, salt, and black pepper.
3. Heat the olive oil in an oven-safe skillet over medium heat. Add the vegetables and sauté for 5-7 minutes until softened.
4. Pour the egg mixture over the vegetables in the skillet. Sprinkle with feta cheese.
5. Cook on the stove for 2-3 minutes, then transfer the skillet to the preheated oven.
6. Bake for 15-20 minutes, or until the frittata is fully set and lightly browned on top.
7. Slice into wedges and serve warm.

Nutritional Facts (per serving):
Calories: 200
Carbohydrates: 5 g
Protein: 13 g
Fats: 14 g
Sugars: 3 g
Salt: 250 mg

15. Chia Seed Pudding with Mango

A creamy and tropical chia seed pudding that's rich in omega-3 fatty acids and fiber. This breakfast can be prepared the night before for a quick and easy morning meal.

- **Servings:** 2
- **Preparation Time:** 5 minutes
- **Cooking Time:** None (Refrigerate overnight)

Ingredients:
1/4 cup (40 g) chia seeds
1 cup (240 ml) unsweetened almond milk
1/2 tsp (2.5 ml) vanilla extract
1 tbsp (20 g) honey or maple syrup (optional)
1/2 cup (75 g) fresh mango, diced

Directions:
1. In a bowl, whisk together chia seeds, almond milk, vanilla extract, and honey or maple syrup.
2. Cover and refrigerate for at least 4 hours or overnight, until the mixture thickens to a pudding-like consistency.
3. Stir well before serving.
4. Divide the pudding into two bowls and top with diced mango.
5. Serve cold.

Nutritional Facts (per serving):
Calories: 200
Carbohydrates: 28 g
Protein: 5 g
Fats: 8 g
Sugars: 15 g
Salt: 50 mg

16. Ricotta Toast with Honey and Almonds

A creamy and crunchy breakfast option that's quick to prepare and packed with protein and healthy fats.

- **Servings:** 1
- **Preparation Time:** 5 minutes
- **Cooking Time:** None

Ingredients:
1 slice whole-grain bread
1/4 cup (60 g) ricotta cheese
1 tbsp (15 ml) honey
1 tbsp (15 g) sliced almonds
1/4 tsp (1.25 ml) ground cinnamon

Directions:
1. Toast the whole-grain bread to your desired level of crispiness.
2. Spread the ricotta cheese evenly over the toast.
3. Drizzle with honey and sprinkle with sliced almonds and ground cinnamon.
4. Serve immediately.

Nutritional Facts (per serving):
Calories: 250
Carbohydrates: 28 g
Protein: 10 g
Fats: 10 g
Sugars: 12 g
Salt: 150 mg

17. Pear and Almond Smoothie

A refreshing smoothie made with ripe pear and almond butter, offering a deliciously creamy texture and a boost of fiber and healthy fats.

- **Servings:** 1
- **Preparation Time:** 5 minutes
- **Cooking Time:** None

Ingredients:

1 ripe pear, cored and chopped
1/2 banana
1 tbsp (15 ml) almond butter
1/2 cup (120 ml) unsweetened almond milk
1/4 tsp (1.25 ml) ground cinnamon
A few ice cubes

Directions:

1. Place all Ingredients In a blender.
2. Blend until smooth and creamy.
3. Pour into a glass and enjoy immediately.

Nutritional Facts (per serving):
Calories: 250
Carbohydrates: 35 g
Protein: 5 g
Fats: 10 g
Sugars: 18 g
Salt: 50 mg

18. Savory Quinoa Breakfast Bowl

A savory quinoa bowl topped with a poached egg and sautéed vegetables, providing a protein-rich and filling start to your day.

- **Servings:** 2
- **Preparation Time:** 10 minutes
- **Cooking Time:** 15 minutes

Ingredients:

1/2 cup (90 g) quinoa, rinsed
1 cup (240 ml) water
1/2 cup (75 g) cherry tomatoes, halved
1 cup (30 g) fresh spinach
2 large eggs
1 tbsp (15 ml) olive oil
1/4 tsp (1.25 ml) black pepper
A pinch of salt

Directions:

1. In a medium saucepan, bring water to a boil. Add the quinoa, reduce heat to low, cover, and simmer for 12-15 minutes, or until the water is absorbed and quinoa is cooked.

2. Meanwhile, heat olive oil in a skillet over medium heat. Add cherry tomatoes and cook for 3-4 minutes, until softened. Add spinach and cook until wilted, about 1-2 minutes.
3. In a separate pot, poach the eggs by bringing water to a gentle simmer. Crack each egg into a small bowl and gently slide them into the water. Cook for 3-4 minutes for a runny yolk or longer for a firmer yolk.
4. Divide the cooked quinoa into two bowls.
5. Top each bowl with sautéed vegetables and a poached egg.
6. Season with salt and pepper and serve immediately.

Nutritional Facts (per serving):
Calories: 280
Carbohydrates: 28 g
Protein: 12 g
Fats: 14 g
Sugars: 3 g
Salt: 150 mg

19. Tropical Smoothie Bowl

A vibrant smoothie bowl packed with tropical fruits and topped with nutrient-rich seeds and nuts, offering a refreshing and energizing breakfast.

- **Servings:** 1
- **Preparation Time:** 10 minutes
- **Cooking Time:** None

Ingredients:

1/2 cup (75 g) frozen mango
1/2 banana
1/4 cup (60 ml) coconut milk
1/4 cup (60 ml) plain Greek yogurt
1 tbsp (15 g) chia seeds
1 tbsp (15 ml) shredded coconut
1 tbsp (15 g) granola

Directions:

1. In a blender, combine frozen mango, banana, coconut milk, and Greek yogurt. Blend until smooth and thick.
2. Pour the smoothie into a bowl.
3. Top with chia seeds, shredded coconut, and granola.
4. Serve immediately with a spoon.

Nutritional Facts (per serving):
Calories: 300
Carbohydrates: 42 g
Protein: 8 g

Fats: 12 g
Sugars: 22 g
Salt: 60 mg

20. Scrambled Eggs with Smoked Salmon

A luxurious breakfast that combines fluffy scrambled eggs with rich smoked salmon, offering a protein-packed and heart-healthy meal.

- **Servings:** 1
- **Preparation Time:** 5 minutes
- **Cooking Time:** 5 minutes

Ingredients:
2 large eggs
1/4 cup (60 ml) low-fat milk
2 oz (60 g) smoked salmon, sliced
1 tbsp (15 ml) chives, chopped
1/4 tsp (1.25 ml) black pepper
A pinch of salt
1 tsp (5 ml) olive oil

Directions:
1. In a bowl, whisk together eggs, milk, salt, and black pepper.
2. Heat the olive oil in a non-stick skillet over medium heat.
3. Pour the egg mixture into the skillet and cook, stirring gently, until the eggs are scrambled and just set.
4. Remove from heat and gently fold in the smoked salmon.
5. Sprinkle with chopped chives and serve immediately.

Nutritional Facts (per serving):
Calories: 250
Carbohydrates: 2 g
Protein: 20 g
Fats: 17 g
Sugars: 1 g
Salt: 500 mg

These ten breakfast recipes offer a variety of options to help you start your day on the right foot. Each dish is designed to be heart-healthy, satisfying, and easy to prepare, ensuring that you can enjoy delicious meals without compromising your cardiovascular health. By incorporating these recipes into your routine, you're taking positive steps toward a healthier lifestyle every morning.

Chapter 12: Hearty and Nourishing Lunches

Lunch is the perfect opportunity to refuel your body with nutritious, heart-healthy meals that sustain you throughout the day. These recipes are designed to be satisfying, easy to prepare, and packed with ingredients that support cardiovascular health. Whether you're at home, at work, or on the go, these lunches will keep you energized and on track with your heart-healthy goals.

1. Quinoa and Black Bean Salad

This vibrant salad is loaded with protein-packed quinoa and fiber-rich black beans, making it a filling and nutritious lunch option.

- **Servings:** 2
- **Preparation Time:** 10 minutes
- **Cooking Time:** 15 minutes

Ingredients:
1/2 cup (90 g) quinoa, rinsed
1 cup (240 ml) water
1/2 cup (120 ml) black beans, drained and rinsed
1/2 cup (75 g) cherry tomatoes, halved
1/2 avocado, diced
1/4 cup (30 g) red bell pepper, diced
1/4 cup (30 g) fresh cilantro, chopped
1 tbsp (15 ml) olive oil
1 tbsp (15 ml) lime juice
1/4 tsp (1.25 ml) cumin
1/4 tsp (1.25 ml) black pepper
A pinch of salt

Directions:
1. In a medium saucepan, bring the water to a boil. Add the quinoa, reduce heat to low, cover, and simmer for 12-15 minutes, or until the water is absorbed and the quinoa is tender. Remove from heat and let cool.
2. In a large bowl, combine the cooked quinoa, black beans, cherry tomatoes, avocado, red bell pepper, and cilantro.
3. In a small bowl, whisk together the olive oil, lime juice, cumin, black pepper, and salt.
4. Pour the dressing over the salad and toss to combine.
5. Serve immediately or refrigerate for up to 2 days.

Nutritional Facts (per serving):
Calories: 320
Carbohydrates: 42 g
Protein: 9 g
Fats: 14 g
Sugars: 3 g
Salt: 150 mg

2. Mediterranean Chickpea Wrap

This wrap is packed with Mediterranean flavors, combining protein-rich chickpeas with fresh vegetables and a tangy yogurt dressing.

- **Servings:** 2
- **Preparation Time:** 10 minutes
- **Cooking Time:** None

Ingredients:
1 cup (240 ml) canned chickpeas, drained and rinsed
1/4 cup (60 ml) plain Greek yogurt
1 tbsp (15 ml) lemon juice
1/2 tsp (2.5 ml) dried oregano
1/4 tsp (1.25 ml) garlic powder
1/4 cup (30 g) cucumber, diced
1/4 cup (30 g) cherry tomatoes, halved
2 whole-grain wraps
1/4 cup (30 g) baby spinach
1 tbsp (15 ml) olive oil
A pinch of salt and pepper

Directions:

1. In a bowl, mash the chickpeas with a fork until slightly chunky.
2. In a separate bowl, mix together the Greek yogurt, lemon juice, oregano, garlic powder, salt, and pepper.
3. Add the yogurt mixture to the mashed chickpeas and stir to combine.
4. Lay the whole-grain wraps flat and divide the chickpea mixture evenly between them.
5. Top with diced cucumber, cherry tomatoes, and baby spinach.
6. Drizzle with olive oil and roll up the wraps tightly.
7. Serve immediately or wrap in foil and refrigerate for later.

Nutritional Facts (per serving):
Calories: 310
Carbohydrates: 45 g
Protein: 12 g
Fats: 10 g
Sugars: 4 g
Salt: 220 mg

3. Grilled Chicken and Avocado Salad

A light yet satisfying salad featuring grilled chicken, creamy avocado, and a zesty lime dressing. Perfect for a heart-healthy lunch.

- **Servings:** 2
- **Preparation Time:** 10 minutes
- **Cooking Time:** 15 minutes

Ingredients:
1 boneless, skinless chicken breast
1 tbsp (15 ml) olive oil
1/2 tsp (2.5 ml) cumin
1/2 tsp (2.5 ml) paprika
1/4 tsp (1.25 ml) black pepper
1/4 tsp (1.25 ml) salt
4 cups (480 g) mixed greens
1 avocado, sliced
1/2 cup (75 g) cherry tomatoes, halved
1/4 cup (30 g) red onion, thinly sliced
2 tbsp (30 ml) lime juice
1 tbsp (15 ml) fresh cilantro, chopped

Directions:
1. Preheat a grill or grill pan over medium heat.
2. Rub the chicken breast with olive oil, cumin, paprika, black pepper, and salt.

3. Grill the chicken for 6-7 minutes on each side, or until fully cooked. Remove from heat and let it rest for 5 minutes before slicing.
4. In a large bowl, combine the mixed greens, avocado, cherry tomatoes, and red onion.
5. Add the sliced chicken on top of the salad.
6. Drizzle with lime juice and sprinkle with fresh cilantro.
7. Toss lightly and serve.

Nutritional Facts (per serving):
Calories: 350
Carbohydrates: 15 g
Protein: 28 g
Fats: 22 g
Sugars: 3 g
Salt: 250 mg

4. Lentil and Vegetable Soup

This hearty soup is packed with fiber-rich lentils and a variety of vegetables, making it a warm and comforting choice for lunch.

- **Servings:** 4
- **Preparation Time:** 10 minutes
- **Cooking Time:** 30 minutes

Ingredients:
1 cup (200 g) dried lentils, rinsed
1 tbsp (15 ml) olive oil
1 onion, diced
2 carrots, sliced
2 celery stalks, sliced
2 garlic cloves, minced
1 zucchini, diced
1 can (400 g) diced tomatoes
4 cups (960 ml) low-sodium vegetable broth
1 tsp (5 ml) dried thyme
1 tsp (5 ml) ground cumin
1/2 tsp (2.5 ml) black pepper
A pinch of salt
2 tbsp (30 ml) fresh parsley, chopped

Directions:
1. In a large pot, heat the olive oil over medium heat. Add the onion, carrots, and celery, and sauté for 5-7 minutes until softened.
2. Add the garlic and zucchini, and cook for another 2 minutes.
3. Stir in the diced tomatoes, vegetable broth, lentils, thyme, cumin, black pepper, and salt.

4. Bring the soup to a boil, then reduce the heat and simmer for 25-30 minutes, or until the lentils are tender.
5. Stir in the fresh parsley before serving.
6. Serve hot.

Nutritional Facts (per serving):
Calories: 250
Carbohydrates: 40 g
Protein: 12 g
Fats: 6 g
Sugars: 7 g
Salt: 150 mg

5. Baked Salmon with Quinoa and Asparagus

A nutritious and delicious lunch that combines baked salmon with fiber-rich quinoa and asparagus for a heart-healthy meal.
- **Servings:** 2
- **Preparation Time:** 10 minutes
- **Cooking Time:** 20 minutes

Ingredients:
2 salmon fillets (about 150 g each)
1 tbsp (15 ml) olive oil
1/2 tsp (2.5 ml) black pepper
1/2 tsp (2.5 ml) dried dill
1 lemon, sliced
1/2 cup (90 g) quinoa, rinsed
1 cup (240 ml) water
1 bunch asparagus, trimmed
1/4 tsp (1.25 ml) salt

Directions:
1. Preheat your oven to 375°F (190°C).
2. Place the salmon fillets on a baking sheet lined with parchment paper. Drizzle with olive oil and sprinkle with black pepper and dried dill. Top with lemon slices.
3. Bake the salmon for 15-20 minutes, or until cooked through and flaky.
4. While the salmon is baking, bring the water to a boil in a medium saucepan. Add the quinoa, reduce heat to low, cover, and simmer for 12-15 minutes until the water is absorbed and the quinoa is tender.
5. Steam the asparagus for 5-7 minutes until tender.
6. Serve the salmon with quinoa and asparagus on the side.

Nutritional Facts (per serving):
Calories: 400
Carbohydrates: 30 g
Protein: 28 g
Fats: 18 g
Sugars: 3 g
Salt: 250 mg

6. Chickpea and Spinach Curry

A flavorful, plant-based curry that's packed with protein-rich chickpeas and nutrient-dense spinach, perfect for a heart-healthy lunch.
- **Servings:** 4
- **Preparation Time:** 10 minutes
- **Cooking Time:** 20 minutes

Ingredients:
1 tbsp (15 ml) olive oil
1 onion, diced
2 garlic cloves, minced
1 tbsp (15 ml) curry powder
1/2 tsp (2.5 ml) ground cumin
1/2 tsp (2.5 ml) ground turmeric
1 can (400 g) diced tomatoes
1 can (400 g) chickpeas, drained and rinsed
4 cups (120 g) fresh spinach
1/2 cup (120 ml) low-fat coconut milk
1/2 tsp (2.5 ml) salt
1/4 tsp (1.25 ml) black pepper
2 tbsp (30 ml) fresh cilantro, chopped

Directions:
1. Heat the olive oil in a large skillet over medium heat. Add the onion and sauté for 5 minutes until softened.
2. Add the garlic, curry powder, cumin, and turmeric, and cook for another 2 minutes, stirring constantly.
3. Stir in the diced tomatoes and chickpeas. Bring to a simmer and cook for 10 minutes.
4. Add the spinach and coconut milk, and cook until the spinach is wilted and the curry is heated through.
5. Season with salt and black pepper, and stir in the fresh cilantro.
6. Serve hot.

Nutritional Facts (per serving):
Calories: 260
Carbohydrates: 35 g
Protein: 9 g
Fats: 11 g

Sugars: 6 g
Salt: 300 mg

7. Turkey and Avocado Sandwich

A quick and healthy sandwich featuring lean turkey breast, creamy avocado, and fresh veggies on whole-grain bread.

- **Servings:** 1
- **Preparation Time:** 5 minutes
- **Cooking Time:** None

Ingredients:

2 slices whole-grain bread
3 oz (85 g) sliced turkey breast
1/2 avocado, mashed
1 slice tomato
1 leaf lettuce
1 tbsp (15 ml) Dijon mustard
A pinch of salt and pepper

Directions:

1. Toast the whole-grain bread if desired.
2. Spread the Dijon mustard on one slice of bread and the mashed avocado on the other.
3. Layer the turkey, tomato, and lettuce on the bread.
4. Sprinkle with a pinch of salt and pepper.
5. Close the sandwich with the second slice of bread and serve immediately.

Nutritional Facts (per serving):

Calories: 320
Carbohydrates: 28 g
Protein: 22 g
Fats: 14 g
Sugars: 2 g
Salt: 300 mg

8. Zucchini Noodles with Pesto and Cherry Tomatoes

A light and flavorful dish made with zucchini noodles, fresh pesto, and cherry tomatoes. It's a delicious low-carb lunch option.

- **Servings:** 2
- **Preparation Time:** 10 minutes
- **Cooking Time:** 5 minutes

Ingredients:

2 medium zucchini, spiralized
1 cup (150 g) cherry tomatoes, halved
1/4 cup (60 ml) fresh basil pesto (store-bought or homemade)
1 tbsp (15 ml) olive oil

1/4 tsp (1.25 ml) black pepper
A pinch of salt
2 tbsp (30 ml) grated Parmesan cheese (optional)

Directions:

1. Heat the olive oil in a large skillet over medium heat. Add the spiralized zucchini and sauté for 2-3 minutes until just tender.
2. Add the cherry tomatoes and cook for another 2 minutes until they are slightly softened.
3. Remove the skillet from heat and stir in the basil pesto. Toss to coat the zucchini noodles evenly.
4. Season with salt and black pepper.
5. Serve immediately, topped with grated Parmesan cheese if desired.

Nutritional Facts (per serving):

Calories: 220
Carbohydrates: 12 g
Protein: 5 g
Fats: 18 g
Sugars: 6 g
Salt: 200 mg

9. Grilled Veggie and Hummus Wrap

A satisfying wrap filled with grilled vegetables, creamy hummus, and fresh greens, perfect for a quick and healthy lunch.

- **Servings:** 2
- **Preparation Time:** 10 minutes
- **Cooking Time:** 10 minutes

Ingredients:

1 red bell pepper, sliced
1 zucchini, sliced
1 red onion, sliced
1 tbsp (15 ml) olive oil
1/2 tsp (2.5 ml) black pepper
A pinch of salt
2 whole-grain wraps
1/2 cup (120 ml) hummus
1/2 cup (30 g) baby spinach

Directions:

1. Preheat a grill or grill pan over medium heat.
2. Toss the sliced vegetables with olive oil, black pepper, and salt.
3. Grill the vegetables for 3-4 minutes on each side until tender and lightly charred.
4. Spread hummus evenly over each whole-grain wrap.
5. Layer the grilled vegetables and baby spinach on top of the hummus.

6. Roll up the wraps tightly and serve immediately.

Nutritional Facts (per serving):
Calories: 300
Carbohydrates: 35 g
Protein: 8 g
Fats: 15 g
Sugars: 6 g
Salt: 220 mg

10. Baked Cod with Lemon and Garlic

A simple and flavorful dish featuring baked cod seasoned with lemon, garlic, and fresh herbs. It's a light and nutritious lunch option.
- **Servings:** 2
- **Preparation Time:** 5 minutes
- **Cooking Time:** 15 minutes

Ingredients:
2 cod fillets (about 150 g each)
1 tbsp (15 ml) olive oil
2 garlic cloves, minced
1 lemon, sliced
1/4 tsp (1.25 ml) black pepper
1/4 tsp (1.25 ml) salt
2 tbsp (30 ml) fresh parsley, chopped

Directions:
1. Preheat your oven to 375°F (190°C).
2. Place the cod fillets on a baking sheet lined with parchment paper.
3. Drizzle with olive oil and sprinkle with minced garlic, black pepper, and salt.
4. Top each fillet with lemon slices.
5. Bake for 12-15 minutes, or until the cod is opaque and flakes easily with a fork.
6. Sprinkle with fresh parsley before serving.

Nutritional Facts (per serving):
Calories: 220
Carbohydrates: 2 g
Protein: 28 g
Fats: 10 g
Sugars: 0 g
Salt: 300 mg

11. Farro Salad with Roasted Vegetables

This hearty salad features nutty farro and a mix of roasted vegetables, making it a filling and delicious lunch option.
- **Servings:** 2
- **Preparation Time:** 10 minutes
- **Cooking Time:** 20 minutes

Ingredients:
1/2 cup (90 g) farro
1 cup (240 ml) water
1 zucchini, diced
1 red bell pepper, diced
1 red onion, diced
1 tbsp (15 ml) olive oil
1/4 tsp (1.25 ml) black pepper
1/4 tsp (1.25 ml) salt
2 tbsp (30 ml) balsamic vinegar
2 tbsp (30 g) crumbled feta cheese (optional)

Directions:
1. Preheat your oven to 400°F (200°C).
2. Toss the diced zucchini, red bell pepper, and red onion with olive oil, black pepper, and salt.
3. Spread the vegetables on a baking sheet and roast for 20 minutes, or until tender and slightly caramelized.
4. While the vegetables are roasting, bring the water to a boil in a medium saucepan. Add the farro, reduce heat, cover, and simmer for 15-20 minutes, or until tender. Drain any excess water.
5. In a large bowl, combine the cooked farro and roasted vegetables.
6. Drizzle with balsamic vinegar and toss to combine.
7. Sprinkle with crumbled feta cheese if desired and serve.

Nutritional Facts (per serving):
Calories: 300
Carbohydrates: 45 g
Protein: 8 g
Fats: 10 g
Sugars: 8 g
Salt: 200 mg

12. Shrimp and Avocado Salad

A light and refreshing salad featuring shrimp, creamy avocado, and a citrusy dressing. It's a perfect choice for a heart-healthy lunch.
- **Servings:** 2
- **Preparation Time:** 10 minutes
- **Cooking Time:** 5 minutes

Ingredients:
8 oz (225 g) cooked shrimp, peeled and deveined
1 avocado, diced
1/2 cup (75 g) cherry tomatoes, halved
1/4 cup (30 g) red onion, thinly sliced
4 cups (480 g) mixed greens

1 tbsp (15 ml) olive oil
1 tbsp (15 ml) lime juice
1/4 tsp (1.25 ml) black pepper
A pinch of salt
2 tbsp (30 ml) fresh cilantro, chopped

Directions:
1. In a large bowl, combine the shrimp, avocado, cherry tomatoes, red onion, and mixed greens.
2. In a small bowl, whisk together the olive oil, lime juice, black pepper, and salt.
3. Pour the dressing over the salad and toss to combine.
4. Sprinkle with fresh cilantro and serve immediately.

Nutritional Facts (per serving):
Calories: 280
Carbohydrates: 12 g
Protein: 20 g
Fats: 18 g
Sugars: 3 g
Salt: 220 mg

13. Tofu Stir-Fry with Broccoli and Carrots

A quick and flavorful stir-fry made with tofu, broccoli, and carrots. This plant-based dish is packed with protein and nutrients.
- **Servings:** 2
- **Preparation Time:** 10 minutes
- **Cooking Time:** 10 minutes

Ingredients:
1 block (200 g) firm tofu, drained and cubed
1 tbsp (15 ml) olive oil
2 cups (180 g) broccoli florets
1 large carrot, julienned
2 garlic cloves, minced
2 tbsp (30 ml) low-sodium soy sauce
1 tbsp (15 ml) rice vinegar
1 tsp (5 ml) honey
1/4 tsp (1.25 ml) black pepper
2 tbsp (30 ml) sesame seeds (optional)

Directions:
1. Heat the olive oil in a large skillet or wok over medium heat. Add the cubed tofu and cook for 5-7 minutes, turning occasionally, until golden brown. Remove from the skillet and set aside.
2. In the same skillet, add the broccoli, carrots, and garlic. Stir-fry for 3-4 minutes until the vegetables are tender-crisp.

3. In a small bowl, whisk together the soy sauce, rice vinegar, honey, and black pepper.
4. Return the tofu to the skillet and pour the sauce over the stir-fry. Toss to coat evenly and cook for another 2 minutes.
5. Sprinkle with sesame seeds if desired and serve.

Nutritional Facts (per serving):
Calories: 280
Carbohydrates: 20 g
Protein: 15 g
Fats: 16 g
Sugars: 6 g
Salt: 300 mg

14. Spinach and Feta Stuffed Chicken Breast

A flavorful and protein-rich dish featuring chicken breasts stuffed with spinach and feta cheese, making it a satisfying and healthy lunch option.
- **Servings:** 2
- **Preparation Time:** 10 minutes
- **Cooking Time:** 25 minutes

Ingredients:
2 boneless, skinless chicken breasts
1 cup (30 g) fresh spinach, chopped
1/4 cup (30 g) feta cheese, crumbled
1 tbsp (15 ml) olive oil
1/4 tsp (1.25 ml) black pepper
1/4 tsp (1.25 ml) garlic powder
A pinch of salt
2 tbsp (30 ml) fresh parsley, chopped

Directions:
1. Preheat your oven to 375°F (190°C).
2. Slice a pocket into each chicken breast, being careful not to cut all the way through.
3. In a small bowl, mix together the chopped spinach and feta cheese. Stuff each chicken breast with the spinach and feta mixture.
4. Secure the openings with toothpicks if needed.
5. Heat the olive oil in an oven-safe skillet over medium heat. Season the chicken breasts with black pepper, garlic powder, and salt. Sear the chicken breasts for 2-3 minutes on each side until golden brown.
6. Transfer the skillet to the preheated oven and bake for 20 minutes, or until the chicken is fully cooked and the internal temperature reaches 165°F (74°C).

7. Remove the toothpicks and sprinkle with fresh parsley before serving.

Nutritional Facts (per serving):
Calories: 320
Carbohydrates: 2 g
Protein: 40 g
Fats: 16 g
Sugars: 0 g
Salt: 350 mg

15. Baked Sweet Potato with Black Beans and Avocado

A nutrient-dense lunch featuring baked sweet potatoes topped with black beans, avocado, and a zesty lime dressing. It's a delicious and filling plant-based meal.
- **Servings:** 2
- **Preparation Time:** 10 minutes
- **Cooking Time:** 45 minutes

Ingredients:
2 medium sweet potatoes
1 cup (240 ml) black beans, drained and rinsed
1 avocado, diced
1 tbsp (15 ml) olive oil
1 tbsp (15 ml) lime juice
1/4 tsp (1.25 ml) cumin
1/4 tsp (1.25 ml) black pepper
A pinch of salt
2 tbsp (30 ml) fresh cilantro, chopped

Directions:
1. Preheat your oven to 400°F (200°C). Pierce the sweet potatoes with a fork and place them on a baking sheet. Bake for 45 minutes, or until tender.
2. While the sweet potatoes are baking, in a small bowl, whisk together the olive oil, lime juice, cumin, black pepper, and salt.
3. Once the sweet potatoes are done, slice them open and fluff the insides with a fork.
4. Top each sweet potato with black beans and diced avocado.
5. Drizzle with the lime dressing and sprinkle with fresh cilantro.
6. Serve immediately.

Nutritional Facts (per serving):
Calories: 350
Carbohydrates: 50 g
Protein: 9 g
Fats: 16 g

Sugars: 8 g
Salt: 200 mg

16. Cauliflower Rice Stir-Fry

A low-carb and vegetable-packed stir-fry made with cauliflower rice, making it a light yet filling lunch option.
- **Servings:** 2
- **Preparation Time:** 10 minutes
- **Cooking Time:** 10 minutes

Ingredients:
2 cups (300 g) cauliflower rice
1/2 cup (75 g) peas
1/2 cup (75 g) diced carrots
1/4 cup (30 g) diced bell pepper
1/4 cup (30 g) diced onion
2 garlic cloves, minced
1 tbsp (15 ml) olive oil
2 tbsp (30 ml) low-sodium soy sauce
1 tsp (5 ml) sesame oil
1/4 tsp (1.25 ml) black pepper
2 tbsp (30 ml) chopped green onions

Directions:
1. Heat the olive oil in a large skillet or wok over medium heat. Add the diced onion and garlic and sauté for 2-3 minutes until softened.
2. Add the cauliflower rice, peas, carrots, and bell pepper to the skillet. Stir-fry for 5-7 minutes until the vegetables are tender.
3. Stir in the soy sauce, sesame oil, and black pepper. Cook for another 2 minutes.
4. Remove from heat and sprinkle with chopped green onions before serving.

Nutritional Facts (per serving):
Calories: 180
Carbohydrates: 20 g
Protein: 5 g
Fats: 9 g
Sugars: 6 g
Salt: 400 mg

17. Grilled Portobello Mushroom Sandwich

A savory sandwich featuring grilled Portobello mushrooms, fresh vegetables, and a tangy balsamic glaze. It's a delicious vegetarian lunch option.
- **Servings:** 2
- **Preparation Time:** 10 minutes
- **Cooking Time:** 10 minutes

Ingredients:
2 large Portobello mushrooms, stems removed
2 tbsp (30 ml) balsamic vinegar
1 tbsp (15 ml) olive oil
1/4 tsp (1.25 ml) black pepper
1/4 tsp (1.25 ml) garlic powder
A pinch of salt
4 slices whole-grain bread
1 tomato, sliced
1/4 cup (30 g) baby spinach
1/4 cup (30 g) roasted red peppers

Directions:
1. Preheat a grill or grill pan over medium heat.
2. In a small bowl, whisk together the balsamic vinegar, olive oil, black pepper, garlic powder, and salt. Brush the mixture onto both sides of the Portobello mushrooms.
3. Grill the mushrooms for 4-5 minutes on each side until tender.
4. Toast the whole-grain bread slices if desired.
5. Assemble the sandwiches by placing the grilled mushrooms on the bread, followed by tomato slices, baby spinach, and roasted red peppers.
6. Close the sandwiches and serve immediately.

Nutritional Facts (per serving):
Calories: 280
Carbohydrates: 35 g
Protein: 8 g
Fats: 12 g
Sugars: 6 g
Salt: 350 mg

18. Roasted Beet and Goat Cheese Salad

A vibrant and flavorful salad featuring roasted beets, creamy goat cheese, and a simple balsamic vinaigrette.
- **Servings:** 2
- **Preparation Time:** 10 minutes
- **Cooking Time:** 40 minutes

Ingredients:
2 medium beets, peeled and diced
1 tbsp (15 ml) olive oil
4 cups (480 g) mixed greens
1/4 cup (30 g) crumbled goat cheese
1/4 cup (30 g) walnuts, toasted
2 tbsp (30 ml) balsamic vinegar
1 tbsp (15 ml) honey
1/4 tsp (1.25 ml) black pepper
A pinch of salt

Directions:
1. Preheat your oven to 400°F (200°C). Toss the diced beets with olive oil, black pepper, and salt. Spread them on a baking sheet and roast for 35-40 minutes, or until tender.
2. In a large bowl, combine the mixed greens, roasted beets, crumbled goat cheese, and toasted walnuts.
3. In a small bowl, whisk together the balsamic vinegar and honey.
4. Drizzle the vinaigrette over the salad and toss to combine.
5. Serve immediately.

Nutritional Facts (per serving):
Calories: 300
Carbohydrates: 25 g
Protein: 9 g
Fats: 20 g
Sugars: 12 g
Salt: 250 mg

19. Spaghetti Squash with Marinara Sauce

A low-carb alternative to pasta, this dish features spaghetti squash topped with a homemade marinara sauce, making it a light yet satisfying lunch.
- **Servings:** 2
- **Preparation Time:** 10 minutes
- **Cooking Time:** 40 minutes

Ingredients:
1 medium spaghetti squash
1 tbsp (15 ml) olive oil
2 cups (480 ml) marinara sauce (store-bought or homemade)
1/4 tsp (1.25 ml) black pepper
1/4 tsp (1.25 ml) garlic powder
1/4 tsp (1.25 ml) dried oregano
1/4 cup (30 g) grated Parmesan cheese (optional)
Fresh basil leaves for garnish

Directions:
1. Preheat your oven to 375°F (190°C). Slice the spaghetti squash in half lengthwise and remove the seeds.
2. Drizzle the cut sides of the squash with olive oil and season with black pepper, garlic powder, and dried oregano.
3. Place the squash halves cut side down on a baking sheet and roast for 35-40 minutes, or until tender.

4. While the squash is roasting, heat the marinara sauce in a saucepan over low heat.
5. Once the squash is done, use a fork to scrape the flesh into spaghetti-like strands.
6. Serve the spaghetti squash topped with marinara sauce, grated Parmesan cheese, and fresh basil leaves.

Nutritional Facts (per serving):
Calories: 280
Carbohydrates: 40 g
Protein: 6 g
Fats: 12 g
Sugars: 12 g
Salt: 300 mg

20. Edamame and Quinoa Salad

A protein-packed salad featuring edamame, quinoa, and a light sesame dressing. It's a refreshing and nutritious lunch option.
- **Servings:** 2
- **Preparation Time:** 10 minutes
- **Cooking Time:** 15 minutes

Ingredients:
1/2 cup (90 g) quinoa, rinsed
1 cup (240 ml) water
1 cup (150 g) shelled edamame, cooked
1/2 cup (75 g) diced cucumber
1/2 cup (75 g) shredded carrots
1 tbsp (15 ml) sesame oil
1 tbsp (15 ml) rice vinegar
1 tsp (5 ml) soy sauce
1 tsp (5 ml) honey
1/4 tsp (1.25 ml) black pepper
2 tbsp (30 ml) sesame seeds

Directions:
1. In a medium saucepan, bring the water to a boil. Add the quinoa, reduce heat to low, cover, and simmer for 12-15 minutes until the water is absorbed and the quinoa is tender. Let cool.
2. In a large bowl, combine the cooked quinoa, edamame, cucumber, and shredded carrots.
3. In a small bowl, whisk together the sesame oil, rice vinegar, soy sauce, honey, and black pepper.
4. Pour the dressing over the salad and toss to combine.
5. Sprinkle with sesame seeds before serving.

Nutritional Facts (per serving):
Calories: 280
Carbohydrates: 34 g
Protein: 10 g
Fats: 12 g
Sugars: 8 g
Salt: 200 mg

These twenty hearty and nourishing lunch recipes are designed to keep you energized and satisfied throughout the day. By incorporating these heart-healthy meals into your routine, you can enjoy delicious, nutritious lunches that support your overall well-being.

Chapter 13: Wholesome and Satisfying Dinners

Dinner is the perfect opportunity to wind down your day with a nutritious and satisfying meal that supports your heart health. In this chapter, I'm excited to share twenty delicious dinner recipes that are both heart-healthy and full of flavor. These recipes are designed to be simple to prepare, using wholesome ingredients that nourish your body and help you stay on track with your health goals.

1. Lemon Herb Grilled Chicken with Steamed Broccoli

This simple yet flavorful dish features tender grilled chicken marinated in lemon and herbs, served with steamed broccoli for a nutrient-rich dinner.
- **Servings:** 2
- **Preparation Time:** 10 minutes
- **Cooking Time:** 20 minutes

Ingredients:
2 boneless, skinless chicken breasts
1 tbsp (15 ml) olive oil
2 tbsp (30 ml) lemon juice
1 tsp (5 ml) dried oregano
1 tsp (5 ml) dried thyme
1/4 tsp (1.25 ml) black pepper
A pinch of salt
2 cups (300 g) broccoli florets, steamed

Directions:
1. In a small bowl, mix the olive oil, lemon juice, oregano, thyme, black pepper, and salt.
2. Place the chicken breasts in a resealable plastic bag and pour the marinade over them. Seal the bag and marinate in the refrigerator for at least 30 minutes.
3. Preheat a grill or grill pan over medium heat. Grill the chicken breasts for 6-7 minutes on each side, or until fully cooked.
4. Steam the broccoli while the chicken is cooking.
5. Serve the grilled chicken with steamed broccoli on the side.

Nutritional Facts (per serving):
Calories: 300
Carbohydrates: 8 g
Protein: 35 g
Fats: 14 g
Sugars: 2 g
Salt: 200 mg

2. Baked Cod with Garlic and Tomatoes

This light and flavorful dish features tender cod baked with garlic, tomatoes, and fresh herbs, making it a heart-healthy and satisfying dinner option.
- **Servings:** 2
- **Preparation Time:** 10 minutes
- **Cooking Time:** 20 minutes

Ingredients:
2 cod fillets (about 150 g each)
1 tbsp (15 ml) olive oil
2 garlic cloves, minced
1 cup (150 g) cherry tomatoes, halved
1 tbsp (15 ml) lemon juice
1 tsp (5 ml) dried basil
1/4 tsp (1.25 ml) black pepper
A pinch of salt

Directions:
1. Preheat your oven to 375°F (190°C).
2. Place the cod fillets in a baking dish. Drizzle with olive oil and lemon juice.
3. Top the cod with minced garlic, cherry tomatoes, basil, black pepper, and salt.
4. Bake for 15-20 minutes, or until the cod is opaque and flakes easily with a fork.

5. Serve hot, garnished with additional fresh herbs if desired.

Nutritional Facts (per serving):
Calories: 250
Carbohydrates: 6 g
Protein: 30 g
Fats: 12 g
Sugars: 4 g
Salt: 200 mg

3. Quinoa-Stuffed Bell Peppers

These colorful bell peppers are stuffed with a flavorful mixture of quinoa, black beans, and vegetables, making for a hearty and nutritious dinner.
- **Servings:** 4
- **Preparation Time:** 15 minutes
- **Cooking Time:** 30 minutes

Ingredients:
4 large bell peppers, tops cut off and seeds removed
1 cup (180 g) quinoa, rinsed
2 cups (480 ml) water
1 can (400 g) black beans, drained and rinsed
1/2 cup (75 g) corn kernels
1/2 cup (75 g) diced tomatoes
1/4 cup (30 g) diced red onion
1 tsp (5 ml) ground cumin
1 tsp (5 ml) smoked paprika
1/4 tsp (1.25 ml) black pepper
A pinch of salt
1/4 cup (30 g) shredded low-fat cheese (optional)

Directions:
1. Preheat your oven to 375°F (190°C).
2. In a medium saucepan, bring the water to a boil. Add the quinoa, reduce heat to low, cover, and simmer for 15 minutes or until the water is absorbed and the quinoa is tender.
3. In a large bowl, combine the cooked quinoa, black beans, corn, diced tomatoes, red onion, cumin, smoked paprika, black pepper, and salt.
4. Stuff each bell pepper with the quinoa mixture and place them in a baking dish.
5. Cover with foil and bake for 25 minutes. If using cheese, sprinkle it on top during the last 5 minutes of baking.
6. Serve hot.

Nutritional Facts (per serving):
Calories: 300
Carbohydrates: 50 g
Protein: 10 g

Fats: 6 g
Sugars: 8 g
Salt: 250 mg

4. Salmon with Asparagus and Lemon-Dill Sauce

A simple yet elegant dish featuring baked salmon paired with tender asparagus and a refreshing lemon-dill sauce.
- **Servings:** 2
- **Preparation Time:** 10 minutes
- **Cooking Time:** 20 minutes

Ingredients:
2 salmon fillets (about 150 g each)
1 tbsp (15 ml) olive oil
1 tbsp (15 ml) lemon juice
1 tsp (5 ml) dried dill
1/4 tsp (1.25 ml) black pepper
A pinch of salt
1 bunch asparagus, trimmed
1/4 cup (60 ml) low-fat Greek yogurt
1 tbsp (15 ml) fresh dill, chopped
1 tsp (5 ml) Dijon mustard

Directions:
1. Preheat your oven to 375°F (190°C).
2. Place the salmon fillets on a baking sheet lined with parchment paper. Drizzle with olive oil, lemon juice, dill, black pepper, and salt.
3. Arrange the asparagus around the salmon and drizzle with a little more olive oil.
4. Bake for 15-20 minutes, or until the salmon is cooked through and the asparagus is tender.
5. While the salmon is baking, mix the Greek yogurt, fresh dill, and Dijon mustard in a small bowl to make the lemon-dill sauce.
6. Serve the salmon and asparagus with the sauce on the side.

Nutritional Facts (per serving):
Calories: 350
Carbohydrates: 8 g
Protein: 30 g
Fats: 20 g
Sugars: 2 g
Salt: 250 mg

5. Lentil and Vegetable Stir-Fry

This hearty stir-fry is packed with fiber-rich lentils and a variety of colorful vegetables, making it a satisfying and heart-healthy dinner.
- **Servings:** 4

- **Preparation Time:** 10 minutes
- **Cooking Time:** 20 minutes

Ingredients:

1 cup (200 g) dried lentils, rinsed
2 cups (480 ml) water
1 tbsp (15 ml) olive oil
1 red bell pepper, sliced
1 zucchini, sliced
1 carrot, julienned
1 cup (150 g) broccoli florets
2 garlic cloves, minced
2 tbsp (30 ml) low-sodium soy sauce
1 tbsp (15 ml) rice vinegar
1 tsp (5 ml) honey
1/4 tsp (1.25 ml) black pepper
2 tbsp (30 ml) chopped green onions

Directions:

1. In a medium saucepan, bring the water to a boil. Add the lentils, reduce heat to low, cover, and simmer for 20 minutes or until tender. Drain any excess water.
2. In a large skillet or wok, heat the olive oil over medium heat. Add the garlic and sauté for 1 minute until fragrant.
3. Add the red bell pepper, zucchini, carrot, and broccoli to the skillet. Stir-fry for 5-7 minutes until the vegetables are tender-crisp.
4. Stir in the cooked lentils, soy sauce, rice vinegar, honey, and black pepper. Cook for another 2 minutes until heated through.
5. Serve hot, garnished with chopped green onions.

Nutritional Facts (per serving):
Calories: 300
Carbohydrates: 48 g
Protein: 12 g
Fats: 7 g
Sugars: 8 g
Salt: 350 mg

6. Baked Chicken with Sweet Potatoes and Brussels Sprouts

This comforting dish combines baked chicken with roasted sweet potatoes and Brussels sprouts, creating a balanced and nutritious dinner.
- **Servings:** 4
- **Preparation Time:** 10 minutes
- **Cooking Time:** 40 minutes

Ingredients:

4 boneless, skinless chicken breasts

2 tbsp (30 ml) olive oil
2 sweet potatoes, peeled and diced
2 cups (300 g) Brussels sprouts, halved
1 tsp (5 ml) dried rosemary
1 tsp (5 ml) dried thyme
1/4 tsp (1.25 ml) black pepper
A pinch of salt

Directions:

1. Preheat your oven to 400°F (200°C).
2. Place the chicken breasts on a baking sheet lined with parchment paper.
3. In a large bowl, toss the sweet potatoes and Brussels sprouts with olive oil, rosemary, thyme, black pepper, and salt.
4. Arrange the vegetables around the chicken on the baking sheet.
5. Bake for 35-40 minutes, or until the chicken is fully cooked and the vegetables are tender.
6. Serve hot.

Nutritional Facts (per serving):
Calories: 350
Carbohydrates: 30 g
Protein: 35 g
Fats: 12 g
Sugars: 6 g
Salt: 200 mg

7. Spinach and Feta Stuffed Salmon

A flavorful dish where tender salmon fillets are stuffed with a creamy spinach and feta mixture, making for a delicious and heart-healthy dinner.
- **Servings:** 2
- **Preparation Time:** 10 minutes
- **Cooking Time:** 20 minutes

Ingredients:

2 salmon fillets (about 150 g each)
1 cup (30 g) fresh spinach, chopped
1/4 cup (30 g) feta cheese, crumbled
1 tbsp (15 ml) olive oil
1/4 tsp (1.25 ml) black pepper
A pinch of salt
2 lemon wedges

Directions:

1. Preheat your oven to 375°F (190°C).
2. In a small bowl, mix the chopped spinach and feta cheese together.
3. Slice a pocket into the side of each salmon fillet and stuff with the spinach and feta mixture.

4. Place the stuffed salmon fillets on a baking sheet lined with parchment paper. Drizzle with olive oil and sprinkle with black pepper and salt.
5. Bake for 15-20 minutes, or until the salmon is cooked through and flakes easily with a fork.
6. Serve hot, garnished with lemon wedges.

Nutritional Facts (per serving):
Calories: 350
Carbohydrates: 4 g
Protein: 30 g
Fats: 22 g
Sugars: 1 g
Salt: 250 mg

8. Whole Wheat Spaghetti with Tomato Basil Sauce

A classic pasta dish made with whole wheat spaghetti and a homemade tomato basil sauce, offering a hearty yet heart-healthy dinner option.
- **Servings:** 4
- **Preparation Time:** 10 minutes
- **Cooking Time:** 20 minutes

Ingredients:
8 oz (225 g) whole wheat spaghetti
1 tbsp (15 ml) olive oil
1 onion, diced
3 garlic cloves, minced
1 can (400 g) diced tomatoes
1/4 cup (60 ml) tomato paste
1 tsp (5 ml) dried basil
1/4 tsp (1.25 ml) black pepper
A pinch of salt
1/4 cup (30 g) grated Parmesan cheese (optional)
Fresh basil leaves for garnish

Directions:
1. Cook the whole wheat spaghetti according to the package instructions. Drain and set aside.
2. In a large skillet, heat the olive oil over medium heat. Add the onion and garlic and sauté for 5 minutes until softened.
3. Stir in the diced tomatoes, tomato paste, dried basil, black pepper, and salt. Simmer for 10-15 minutes until the sauce thickens.
4. Toss the cooked spaghetti with the tomato basil sauce.
5. Serve hot, topped with grated Parmesan cheese and fresh basil leaves if desired.

Nutritional Facts (per serving):
Calories: 320

Carbohydrates: 60 g
Protein: 12 g
Fats: 6 g
Sugars: 8 g
Salt: 200 mg

9. Chicken and Vegetable Stir-Fry with Brown Rice

A quick and easy stir-fry featuring chicken and colorful vegetables served over brown rice, making for a balanced and satisfying dinner.
- **Servings:** 4
- **Preparation Time:** 10 minutes
- **Cooking Time:** 20 minutes

Ingredients:
1 cup (200 g) brown rice, cooked
2 boneless, skinless chicken breasts, sliced
1 tbsp (15 ml) olive oil
1 red bell pepper, sliced
1 yellow bell pepper, sliced
1 cup (150 g) snap peas
1 carrot, julienned
2 garlic cloves, minced
2 tbsp (30 ml) low-sodium soy sauce
1 tbsp (15 ml) rice vinegar
1 tsp (5 ml) honey
1/4 tsp (1.25 ml) black pepper
2 tbsp (30 ml) sesame seeds (optional)

Directions:
1. In a large skillet or wok, heat the olive oil over medium heat. Add the sliced chicken and cook for 5-7 minutes until browned and cooked through. Remove from the skillet and set aside.
2. In the same skillet, add the garlic and sauté for 1 minute until fragrant.
3. Add the red and yellow bell peppers, snap peas, and carrot. Stir-fry for 5-7 minutes until the vegetables are tender-crisp.
4. Return the chicken to the skillet and stir in the soy sauce, rice vinegar, honey, and black pepper. Cook for another 2 minutes until heated through.
5. Serve the stir-fry over cooked brown rice, garnished with sesame seeds if desired.

Nutritional Facts (per serving):
Calories: 350
Carbohydrates: 45 g
Protein: 25 g
Fats: 10 g

Sugars: 6 g
Salt: 300 mg

10. Baked Eggplant Parmesan

A healthier take on a classic Italian dish, this baked eggplant parmesan is light on calories but big on flavor, making it a perfect heart-healthy dinner.

- **Servings:** 4
- **Preparation Time:** 15 minutes
- **Cooking Time:** 30 minutes

Ingredients:
1 large eggplant, sliced into rounds
1 tbsp (15 ml) olive oil
1 cup (240 ml) marinara sauce
1/2 cup (60 g) shredded low-fat mozzarella cheese
1/4 cup (30 g) grated Parmesan cheese
1 tsp (5 ml) dried basil
1/4 tsp (1.25 ml) black pepper
A pinch of salt
Fresh basil leaves for garnish

Directions:
1. Preheat your oven to 375°F (190°C).
2. Lightly brush the eggplant slices with olive oil and arrange them on a baking sheet.
3. Bake for 15 minutes, flipping halfway through, until the eggplant is tender.
4. In a baking dish, layer half of the eggplant slices.
5. Spread half of the marinara sauce over the eggplant, followed by half of the mozzarella cheese.
6. Repeat with the remaining eggplant, marinara sauce, and mozzarella cheese.
7. Sprinkle the top with grated Parmesan cheese, dried basil, black pepper, and salt.
8. Bake for another 15 minutes until the cheese is melted and bubbly.
9. Serve hot, garnished with fresh basil leaves.

Nutritional Facts (per serving):
Calories: 280
Carbohydrates: 28 g
Protein: 12 g
Fats: 14 g
Sugars: 10 g
Salt: 350 mg

11. Grilled Shrimp Skewers with Quinoa

These flavorful shrimp skewers are grilled to perfection and served with a side of quinoa for a protein-packed and heart-healthy dinner.

- **Servings:** 2
- **Preparation Time:** 10 minutes
- **Cooking Time:** 10 minutes

Ingredients:
12 large shrimp, peeled and deveined
1 tbsp (15 ml) olive oil
1 tbsp (15 ml) lemon juice
1 tsp (5 ml) paprika
1/2 tsp (2.5 ml) garlic powder
1/4 tsp (1.25 ml) black pepper
A pinch of salt
1/2 cup (90 g) quinoa, rinsed
1 cup (240 ml) water
2 tbsp (30 ml) fresh parsley, chopped

Directions:
1. In a small bowl, mix the olive oil, lemon juice, paprika, garlic powder, black pepper, and salt.
2. Toss the shrimp in the marinade and let it sit for 10 minutes.
3. Preheat a grill or grill pan over medium heat. Thread the shrimp onto skewers and grill for 2-3 minutes on each side until pink and opaque.
4. In a medium saucepan, bring the water to a boil. Add the quinoa, reduce heat to low, cover, and simmer for 12-15 minutes until the water is absorbed and the quinoa is tender.
5. Serve the grilled shrimp skewers over the cooked quinoa, garnished with fresh parsley.

Nutritional Facts (per serving):
Calories: 320
Carbohydrates: 30 g
Protein: 22 g
Fats: 12 g
Sugars: 1 g
Salt: 300 mg

12. Turkey and Vegetable Meatloaf

A lighter version of a classic comfort food, this turkey and vegetable meatloaf is both flavorful and heart-healthy.

- **Servings:** 4
- **Preparation Time:** 15 minutes
- **Cooking Time:** 45 minutes

Ingredients:
1 lb (450 g) ground turkey
1/2 cup (75 g) diced onion
1/2 cup (75 g) diced carrots
1/2 cup (75 g) diced zucchini
1/2 cup (60 g) whole wheat breadcrumbs
1/4 cup (60 ml) low-sodium ketchup

1 large egg, beaten
1 tsp (5 ml) dried thyme
1/4 tsp (1.25 ml) black pepper
A pinch of salt

Directions:
1. Preheat your oven to 375°F (190°C).
2. In a large bowl, combine the ground turkey, diced onion, carrots, zucchini, breadcrumbs, ketchup, egg, thyme, black pepper, and salt. Mix well.
3. Press the mixture into a loaf pan and smooth the top.
4. Bake for 40-45 minutes, or until the meatloaf is cooked through and a meat thermometer reads 165°F (74°C).
5. Let the meatloaf rest for 5 minutes before slicing and serving.

Nutritional Facts (per serving):
Calories: 280
Carbohydrates: 18 g
Protein: 28 g
Fats: 10 g
Sugars: 4 g
Salt: 300 mg

13. Baked Tofu with Stir-Fried Vegetables

A flavorful and protein-rich dish featuring baked tofu served with a medley of stir-fried vegetables.
- **Servings:** 4
- **Preparation Time:** 10 minutes
- **Cooking Time:** 30 minutes

Ingredients:
1 block (400 g) firm tofu, drained and cubed
2 tbsp (30 ml) olive oil
2 tbsp (30 ml) low-sodium soy sauce
1 tbsp (15 ml) rice vinegar
1 tsp (5 ml) honey
1 tsp (5 ml) sesame oil
1 red bell pepper, sliced
1 yellow bell pepper, sliced
1 zucchini, sliced
1 carrot, julienned
2 garlic cloves, minced
1 tsp (5 ml) grated ginger
1/4 tsp (1.25 ml) black pepper
2 tbsp (30 ml) sesame seeds (optional)

Directions:
1. Preheat your oven to 375°F (190°C).

2. Toss the cubed tofu in 1 tbsp of olive oil and spread on a baking sheet. Bake for 25-30 minutes until golden and crispy.
3. In a large skillet or wok, heat the remaining olive oil over medium heat. Add the garlic and ginger, and sauté for 1 minute.
4. Add the red and yellow bell peppers, zucchini, and carrot to the skillet. Stir-fry for 5-7 minutes until the vegetables are tender-crisp.
5. In a small bowl, whisk together the soy sauce, rice vinegar, honey, sesame oil, and black pepper.
6. Add the baked tofu to the skillet and pour the sauce over the stir-fry. Toss to coat evenly and cook for another 2 minutes.
7. Serve hot, garnished with sesame seeds if desired.

Nutritional Facts (per serving):
Calories: 250
Carbohydrates: 15 g
Protein: 15 g
Fats: 14 g
Sugars: 6 g
Salt: 300 mg

14. Moroccan-Spiced Chickpea Stew

A warm and comforting stew made with chickpeas and a blend of Moroccan spices, perfect for a heart-healthy dinner.
- **Servings:** 4
- **Preparation Time:** 10 minutes
- **Cooking Time:** 30 minutes

Ingredients:
1 tbsp (15 ml) olive oil
1 onion, diced
2 garlic cloves, minced
1 tsp (5 ml) ground cumin
1 tsp (5 ml) ground coriander
1/2 tsp (2.5 ml) ground cinnamon
1/2 tsp (2.5 ml) ground turmeric
1/4 tsp (1.25 ml) ground black pepper
1 can (400 g) chickpeas, drained and rinsed
1 can (400 g) diced tomatoes
2 cups (480 ml) low-sodium vegetable broth
1 cup (150 g) diced carrots
1/2 cup (75 g) diced zucchini
1/4 cup (30 g) dried apricots, chopped
2 tbsp (30 ml) fresh cilantro, chopped

Directions:

1. In a large pot, heat the olive oil over medium heat. Add the onion and garlic, and sauté for 5 minutes until softened.
2. Stir in the cumin, coriander, cinnamon, turmeric, and black pepper, and cook for 1 minute until fragrant.
3. Add the chickpeas, diced tomatoes, vegetable broth, carrots, zucchini, and dried apricots. Bring to a boil, then reduce heat and simmer for 25-30 minutes until the vegetables are tender.
4. Serve hot, garnished with fresh cilantro.

Nutritional Facts (per serving):
Calories: 300
Carbohydrates: 50 g
Protein: 10 g
Fats: 6 g
Sugars: 15 g
Salt: 250 mg

15. Grilled Chicken with Mango Salsa

A refreshing and tropical dish featuring grilled chicken topped with a vibrant mango salsa, perfect for a light and satisfying dinner.

- **Servings:** 2
- **Preparation Time:** 10 minutes
- **Cooking Time:** 15 minutes

Ingredients:
2 boneless, skinless chicken breasts
1 tbsp (15 ml) olive oil
1 tsp (5 ml) ground cumin
1 tsp (5 ml) ground paprika
1/4 tsp (1.25 ml) black pepper
A pinch of salt
1 ripe mango, diced
1/4 cup (30 g) red onion, diced
1/4 cup (30 g) red bell pepper, diced
1 tbsp (15 ml) lime juice
1 tbsp (15 ml) fresh cilantro, chopped

Directions:

1. Preheat a grill or grill pan over medium heat.
2. Rub the chicken breasts with olive oil, cumin, paprika, black pepper, and salt.
3. Grill the chicken for 6-7 minutes on each side until fully cooked.
4. In a small bowl, combine the diced mango, red onion, red bell pepper, lime juice, and cilantro to make the mango salsa.
5. Serve the grilled chicken topped with mango salsa.

Nutritional Facts (per serving):
Calories: 300
Carbohydrates: 20 g
Protein: 28 g
Fats: 12 g
Sugars: 15 g
Salt: 250 mg

16. Spaghetti Squash with Pesto and Cherry Tomatoes

A low-carb alternative to pasta, this dish features spaghetti squash topped with a fresh basil pesto and cherry tomatoes.

- **Servings:** 2
- **Preparation Time:** 10 minutes
- **Cooking Time:** 40 minutes

Ingredients:
1 medium spaghetti squash
1 tbsp (15 ml) olive oil
1/2 cup (120 ml) fresh basil pesto (store-bought or homemade)
1 cup (150 g) cherry tomatoes, halved
1/4 tsp (1.25 ml) black pepper
A pinch of salt
2 tbsp (30 ml) grated Parmesan cheese (optional)

Directions:

1. Preheat your oven to 375°F (190°C). Slice the spaghetti squash in half lengthwise and remove the seeds.
2. Drizzle the cut sides of the squash with olive oil and season with black pepper and salt.
3. Place the squash halves cut side down on a baking sheet and roast for 35-40 minutes, or until tender.
4. Once the squash is done, use a fork to scrape the flesh into spaghetti-like strands.
5. Toss the spaghetti squash with fresh basil pesto and cherry tomatoes.
6. Serve hot, topped with grated Parmesan cheese if desired.

Nutritional Facts (per serving):
Calories: 250
Carbohydrates: 30 g
Protein: 5 g
Fats: 12 g
Sugars: 8 g
Salt: 200 mg

17. Herb-Roasted Chicken with Root Vegetables

A comforting dish featuring herb-roasted chicken served with a medley of root vegetables, perfect for a cozy and nutritious dinner.

- **Servings:** 4
- **Preparation Time:** 10 minutes
- **Cooking Time:** 50 minutes

Ingredients:
4 bone-in, skin-on chicken thighs
2 tbsp (30 ml) olive oil
2 carrots, peeled and diced
2 parsnips, peeled and diced
1 sweet potato, peeled and diced
1 tsp (5 ml) dried rosemary
1 tsp (5 ml) dried thyme
1/4 tsp (1.25 ml) black pepper
A pinch of salt

Directions:
1. Preheat your oven to 400°F (200°C).
2. In a large bowl, toss the diced carrots, parsnips, and sweet potato with 1 tbsp of olive oil, rosemary, thyme, black pepper, and salt.
3. Spread the vegetables on a baking sheet and roast for 20 minutes.
4. Meanwhile, rub the chicken thighs with the remaining olive oil, rosemary, thyme, black pepper, and salt.
5. After 20 minutes, add the chicken thighs to the baking sheet with the vegetables and continue roasting for another 30 minutes, or until the chicken is cooked through and the skin is crispy.
6. Serve hot.

Nutritional Facts (per serving):
Calories: 400
Carbohydrates: 35 g
Protein: 25 g
Fats: 20 g
Sugars: 10 g
Salt: 250 mg

18. Baked Cod with Roasted Cherry Tomatoes

A light and flavorful dish featuring baked cod topped with roasted cherry tomatoes and fresh herbs, making for a healthy and satisfying dinner.

- **Servings:** 2
- **Preparation Time:** 10 minutes
- **Cooking Time:** 20 minutes

Ingredients:
2 cod fillets (about 150 g each)
1 tbsp (15 ml) olive oil
1 cup (150 g) cherry tomatoes, halved
2 garlic cloves, minced
1 tbsp (15 ml) lemon juice
1 tsp (5 ml) dried basil
1/4 tsp (1.25 ml) black pepper
A pinch of salt

Directions:
1. Preheat your oven to 375°F (190°C).
2. Place the cod fillets in a baking dish. Drizzle with olive oil and lemon juice.
3. Top the cod with minced garlic, cherry tomatoes, basil, black pepper, and salt.
4. Bake for 15-20 minutes, or until the cod is opaque and flakes easily with a fork.
5. Serve hot, garnished with additional fresh herbs if desired.

Nutritional Facts (per serving):
Calories: 250
Carbohydrates: 6 g
Protein: 30 g
Fats: 12 g
Sugars: 4 g
Salt: 200 mg

19. Thai-Inspired Chicken Curry with Brown Rice

A fragrant and flavorful Thai-inspired chicken curry served with brown rice, offering a satisfying and heart-healthy dinner.

- **Servings:** 4
- **Preparation Time:** 10 minutes
- **Cooking Time:** 20 minutes

Ingredients:
1 lb (450 g) boneless, skinless chicken thighs, cut into bite-sized pieces
1 tbsp (15 ml) olive oil
1 onion, diced
2 garlic cloves, minced
1 tbsp (15 ml) red curry paste
1 can (400 ml) light coconut milk
1 red bell pepper, sliced
1 cup (150 g) snap peas
1/2 cup (75 g) carrots, julienned
1 tbsp (15 ml) fish sauce
1 tbsp (15 ml) lime juice

1/4 tsp (1.25 ml) black pepper
2 cups (400 g) cooked brown rice
Fresh cilantro for garnish

Directions:
1. In a large skillet, heat the olive oil over medium heat. Add the onion and garlic, and sauté for 5 minutes until softened.
2. Stir in the red curry paste and cook for 1 minute until fragrant.
3. Add the chicken pieces and cook for 5-7 minutes until browned.
4. Pour in the coconut milk, red bell pepper, snap peas, carrots, fish sauce, lime juice, and black pepper. Bring to a simmer and cook for 10 minutes until the chicken is fully cooked and the vegetables are tender.
5. Serve the curry over cooked brown rice, garnished with fresh cilantro.

Nutritional Facts (per serving):
Calories: 400
Carbohydrates: 45 g
Protein: 25 g
Fats: 15 g
Sugars: 6 g
Salt: 400 mg

20. Mushroom and Spinach Stuffed Chicken Breast

A flavorful dish featuring chicken breasts stuffed with a savory mixture of mushrooms and spinach, making it a delicious and heart-healthy dinner option.
- **Servings:** 2
- **Preparation Time:** 10 minutes
- **Cooking Time:** 25 minutes

Ingredients:
2 boneless, skinless chicken breasts
1 tbsp (15 ml) olive oil
1 cup (75 g) mushrooms, chopped
1 cup (30 g) fresh spinach, chopped
1 garlic clove, minced
1/4 cup (30 g) shredded mozzarella cheese
1/4 tsp (1.25 ml) black pepper
A pinch of salt
2 lemon wedges

Directions:
1. Preheat your oven to 375°F (190°C).
2. In a skillet, heat half of the olive oil over medium heat. Add the garlic and mushrooms and sauté for 5 minutes until softened. Add the spinach and cook until wilted. Remove from heat and stir in the mozzarella cheese.
3. Slice a pocket into each chicken breast and stuff with the mushroom and spinach mixture.
4. Heat the remaining olive oil in a skillet over medium heat. Sear the chicken breasts for 2-3 minutes on each side until golden brown.
5. Transfer the chicken to a baking dish and bake for 15-20 minutes, or until the chicken is fully cooked.
6. Serve hot, garnished with lemon wedges.

Nutritional Facts (per serving):
Calories: 350
Carbohydrates: 5 g
Protein: 35 g
Fats: 20 g
Sugars: 2 g
Salt: 250 mg

These twenty wholesome and satisfying dinner recipes are designed to make your evenings both nutritious and delicious. By incorporating these meals into your routine, you can enjoy heart-healthy dinners that are easy to prepare and packed with flavor, ensuring that your diet supports your overall well-being.

Chapter 14: Snacks and Small Bites

Snacks and small bites play a crucial role in maintaining your energy levels throughout the day, especially when you're on a heart-healthy diet. Choosing the right snacks can help keep your hunger in check, provide essential nutrients, and support your overall cardiovascular health. Here, I present 20 simple, delicious, and heart-healthy snack recipes that are perfect for any time of the day.

1. Almond Butter Apple Slices

A classic snack that combines the crisp sweetness of apples with the rich creaminess of almond butter, offering a quick energy boost with healthy fats and fiber.
- **Servings:** 1
- **Preparation Time:** 5 minutes
- **Cooking Time:** None

Ingredients:
1 medium apple, sliced
1 tbsp (15 g) almond butter
1/4 tsp (1.25 ml) ground cinnamon

Directions:
1. Slice the apple into thin wedges.
2. Spread the almond butter evenly on each slice.
3. Sprinkle with ground cinnamon.
4. Serve immediately.

Nutritional Facts (per serving):
Calories: 200
Carbohydrates: 30 g
Protein: 2 g
Fats: 8 g
Sugars: 18 g
Salt: 2 mg

2. Greek Yogurt with Berries and Chia Seeds

This creamy and refreshing snack is rich in protein, antioxidants, and omega-3 fatty acids, making it a heart-healthy option that satisfies your sweet tooth.
- **Servings:** 1
- **Preparation Time:** 5 minutes
- **Cooking Time:** None

Ingredients:
1/2 cup (120 ml) plain Greek yogurt
1/4 cup (50 g) mixed berries (blueberries, strawberries, raspberries)
1 tsp (5 ml) chia seeds
1 tsp (5 ml) honey (optional)

Directions:
1. Spoon the Greek yogurt into a bowl.
2. Top with mixed berries and sprinkle with chia seeds.
3. Drizzle with honey if desired.
4. Serve immediately.

Nutritional Facts (per serving):
Calories: 150
Carbohydrates: 20 g
Protein: 10 g
Fats: 4 g
Sugars: 12 g
Salt: 60 mg

3. Roasted Chickpeas

Crispy roasted chickpeas are a savory snack packed with protein and fiber, perfect for curbing your midday cravings.

- **Servings:** 4
- **Preparation Time:** 5 minutes
- **Cooking Time:** 40 minutes

Ingredients:

1 can (400 g) chickpeas, drained and rinsed
1 tbsp (15 ml) olive oil
1/2 tsp (2.5 ml) paprika
1/2 tsp (2.5 ml) ground cumin
1/4 tsp (1.25 ml) black pepper
A pinch of salt

Directions:

1. Preheat your oven to 400°F (200°C).
2. Pat the chickpeas dry with a paper towel.
3. In a bowl, toss the chickpeas with olive oil, paprika, cumin, black pepper, and salt.
4. Spread the chickpeas in a single layer on a baking sheet.
5. Roast for 35-40 minutes, shaking the pan occasionally, until the chickpeas are golden and crispy.
6. Allow to cool before serving.

Nutritional Facts (per serving):
Calories: 150
Carbohydrates: 20 g
Protein: 5 g
Fats: 5 g
Sugars: 1 g
Salt: 150 mg

4. Avocado Toast with Cherry Tomatoes

A simple yet satisfying snack that combines creamy avocado with the fresh burst of cherry tomatoes on whole-grain toast.

- **Servings:** 1
- **Preparation Time:** 5 minutes
- **Cooking Time:** None

Ingredients:

1 slice whole-grain bread
1/2 ripe avocado, mashed
1/4 cup (50 g) cherry tomatoes, halved
1/4 tsp (1.25 ml) black pepper
A pinch of salt

Directions:

1. Toast the whole-grain bread to your desired level of crispiness.
2. Spread the mashed avocado evenly over the toast.
3. Top with halved cherry tomatoes.
4. Sprinkle with black pepper and a pinch of salt.
5. Serve immediately.

Nutritional Facts (per serving):
Calories: 220
Carbohydrates: 26 g
Protein: 5 g
Fats: 12 g
Sugars: 3 g
Salt: 200 mg

5. Veggie Sticks with Hummus

A colorful and crunchy snack that pairs fresh vegetable sticks with creamy hummus, offering a satisfying mix of flavors and textures.

- **Servings:** 2
- **Preparation Time:** 10 minutes
- **Cooking Time:** None

Ingredients:

1/2 cup (120 ml) hummus
1 carrot, cut into sticks
1 cucumber, cut into sticks
1 red bell pepper, sliced
1 celery stalk, cut into sticks

Directions:

1. Arrange the vegetable sticks on a plate.
2. Serve with hummus on the side for dipping.
3. Enjoy as a healthy and refreshing snack.

Nutritional Facts (per serving):
Calories: 150
Carbohydrates: 18 g
Protein: 5 g
Fats: 7 g
Sugars: 6 g
Salt: 150 mg

6. Baked Sweet Potato Chips

These crispy baked sweet potato chips are a healthier alternative to regular chips, offering a satisfying crunch with a touch of natural sweetness.

- **Servings:** 2
- **Preparation Time:** 5 minutes
- **Cooking Time:** 20 minutes

Ingredients:
1 large sweet potato, thinly sliced
1 tbsp (15 ml) olive oil
1/2 tsp (2.5 ml) paprika
1/4 tsp (1.25 ml) black pepper
A pinch of salt

Directions:
1. Preheat your oven to 375°F (190°C).
2. Toss the sweet potato slices in olive oil, paprika, black pepper, and salt.
3. Arrange the slices in a single layer on a baking sheet.
4. Bake for 15-20 minutes, flipping halfway through, until crispy and golden.
5. Allow to cool before serving.

Nutritional Facts (per serving):
Calories: 140
Carbohydrates: 22 g
Protein: 2 g
Fats: 5 g
Sugars: 6 g
Salt: 100 mg

7. Cottage Cheese with Pineapple

A light and refreshing snack that combines protein-rich cottage cheese with sweet and tangy pineapple for a delicious and nutritious treat.
- **Servings:** 1
- **Preparation Time:** 5 minutes
- **Cooking Time:** None

Ingredients:
1/2 cup (120 ml) low-fat cottage cheese
1/4 cup (50 g) pineapple chunks (fresh or canned in juice, drained)
1/4 tsp (1.25 ml) ground cinnamon (optional)

Directions:
1. Spoon the cottage cheese into a bowl.
2. Top with pineapple chunks.
3. Sprinkle with ground cinnamon if desired.
4. Serve immediately.

Nutritional Facts (per serving):
Calories: 110
Carbohydrates: 12 g
Protein: 10 g
Fats: 2 g
Sugars: 8 g
Salt: 300 mg

8. Peanut Butter Banana Bites

A simple and tasty snack that combines banana slices with peanut butter for a quick boost of energy and nutrients.
- **Servings:** 1
- **Preparation Time:** 5 minutes
- **Cooking Time:** None

Ingredients:
1 banana, sliced
1 tbsp (15 g) natural peanut butter
1/4 tsp (1.25 ml) ground cinnamon

Directions:
1. Spread a small amount of peanut butter on each banana slice.
2. Sprinkle with ground cinnamon.
3. Enjoy as a quick and satisfying snack.

Nutritional Facts (per serving):
Calories: 200
Carbohydrates: 30 g
Protein: 4 g
Fats: 8 g
Sugars: 14 g
Salt: 50 mg

9. Whole-Grain Crackers with Avocado and Tuna

A protein-packed snack that combines whole-grain crackers with creamy avocado and tuna for a savory and satisfying bite.
- **Servings:** 2
- **Preparation Time:** 5 minutes
- **Cooking Time:** None

Ingredients:
8 whole-grain crackers
1/2 ripe avocado, mashed
1/2 can (60 g) tuna in water, drained
1/4 tsp (1.25 ml) black pepper
A pinch of salt

Directions:
1. Spread the mashed avocado evenly on each cracker.
2. Top with a small amount of tuna.
3. Sprinkle with black pepper and a pinch of salt.
4. Serve immediately.

Nutritional Facts (per serving):
Calories: 180

Carbohydrates: 15 g
Protein: 10 g
Fats: 10 g
Sugars: 1 g
Salt: 200 mg

10. Edamame with Sea Salt

Edamame, or young soybeans, are a protein-rich snack that's easy to prepare and perfect for curbing your hunger between meals.

- **Servings:** 2
- **Preparation Time:** 5 minutes
- **Cooking Time:** 5 minutes

Ingredients:
1 cup (150 g) shelled edamame
1/4 tsp (1.25 ml) sea salt

Directions:
1. Bring a pot of water to a boil. Add the edamame and cook for 3-5 minutes until tender.
2. Drain the edamame and sprinkle with sea salt.
3. Serve warm or cold as a snack.

Nutritional Facts (per serving):
Calories: 120
Carbohydrates: 10 g
Protein: 10 g
Fats: 5 g
Sugars: 2 g
Salt: 150 mg

11. Oat and Nut Energy Bites

These no-bake energy bites are made with oats, nuts, and a touch of honey, offering a sweet and satisfying snack that's perfect for on-the-go.

- **Servings:** 10
- **Preparation Time:** 10 minutes
- **Cooking Time:** None

Ingredients:
1 cup (90 g) rolled oats
1/2 cup (120 ml) almond butter
1/4 cup (60 ml) honey
1/4 cup (30 g) chopped nuts (almonds, walnuts, or pecans)
1/4 cup (30 g) dark chocolate chips (optional)
1/4 tsp (1.25 ml) vanilla extract

Directions:
1. In a large bowl, mix together all the ingredients until well combined.

2. Roll the mixture into small balls, about 1 inch (2.5 cm) in diameter.
3. Place the bites on a baking sheet and refrigerate for at least 30 minutes to firm up.
4. Store in an airtight container in the refrigerator.

Nutritional Facts (per serving):
Calories: 120
Carbohydrates: 15 g
Protein: 3 g
Fats: 6 g
Sugars: 8 g
Salt: 40 mg

12. Carrot Sticks with Tahini Dip

A simple and nutritious snack featuring crunchy carrot sticks paired with a creamy tahini dip, offering a boost of healthy fats and fiber.

- **Servings:** 2
- **Preparation Time:** 5 minutes
- **Cooking Time:** None

Ingredients:
2 large carrots, cut into sticks
2 tbsp (30 ml) tahini
1 tbsp (15 ml) lemon juice
1/2 tsp (2.5 ml) garlic powder
1/4 tsp (1.25 ml) cumin
1/4 tsp (1.25 ml) black pepper
A pinch of salt

Directions:
1. In a small bowl, mix together the tahini, lemon juice, garlic powder, cumin, black pepper, and salt. Add a little water if needed to reach your desired consistency.
2. Serve the tahini dip with carrot sticks on the side.
3. Enjoy as a healthy and satisfying snack.

Nutritional Facts (per serving):
Calories: 130
Carbohydrates: 10 g
Protein: 3 g
Fats: 9 g
Sugars: 5 g
Salt: 80 mg

13. Frozen Yogurt Bark with Berries

A refreshing and healthy snack, this frozen yogurt bark is topped with berries and nuts, making it a delicious treat for hot days.
- **Servings:** 8
- **Preparation Time:** 10 minutes
- **Cooking Time:** None
- **Freezing Time:** 2 hours

Ingredients:
2 cups (480 ml) plain Greek yogurt
1 tbsp (15 ml) honey
1/2 cup (100 g) mixed berries (blueberries, strawberries, raspberries)
1/4 cup (30 g) chopped nuts (almonds, walnuts, or pistachios)

Directions:
1. In a bowl, mix the Greek yogurt with honey until well combined.
2. Spread the yogurt mixture evenly on a baking sheet lined with parchment paper.
3. Sprinkle the mixed berries and chopped nuts over the yogurt.
4. Freeze for at least 2 hours or until fully hardened.
5. Once frozen, break the yogurt bark into pieces and serve immediately.

Nutritional Facts (per serving):
Calories: 90
Carbohydrates: 8 g
Protein: 6 g
Fats: 3 g
Sugars: 6 g
Salt: 30 mg

14. Spiced Pumpkin Seeds

These crunchy and flavorful pumpkin seeds are roasted with a blend of spices, making them a perfect snack for any time of the day.
- **Servings:** 4
- **Preparation Time:** 5 minutes
- **Cooking Time:** 15 minutes

Ingredients:
1 cup (120 g) raw pumpkin seeds
1 tbsp (15 ml) olive oil
1/2 tsp (2.5 ml) paprika
1/2 tsp (2.5 ml) ground cumin
1/4 tsp (1.25 ml) cayenne pepper (optional)
1/4 tsp (1.25 ml) black pepper
A pinch of salt

Directions:
1. Preheat your oven to 350°F (175°C).
2. In a bowl, toss the pumpkin seeds with olive oil, paprika, cumin, cayenne pepper, black pepper, and salt.
3. Spread the seeds in a single layer on a baking sheet.
4. Roast for 12-15 minutes, stirring occasionally, until golden and crispy.
5. Allow to cool before serving.

Nutritional Facts (per serving):
Calories: 120
Carbohydrates: 4 g
Protein: 5 g
Fats: 10 g
Sugars: 0 g
Salt: 100 mg

15. Cucumber Slices with Feta and Olive Oil

A refreshing and light snack, these cucumber slices topped with crumbled feta and a drizzle of olive oil are both hydrating and satisfying.
- **Servings:** 2
- **Preparation Time:** 5 minutes
- **Cooking Time:** None

Ingredients:
1/2 cucumber, sliced
2 tbsp (30 g) crumbled feta cheese
1 tsp (5 ml) olive oil
1/4 tsp (1.25 ml) black pepper
A pinch of salt

Directions:
1. Arrange the cucumber slices on a plate.
2. Top with crumbled feta cheese.
3. Drizzle with olive oil and sprinkle with black pepper and a pinch of salt.
4. Serve immediately.

Nutritional Facts (per serving):
Calories: 80
Carbohydrates: 4 g
Protein: 3 g
Fats: 6 g
Sugars: 2 g
Salt: 200 mg

16. Mixed Berry Smoothie

This vibrant and refreshing smoothie is packed with antioxidants and fiber from mixed berries, making it a perfect heart-healthy snack.

- **Servings:** 1
- **Preparation Time:** 5 minutes
- **Cooking Time:** None

Ingredients:
1/2 cup (75 g) mixed berries (blueberries, strawberries, raspberries)
1/2 banana
1/4 cup (60 ml) low-fat milk or almond milk
1/4 cup (60 ml) plain Greek yogurt
1 tsp (5 ml) honey (optional)

Directions:
1. In a blender, combine all the ingredients and blend until smooth.
2. Pour into a glass and serve immediately.

Nutritional Facts (per serving):
Calories: 150
Carbohydrates: 30 g
Protein: 6 g
Fats: 2 g
Sugars: 18 g
Salt: 60 mg

17. Dark Chocolate Almonds

A sweet and satisfying snack that combines the richness of dark chocolate with the crunch of almonds, offering a heart-healthy treat.

- **Servings:** 4
- **Preparation Time:** 5 minutes
- **Cooking Time:** None

Ingredients:
1/2 cup (60 g) raw almonds
1/4 cup (30 g) dark chocolate chips (70% cocoa or higher)

Directions:
1. Melt the dark chocolate chips in the microwave or over a double boiler.
2. Dip the almonds in the melted chocolate and place them on a baking sheet lined with parchment paper.
3. Allow the chocolate to set at room temperature or in the refrigerator.
4. Serve as a sweet and crunchy snack.

Nutritional Facts (per serving):
Calories: 150

Carbohydrates: 10 g
Protein: 4 g
Fats: 12 g
Sugars: 6 g
Salt: 0 mg

18. Apple Nachos with Peanut Butter and Nuts

A fun and healthy twist on nachos, this snack features apple slices drizzled with peanut butter and topped with nuts and raisins.

- **Servings:** 2
- **Preparation Time:** 5 minutes
- **Cooking Time:** None

Ingredients:
1 large apple, sliced
2 tbsp (30 g) natural peanut butter
1 tbsp (15 g) chopped nuts (almonds, walnuts, or pecans)
1 tbsp (15 g) raisins
1/4 tsp (1.25 ml) ground cinnamon

Directions:
1. Arrange the apple slices on a plate.
2. Drizzle with peanut butter.
3. Sprinkle with chopped nuts, raisins, and ground cinnamon.
4. Serve immediately.

Nutritional Facts (per serving):
Calories: 200
Carbohydrates: 30 g
Protein: 4 g
Fats: 8 g
Sugars: 18 g
Salt: 20 mg

19. Cherry Tomato and Mozzarella Skewers

A light and flavorful snack, these skewers combine juicy cherry tomatoes with fresh mozzarella and basil for a refreshing bite.

- **Servings:** 2
- **Preparation Time:** 5 minutes
- **Cooking Time:** None

Ingredients:
10 cherry tomatoes
10 small fresh mozzarella balls (bocconcini)
10 fresh basil leaves
1 tbsp (15 ml) balsamic glaze (optional)

Directions:

1. Thread each cherry tomato, mozzarella ball, and basil leaf onto small skewers or toothpicks.
2. Drizzle with balsamic glaze if desired.
3. Serve immediately.

Nutritional Facts (per serving):

Calories: 100
Carbohydrates: 5 g
Protein: 5 g
Fats: 7 g
Sugars: 3 g
Salt: 60 mg

20. Banana Oat Cookies

These simple and healthy cookies are made with just bananas and oats, offering a naturally sweet and satisfying snack.

- **Servings:** 10
- **Preparation Time:** 10 minutes
- **Cooking Time:** 15 minutes

Ingredients:

2 ripe bananas, mashed
1 cup (90 g) rolled oats
1/4 cup (30 g) dark chocolate chips (optional)
1/4 tsp (1.25 ml) ground cinnamon

Directions:

1. Preheat your oven to 350°F (175°C).
2. In a bowl, mix the mashed bananas with rolled oats, dark chocolate chips, and ground cinnamon.
3. Drop spoonfuls of the mixture onto a baking sheet lined with parchment paper.
4. Bake for 12-15 minutes until golden brown.
5. Allow to cool before serving.

Nutritional Facts (per serving):

Calories: 90
Carbohydrates: 18 g
Protein: 2 g
Fats: 2 g
Sugars: 6 g
Salt: 5 mg

These twenty snack and small bite recipes are designed to keep you energized and satisfied between meals, all while supporting your heart health. By incorporating these snacks into your daily routine, you can enjoy delicious, nutritious bites that align with your overall well-being and dietary goals.

Chapter 15: Healthy Indulgences: Desserts and Treats

Even when following a heart-healthy diet, there's no need to completely give up on indulgences. The key is to enjoy treats made with wholesome ingredients that satisfy your sweet tooth without compromising your health. In this chapter, I present twenty delicious and guilt-free desserts and treats that will allow you to indulge while still supporting your heart health.

1. Dark Chocolate Avocado Mousse

This creamy and decadent mousse combines the richness of dark chocolate with the healthy fats of avocado for a heart-healthy indulgence.
- **Servings:** 4
- **Preparation Time:** 10 minutes
- **Cooking Time:** None

Ingredients:
2 ripe avocados
1/4 cup (30 g) cocoa powder
1/4 cup (60 ml) honey or maple syrup
1/4 cup (60 ml) almond milk
1 tsp (5 ml) vanilla extract
A pinch of sea salt

Directions:
1. In a blender or food processor, combine the avocados, cocoa powder, honey or maple syrup, almond milk, vanilla extract, and sea salt.
2. Blend until smooth and creamy, scraping down the sides as needed.
3. Spoon the mousse into individual serving bowls and chill in the refrigerator for at least 30 minutes before serving.

Nutritional Facts (per serving):
Calories: 220
Carbohydrates: 25 g
Protein: 3 g
Fats: 14 g
Sugars: 18 g
Salt: 40 mg

2. Baked Apple with Cinnamon and Walnuts

This warm and comforting dessert features baked apples stuffed with cinnamon, walnuts, and a touch of honey, making it a perfect heart-healthy treat.
- **Servings:** 2
- **Preparation Time:** 5 minutes
- **Cooking Time:** 25 minutes

Ingredients:
2 medium apples
2 tbsp (30 ml) chopped walnuts
1 tbsp (15 ml) honey
1 tsp (5 ml) ground cinnamon

Directions:
1. Preheat your oven to 350°F (175°C).
2. Core the apples and place them in a baking dish.
3. In a small bowl, mix together the chopped walnuts, honey, and ground cinnamon.
4. Stuff the mixture into the cored apples.
5. Bake for 20-25 minutes, or until the apples are tender.
6. Serve warm.

Nutritional Facts (per serving):
Calories: 180
Carbohydrates: 38 g
Protein: 2 g
Fats: 5 g
Sugars: 30 g
Salt: 0 mg

3. Chia Seed Pudding with Berries

A creamy and satisfying chia seed pudding, layered with fresh berries, offers a nutritious and heart-healthy dessert option.

- **Servings:** 2
- **Preparation Time:** 5 minutes
- **Cooking Time:** None
- **Chilling Time:** 4 hours or overnight

Ingredients:
1/4 cup (40 g) chia seeds
1 cup (240 ml) almond milk
1 tbsp (15 ml) honey or maple syrup
1/2 tsp (2.5 ml) vanilla extract
1/2 cup (75 g) mixed berries

Directions:
1. In a bowl, whisk together the chia seeds, almond milk, honey or maple syrup, and vanilla extract.
2. Cover and refrigerate for at least 4 hours or overnight, until the mixture thickens into a pudding-like consistency.
3. Stir the pudding and layer it in serving glasses with mixed berries.
4. Serve chilled.

Nutritional Facts (per serving):
Calories: 180
Carbohydrates: 20 g
Protein: 5 g
Fats: 9 g
Sugars: 10 g
Salt: 40 mg

4. Banana Oat Cookies

These simple, healthy cookies are made with just bananas, oats, and a few add-ins, making them a naturally sweet treat.

- **Servings:** 10
- **Preparation Time:** 10 minutes
- **Cooking Time:** 15 minutes

Ingredients:
2 ripe bananas, mashed
1 cup (90 g) rolled oats
1/4 cup (30 g) dark chocolate chips or raisins (optional)
1/4 tsp (1.25 ml) ground cinnamon

Directions:
1. Preheat your oven to 350°F (175°C).
2. In a bowl, mix the mashed bananas with rolled oats, dark chocolate chips or raisins, and ground cinnamon.
3. Drop spoonfuls of the mixture onto a baking sheet lined with parchment paper.
4. Bake for 12-15 minutes, until golden brown.
5. Allow to cool before serving.

Nutritional Facts (per serving):
Calories: 90
Carbohydrates: 18 g
Protein: 2 g
Fats: 2 g
Sugars: 6 g
Salt: 5 mg

5. Greek Yogurt Parfait with Granola and Honey

A layered parfait of creamy Greek yogurt, crunchy granola, and a drizzle of honey, offering a delicious balance of textures and flavors.

- **Servings:** 2
- **Preparation Time:** 5 minutes
- **Cooking Time:** None

Ingredients:
1 cup (240 ml) plain Greek yogurt
1/4 cup (30 g) granola
2 tbsp (30 ml) honey
1/2 cup (75 g) mixed berries

Directions:
1. In serving glasses, layer the Greek yogurt, granola, and mixed berries.
2. Drizzle with honey.
3. Serve immediately.

Nutritional Facts (per serving):
Calories: 220
Carbohydrates: 35 g
Protein: 10 g
Fats: 5 g
Sugars: 25 g
Salt: 50 mg

6. Avocado Chocolate Brownies

These rich, fudgy brownies are made with avocado for added moisture and heart-healthy fats, making them a deliciously guilt-free indulgence.

- **Servings:** 12
- **Preparation Time:** 10 minutes
- **Cooking Time:** 25 minutes

Ingredients:
1 ripe avocado, mashed
1/2 cup (120 ml) honey or maple syrup
2 large eggs
1/2 cup (60 g) cocoa powder
1/4 cup (60 ml) almond milk
1 tsp (5 ml) vanilla extract
1/2 cup (60 g) whole wheat flour
1/2 tsp (2.5 ml) baking powder
1/4 tsp (1.25 ml) salt

Directions:
1. Preheat your oven to 350°F (175°C). Grease an 8x8-inch (20x20 cm) baking dish.
2. In a large bowl, mix the mashed avocado with honey or maple syrup until smooth.
3. Add the eggs, cocoa powder, almond milk, and vanilla extract, and mix until well combined.
4. Stir in the whole wheat flour, baking powder, and salt until just combined.
5. Pour the batter into the prepared baking dish and smooth the top.
6. Bake for 20-25 minutes, or until a toothpick inserted into the center comes out clean.
7. Allow to cool before cutting into squares.

Nutritional Facts (per serving):
Calories: 150
Carbohydrates: 20 g
Protein: 3 g
Fats: 7 g
Sugars: 12 g
Salt: 80 mg

7. Coconut Macaroons

These light and chewy coconut macaroons are made with just a few simple ingredients, making them a satisfying and heart-healthy treat.
- **Servings:** 12
- **Preparation Time:** 10 minutes
- **Cooking Time:** 15 minutes

Ingredients:
2 cups (150 g) unsweetened shredded coconut
2 large egg whites
1/4 cup (60 ml) honey or maple syrup
1 tsp (5 ml) vanilla extract
A pinch of sea salt

Directions:
1. Preheat your oven to 350°F (175°C). Line a baking sheet with parchment paper.
2. In a bowl, whisk the egg whites until frothy.

3. Stir in the shredded coconut, honey or maple syrup, vanilla extract, and sea salt until well combined.
4. Drop spoonfuls of the mixture onto the prepared baking sheet.
5. Bake for 12-15 minutes, until the edges are golden brown.
6. Allow to cool before serving.

Nutritional Facts (per serving):
Calories: 80
Carbohydrates: 10 g
Protein: 1 g
Fats: 4 g
Sugars: 8 g
Salt: 30 mg

8. Baked Pears with Honey and Almonds

These tender baked pears are drizzled with honey and topped with sliced almonds, making for a light and elegant dessert.
- **Servings:** 4
- **Preparation Time:** 5 minutes
- **Cooking Time:** 25 minutes

Ingredients:
2 ripe pears, halved and cored
2 tbsp (30 ml) honey
1/4 cup (30 g) sliced almonds
1/2 tsp (2.5 ml) ground cinnamon

Directions:
1. Preheat your oven to 350°F (175°C).
2. Place the pear halves cut side up in a baking dish.
3. Drizzle with honey and sprinkle with sliced almonds and ground cinnamon.
4. Bake for 20-25 minutes, or until the pears are tender.
5. Serve warm.

Nutritional Facts (per serving):
Calories: 150
Carbohydrates: 25 g
Protein: 2 g
Fats: 5 g
Sugars: 20 g
Salt: 5 mg

9. Dark Chocolate-Covered Strawberries

These elegant and simple treats feature fresh strawberries dipped in dark chocolate, offering a sweet and heart-healthy indulgence.

- **Servings:** 10
- **Preparation Time:** 10 minutes
- **Cooking Time:** None

Ingredients:
10 large strawberries
1/2 cup (60 g) dark chocolate chips (70% cocoa or higher)

Directions:
1. Melt the dark chocolate chips in the microwave or over a double boiler.
2. Dip each strawberry into the melted chocolate, allowing the excess to drip off.
3. Place the strawberries on a baking sheet lined with parchment paper.
4. Allow the chocolate to set at room temperature or in the refrigerator.
5. Serve as a sweet and satisfying treat.

Nutritional Facts (per serving):
Calories: 50
Carbohydrates: 8 g
Protein: 1 g
Fats: 3 g
Sugars: 6 g
Salt: 0 mg

10. Mango Sorbet

This refreshing and naturally sweet mango sorbet is a simple and healthy dessert that's perfect for warm weather.

- **Servings:** 4
- **Preparation Time:** 5 minutes
- **Cooking Time:** None
- **Freezing Time:** 2 hours

Ingredients:
2 ripe mangoes, peeled and chopped
1 tbsp (15 ml) lime juice
1 tbsp (15 ml) honey or maple syrup
1/4 cup (60 ml) water

Directions:
1. In a blender, combine the chopped mangoes, lime juice, honey or maple syrup, and water.
2. Blend until smooth.
3. Pour the mixture into a freezer-safe container and freeze for at least 2 hours, or until firm.

4. Scoop and serve as a refreshing sorbet.

Nutritional Facts (per serving):
Calories: 80
Carbohydrates: 20 g
Protein: 1 g
Fats: 0 g
Sugars: 18 g
Salt: 0 mg

11. Banana Ice Cream

A creamy and dairy-free ice cream made with just bananas, offering a naturally sweet and satisfying treat.

- **Servings:** 2
- **Preparation Time:** 5 minutes
- **Cooking Time:** None
- **Freezing Time:** 2 hours

Ingredients:
2 ripe bananas, sliced and frozen
1/4 tsp (1.25 ml) vanilla extract (optional)

Directions:
1. In a food processor, blend the frozen banana slices until smooth and creamy.
2. Add vanilla extract if desired and blend again.
3. Serve immediately as soft-serve or freeze for an additional hour for a firmer texture.

Nutritional Facts (per serving):
Calories: 100
Carbohydrates: 27 g
Protein: 1 g
Fats: 0 g
Sugars: 14 g
Salt: 0 mg

12. Almond Butter Chocolate Cups

These rich and satisfying almond butter cups are made with dark chocolate and almond butter, offering a healthier twist on a classic treat.

- **Servings:** 6
- **Preparation Time:** 10 minutes
- **Cooking Time:** None
- **Chilling Time:** 30 minutes

Ingredients:
1/2 cup (60 g) dark chocolate chips (70% cocoa or higher)
1/4 cup (60 ml) almond butter
1 tbsp (15 ml) honey or maple syrup

Directions:

1. Melt the dark chocolate chips in the microwave or over a double boiler.
2. Line a muffin tin with paper liners.
3. Pour a small amount of melted chocolate into each liner to cover the bottom.
4. In a small bowl, mix the almond butter with honey or maple syrup.
5. Spoon a small amount of the almond butter mixture onto the chocolate layer in each liner.
6. Cover with the remaining melted chocolate.
7. Chill in the refrigerator for at least 30 minutes, or until set.
8. Serve chilled.

Nutritional Facts (per serving):
Calories: 120
Carbohydrates: 10 g
Protein: 2 g
Fats: 9 g
Sugars: 7 g
Salt: 0 mg

13. Berry Crumble

A warm and comforting berry crumble made with oats and almond flour, offering a sweet and tart dessert that's both heart-healthy and satisfying.

- **Servings:** 4
- **Preparation Time:** 10 minutes
- **Cooking Time:** 25 minutes

Ingredients:
2 cups (300 g) mixed berries (blueberries, strawberries, raspberries)
1 tbsp (15 ml) honey or maple syrup
1/2 cup (45 g) rolled oats
1/4 cup (30 g) almond flour
1/4 cup (60 ml) almond butter
1 tsp (5 ml) ground cinnamon

Directions:

1. Preheat your oven to 350°F (175°C).
2. In a baking dish, toss the mixed berries with honey or maple syrup.
3. In a small bowl, mix the rolled oats, almond flour, almond butter, and ground cinnamon until crumbly.
4. Sprinkle the oat mixture over the berries.
5. Bake for 20-25 minutes, or until the topping is golden brown and the berries are bubbling.
6. Serve warm.

Nutritional Facts (per serving):
Calories: 180
Carbohydrates: 25 g
Protein: 4 g
Fats: 8 g
Sugars: 15 g
Salt: 0 mg

14. Zucchini Chocolate Cake

A moist and rich chocolate cake made with zucchini for added moisture and nutrients, offering a heart-healthy indulgence.

- **Servings:** 12
- **Preparation Time:** 15 minutes
- **Cooking Time:** 25 minutes

Ingredients:
1 cup (120 g) grated zucchini
1/2 cup (120 ml) honey or maple syrup
2 large eggs
1/2 cup (120 ml) olive oil
1 tsp (5 ml) vanilla extract
1/2 cup (60 g) cocoa powder
1 cup (120 g) whole wheat flour
1 tsp (5 ml) baking powder
1/4 tsp (1.25 ml) salt

Directions:

1. Preheat your oven to 350°F (175°C). Grease a 9x9-inch (23x23 cm) baking dish.
2. In a large bowl, mix the grated zucchini, honey or maple syrup, eggs, olive oil, and vanilla extract.
3. Stir in the cocoa powder, whole wheat flour, baking powder, and salt until well combined.
4. Pour the batter into the prepared baking dish and smooth the top.
5. Bake for 20-25 minutes, or until a toothpick inserted into the center comes out clean.
6. Allow to cool before cutting into squares.

Nutritional Facts (per serving):
Calories: 180
Carbohydrates: 22 g
Protein: 3 g
Fats: 9 g
Sugars: 14 g
Salt: 50 mg

15. Raspberry Chia Jam

A simple and healthy chia seed jam made with fresh raspberries, offering a naturally sweet spread for toast or desserts.

- **Servings:** 8
- **Preparation Time:** 5 minutes
- **Cooking Time:** None
- **Chilling Time:** 1 hour

Ingredients:
2 cups (300 g) fresh raspberries
2 tbsp (30 ml) honey or maple syrup
2 tbsp (30 ml) chia seeds
1 tsp (5 ml) lemon juice

Directions:
1. In a bowl, mash the raspberries with a fork until smooth.
2. Stir in the honey or maple syrup, chia seeds, and lemon juice.
3. Cover and refrigerate for at least 1 hour, or until thickened to a jam-like consistency.
4. Serve as a spread on toast or as a topping for desserts.

Nutritional Facts (per serving):
Calories: 40
Carbohydrates: 7 g
Protein: 1 g
Fats: 1 g
Sugars: 5 g
Salt: 0 mg

16. Oatmeal Raisin Cookies

These classic oatmeal raisin cookies are made with whole grains and natural sweeteners, offering a heart-healthy treat that's perfect with a cup of tea.

- **Servings:** 12
- **Preparation Time:** 10 minutes
- **Cooking Time:** 12 minutes

Ingredients:
1 cup (90 g) rolled oats
1/2 cup (60 g) whole wheat flour
1/2 tsp (2.5 ml) baking powder
1/2 tsp (2.5 ml) ground cinnamon
1/4 cup (60 ml) olive oil
1/4 cup (60 ml) honey or maple syrup
1 large egg
1 tsp (5 ml) vanilla extract
1/4 cup (30 g) raisins

Directions:
1. Preheat your oven to 350°F (175°C). Line a baking sheet with parchment paper.
2. In a bowl, mix the rolled oats, whole wheat flour, baking powder, and ground cinnamon.
3. In another bowl, whisk together the olive oil, honey or maple syrup, egg, and vanilla extract.
4. Stir the wet ingredients into the dry ingredients until combined.
5. Fold in the raisins.
6. Drop spoonfuls of the dough onto the prepared baking sheet.
7. Bake for 10-12 minutes, or until the edges are golden brown.
8. Allow to cool before serving.

Nutritional Facts (per serving):
Calories: 90
Carbohydrates: 15 g
Protein: 2 g
Fats: 3 g
Sugars: 8 g
Salt: 50 mg

17. Peanut Butter and Banana Quesadilla

A fun and sweet quesadilla filled with peanut butter and banana slices, offering a quick and satisfying dessert or snack.

- **Servings:** 1
- **Preparation Time:** 5 minutes
- **Cooking Time:** 5 minutes

Ingredients:
1 whole-grain tortilla
1 tbsp (15 g) natural peanut butter
1 banana, sliced
1/4 tsp (1.25 ml) ground cinnamon

Directions:
1. Spread the peanut butter evenly on one side of the tortilla.
2. Arrange the banana slices over the peanut butter.
3. Sprinkle with ground cinnamon.
4. Fold the tortilla in half and cook in a skillet over medium heat for 2-3 minutes on each side, until golden brown.
5. Slice into wedges and serve warm.

Nutritional Facts (per serving):
Calories: 220
Carbohydrates: 35 g
Protein: 6 g
Fats: 8 g

Sugars: 12 g
Salt: 150 mg

18. Lemon Blueberry Muffins

These light and fluffy muffins are bursting with fresh blueberries and a hint of lemon, making them a delightful and heart-healthy treat.
- **Servings:** 12
- **Preparation Time:** 10 minutes
- **Cooking Time:** 20 minutes

Ingredients:
1 cup (120 g) whole wheat flour
1/2 cup (60 g) almond flour
1/2 tsp (2.5 ml) baking powder
1/4 tsp (1.25 ml) baking soda
1/4 tsp (1.25 ml) salt
1/2 cup (120 ml) honey or maple syrup
1/4 cup (60 ml) olive oil
1 large egg
1/2 cup (120 ml) low-fat milk or almond milk
1 tsp (5 ml) vanilla extract
1 tbsp (15 ml) lemon zest
1 cup (150 g) fresh or frozen blueberries

Directions:
1. Preheat your oven to 350°F (175°C). Line a muffin tin with paper liners.
2. In a large bowl, whisk together the whole wheat flour, almond flour, baking powder, baking soda, and salt.
3. In another bowl, whisk together the honey or maple syrup, olive oil, egg, milk, vanilla extract, and lemon zest.
4. Pour the wet ingredients into the dry ingredients and stir until just combined.
5. Fold in the blueberries.
6. Divide the batter evenly among the muffin cups.
7. Bake for 18-20 minutes, or until a toothpick inserted into the center comes out clean.
8. Allow to cool before serving.

Nutritional Facts (per serving):
Calories: 150
Carbohydrates: 25 g
Protein: 3 g
Fats: 5 g
Sugars: 15 g
Salt: 100 mg

19. Strawberry Banana Smoothie

A creamy and refreshing smoothie made with strawberries and bananas, offering a sweet and nutritious treat that's perfect for any time of day.
- **Servings:** 2
- **Preparation Time:** 5 minutes
- **Cooking Time:** None

Ingredients:
1 banana
1 cup (150 g) strawberries, fresh or frozen
1/2 cup (120 ml) low-fat milk or almond milk
1/4 cup (60 ml) plain Greek yogurt
1 tsp (5 ml) honey (optional)

Directions:
1. In a blender, combine all the ingredients and blend until smooth.
2. Pour into glasses and serve immediately.

Nutritional Facts (per serving):
Calories: 150
Carbohydrates: 32 g
Protein: 5 g
Fats: 2 g
Sugars: 22 g
Salt: 60 mg

20. Cinnamon Baked Apple Chips

These crispy baked apple chips are lightly seasoned with cinnamon, offering a sweet and healthy snack that's perfect for munching.
- **Servings:** 4
- **Preparation Time:** 10 minutes
- **Cooking Time:** 2 hours

Ingredients:
2 large apples, thinly sliced
1 tsp (5 ml) ground cinnamon

Directions:
1. Preheat your oven to 200°F (95°C). Line a baking sheet with parchment paper.
2. Arrange the apple slices in a single layer on the baking sheet.
3. Sprinkle with ground cinnamon.
4. Bake for 2 hours, flipping halfway through, until the apples are crispy.
5. Allow to cool before serving.

Nutritional Facts (per serving):
Calories: 50
Carbohydrates: 14 g

Protein: 0 g
Fats: 0 g
Sugars: 10 g
Salt: 0 mg

These twenty healthy indulgences offer a range of flavors and textures, from rich and chocolatey to light and fruity, ensuring that you can enjoy desserts and treats while still supporting your heart health. By incorporating these recipes into your routine, you can satisfy your cravings without compromising your commitment to a heart-healthy lifestyle.

Chapter 16: Refreshing Smoothies and Beverages

Staying hydrated and nourished is key to maintaining a healthy heart. Smoothies and beverages can be a delicious and easy way to get essential nutrients while keeping your taste buds satisfied. In this chapter, I'll share twenty refreshing smoothie and beverage recipes that are not only delicious but also heart-healthy. These drinks are designed to provide a balance of vitamins, minerals, and antioxidants to support your cardiovascular health.

1. Berry Green Smoothie

This vibrant smoothie combines the antioxidant power of mixed berries with nutrient-dense spinach for a refreshing and heart-healthy drink.

- **Servings:** 2
- **Preparation Time:** 5 minutes
- **Cooking Time:** None

Ingredients:
1 cup (150 g) mixed berries (blueberries, strawberries, raspberries)
1 cup (30 g) fresh spinach
1/2 banana
1/2 cup (120 ml) unsweetened almond milk
1/2 cup (120 ml) water
1 tbsp (15 ml) chia seeds

Directions:
1. In a blender, combine all the ingredients and blend until smooth.
2. Pour into glasses and serve immediately.

Nutritional Facts (per serving):
Calories: 100
Carbohydrates: 22 g
Protein: 2 g
Fats: 2 g
Sugars: 12 g
Salt: 70 mg

2. Tropical Mango Smoothie

This tropical smoothie is packed with the bright flavors of mango and pineapple, providing a burst of vitamin C and other heart-healthy nutrients.

- **Servings:** 2
- **Preparation Time:** 5 minutes
- **Cooking Time:** None

Ingredients:
1 cup (165 g) frozen mango chunks
1/2 cup (80 g) frozen pineapple chunks
1/2 banana
1/2 cup (120 ml) orange juice
1/2 cup (120 ml) coconut water
1 tsp (5 ml) flaxseed oil (optional)

Directions:
1. In a blender, combine all the ingredients and blend until smooth.
2. Pour into glasses and serve immediately.

Nutritional Facts (per serving):
Calories: 150
Carbohydrates: 35 g
Protein: 2 g
Fats: 1 g
Sugars: 28 g
Salt: 50 mg

3. Strawberry Banana Smoothie

A classic smoothie that's creamy and satisfying, made with sweet strawberries and bananas, perfect for a quick and nutritious beverage.

- **Servings:** 2
- **Preparation Time:** 5 minutes
- **Cooking Time:** None

Ingredients:
1 banana
1 cup (150 g) strawberries, fresh or frozen
1/2 cup (120 ml) low-fat milk or almond milk
1/4 cup (60 ml) plain Greek yogurt
1 tsp (5 ml) honey (optional)

Directions:
1. In a blender, combine all the ingredients and blend until smooth.
2. Pour into glasses and serve immediately.

Nutritional Facts (per serving):
Calories: 150
Carbohydrates: 32 g
Protein: 5 g
Fats: 2 g
Sugars: 22 g
Salt: 60 mg

4. Blueberry Almond Smoothie

This smoothie features antioxidant-rich blueberries blended with creamy almond butter and almond milk, making for a heart-healthy and delicious drink.

- **Servings:** 2
- **Preparation Time:** 5 minutes
- **Cooking Time:** None

Ingredients:
1 cup (150 g) blueberries, fresh or frozen
1/2 banana
1 tbsp (15 g) almond butter
1 cup (240 ml) unsweetened almond milk
1/4 tsp (1.25 ml) vanilla extract

Directions:
1. In a blender, combine all the ingredients and blend until smooth.
2. Pour into glasses and serve immediately.

Nutritional Facts (per serving):
Calories: 160
Carbohydrates: 25 g
Protein: 3 g
Fats: 6 g

Sugars: 15 g
Salt: 80 mg

5. Green Tea Citrus Cooler

A refreshing beverage made with green tea and fresh citrus, offering a boost of antioxidants and a zesty flavor that's perfect for any time of day.

- **Servings:** 2
- **Preparation Time:** 5 minutes
- **Cooking Time:** None

Ingredients:
2 green tea bags
2 cups (480 ml) boiling water
1 orange, juiced
1 lemon, juiced
1 tsp (5 ml) honey (optional)
Ice cubes

Directions:
1. Steep the green tea bags in boiling water for 3-5 minutes.
2. Remove the tea bags and allow the tea to cool.
3. Stir in the orange juice, lemon juice, and honey if using.
4. Pour over ice and serve immediately.

Nutritional Facts (per serving):
Calories: 40
Carbohydrates: 10 g
Protein: 0 g
Fats: 0 g
Sugars: 8 g
Salt: 5 mg

6. Pineapple Mint Smoothie

This refreshing smoothie combines sweet pineapple with cooling mint, creating a delicious and hydrating beverage that's perfect for hot days.

- **Servings:** 2
- **Preparation Time:** 5 minutes
- **Cooking Time:** None

Ingredients:
1 cup (165 g) frozen pineapple chunks
1/2 cup (120 ml) coconut water
1/2 cup (120 ml) unsweetened almond milk
1 tbsp (15 ml) fresh mint leaves
1 tsp (5 ml) honey (optional)

Directions:
1. In a blender, combine all the ingredients and blend until smooth.

2. Pour into glasses and serve immediately.

Nutritional Facts (per serving):
Calories: 80
Carbohydrates: 20 g
Protein: 1 g
Fats: 1 g
Sugars: 15 g
Salt: 30 mg

7. Avocado Green Smoothie

This creamy green smoothie features heart-healthy avocado, spinach, and a touch of lime, providing a nutrient-dense and satisfying drink.
- **Servings:** 2
- **Preparation Time:** 5 minutes
- **Cooking Time:** None

Ingredients:
1/2 avocado
1 cup (30 g) fresh spinach
1/2 banana
1/2 cup (120 ml) unsweetened almond milk
1/2 cup (120 ml) water
1 tbsp (15 ml) lime juice

Directions:
1. In a blender, combine all the ingredients and blend until smooth.
2. Pour into glasses and serve immediately.

Nutritional Facts (per serving):
Calories: 120
Carbohydrates: 15 g
Protein: 2 g
Fats: 6 g
Sugars: 8 g
Salt: 40 mg

8. Orange Carrot Ginger Juice

A vibrant and zesty juice made with fresh oranges, carrots, and ginger, offering a refreshing and immune-boosting beverage.
- **Servings:** 2
- **Preparation Time:** 5 minutes
- **Cooking Time:** None

Ingredients:
2 large oranges, juiced
2 medium carrots, peeled and juiced
1 tsp (5 ml) fresh ginger, grated
Ice cubes

Directions:
1. In a juicer, process the oranges, carrots, and ginger.
2. Stir the juice and pour over ice.
3. Serve immediately.

Nutritional Facts (per serving):
Calories: 90
Carbohydrates: 22 g
Protein: 1 g
Fats: 0 g
Sugars: 18 g
Salt: 30 mg

9. Raspberry Lemonade

A refreshing and slightly tart lemonade made with fresh raspberries and lemon juice, perfect for a heart-healthy and hydrating drink.
- **Servings:** 4
- **Preparation Time:** 10 minutes
- **Cooking Time:** None

Ingredients:
1/2 cup (75 g) fresh raspberries
1/2 cup (120 ml) lemon juice (from about 4 lemons)
3 cups (720 ml) cold water
1 tbsp (15 ml) honey or maple syrup
Ice cubes

Directions:
1. In a blender, combine the raspberries, lemon juice, water, and honey.
2. Blend until smooth and strain through a fine mesh sieve to remove seeds.
3. Pour over ice and serve immediately.

Nutritional Facts (per serving):
Calories: 35
Carbohydrates: 9 g
Protein: 0 g
Fats: 0 g
Sugars: 6 g
Salt: 0 mg

10. Cherry Vanilla Smoothie

A sweet and creamy smoothie featuring ripe cherries and a hint of vanilla, offering a delicious treat that's also heart-healthy.
- **Servings:** 2
- **Preparation Time:** 5 minutes
- **Cooking Time:** None

Ingredients:
1 cup (150 g) cherries, pitted and frozen
1/2 banana
1/2 cup (120 ml) low-fat milk or almond milk
1/4 tsp (1.25 ml) vanilla extract
1 tsp (5 ml) honey (optional)

Directions:
1. In a blender, combine all the ingredients and blend until smooth.
2. Pour into glasses and serve immediately.

Nutritional Facts (per serving):
Calories: 120
Carbohydrates: 26 g
Protein: 2 g
Fats: 1 g
Sugars: 20 g
Salt: 40 mg

11. Watermelon Lime Cooler

A light and refreshing cooler made with sweet watermelon and tangy lime, perfect for staying hydrated on hot days.
- **Servings:** 2
- **Preparation Time:** 5 minutes
- **Cooking Time:** None

Ingredients:
2 cups (300 g) watermelon, diced
1 tbsp (15 ml) lime juice
1 cup (240 ml) cold water
Ice cubes
Fresh mint leaves for garnish

Directions:
1. In a blender, combine the watermelon, lime juice, and cold water.
2. Blend until smooth and pour over ice.
3. Garnish with fresh mint leaves and serve immediately.

Nutritional Facts (per serving):
Calories: 50
Carbohydrates: 13 g
Protein: 1 g
Fats: 0 g
Sugars: 10 g
Salt: 5 mg

12. Cucumber Mint Smoothie

This hydrating smoothie features crisp cucumber, fresh mint, and a touch of lime, creating a refreshing drink that's perfect for hot weather.
- **Servings:** 2
- **Preparation Time:** 5 minutes
- **Cooking Time:** None

Ingredients:
1 cucumber, peeled and chopped
1/2 cup (120 ml) unsweetened almond milk
1/2 cup (120 ml) water
1 tbsp (15 ml) fresh mint leaves
1 tbsp (15 ml) lime juice
1 tsp (5 ml) honey (optional)

Directions:
1. In a blender, combine all the ingredients and blend until smooth.
2. Pour into glasses and serve immediately.

Nutritional Facts (per serving):
Calories: 40
Carbohydrates: 10 g
Protein: 1 g
Fats: 1 g
Sugars: 6 g
Salt: 15 mg

13. Spinach Pear Smoothie

A nutrient-packed smoothie featuring spinach, pear, and a hint of ginger, offering a delicious and heart-healthy way to start your day.
- **Servings:** 2
- **Preparation Time:** 5 minutes
- **Cooking Time:** None

Ingredients:
1 pear, cored and chopped
1 cup (30 g) fresh spinach
1/2 banana
1/2 cup (120 ml) unsweetened almond milk
1/2 cup (120 ml) water
1 tsp (5 ml) fresh ginger, grated

Directions:
1. In a blender, combine all the ingredients and blend until smooth.
2. Pour into glasses and serve immediately.

Nutritional Facts (per serving):
Calories: 100
Carbohydrates: 25 g

Protein: 2 g
Fats: 1 g
Sugars: 15 g
Salt: 30 mg

14. Matcha Coconut Latte

A creamy latte made with matcha green tea and coconut milk, offering a boost of antioxidants and a deliciously rich flavor.

- **Servings:** 2
- **Preparation Time:** 5 minutes
- **Cooking Time:** 5 minutes

Ingredients:
1 tsp (5 ml) matcha green tea powder
1 cup (240 ml) unsweetened coconut milk
1/2 cup (120 ml) water
1 tsp (5 ml) honey or maple syrup (optional)

Directions:
1. In a small saucepan, heat the coconut milk and water over medium heat until warm.
2. Whisk in the matcha green tea powder and honey or maple syrup if using.
3. Pour into cups and serve warm.

Nutritional Facts (per serving):
Calories: 60
Carbohydrates: 5 g
Protein: 1 g
Fats: 5 g
Sugars: 4 g
Salt: 15 mg

15. Cranberry Ginger Fizz

A sparkling and festive beverage made with tart cranberry juice and spicy ginger, perfect for special occasions or just as a refreshing treat.

- **Servings:** 2
- **Preparation Time:** 5 minutes
- **Cooking Time:** None

Ingredients:
1/2 cup (120 ml) unsweetened cranberry juice
1/2 tsp (2.5 ml) fresh ginger, grated
1/2 cup (120 ml) sparkling water
Ice cubes
Fresh cranberries for garnish (optional)

Directions:
1. In a glass, combine the cranberry juice and fresh ginger.
2. Add ice cubes and top with sparkling water.

3. Garnish with fresh cranberries if desired.
4. Serve immediately.

Nutritional Facts (per serving):
Calories: 25
Carbohydrates: 6 g
Protein: 0 g
Fats: 0 g
Sugars: 5 g
Salt: 5 mg

16. Peach Basil Smoothie

This unique smoothie combines sweet peaches with fresh basil for a flavorful and refreshing beverage that's perfect for summer.

- **Servings:** 2
- **Preparation Time:** 5 minutes
- **Cooking Time:** None

Ingredients:
1 cup (150 g) frozen peach slices
1/2 banana
1 tbsp (15 ml) fresh basil leaves
1/2 cup (120 ml) unsweetened almond milk
1/2 cup (120 ml) water
1 tsp (5 ml) honey (optional)

Directions:
1. In a blender, combine all the ingredients and blend until smooth.
2. Pour into glasses and serve immediately.

Nutritional Facts (per serving):
Calories: 90
Carbohydrates: 22 g
Protein: 1 g
Fats: 1 g
Sugars: 18 g
Salt: 15 mg

17. Spiced Apple Cider

A warm and comforting beverage made with apple cider and warming spices, perfect for cozying up on a chilly day.

- **Servings:** 2
- **Preparation Time:** 5 minutes
- **Cooking Time:** 10 minutes

Ingredients:
2 cups (480 ml) apple cider
1 cinnamon stick
2 cloves
1/4 tsp (1.25 ml) ground nutmeg
1/2 tsp (2.5 ml) fresh ginger, grated

Directions:

1. In a small saucepan, combine the apple cider, cinnamon stick, cloves, nutmeg, and ginger.
2. Bring to a simmer over medium heat and let steep for 5-10 minutes.
3. Remove the spices and pour into mugs.
4. Serve warm.

Nutritional Facts (per serving):
Calories: 120
Carbohydrates: 30 g
Protein: 0 g
Fats: 0 g
Sugars: 24 g
Salt: 0 mg

18. Almond Date Smoothie

A creamy and naturally sweet smoothie made with almonds, dates, and a hint of cinnamon, offering a satisfying and energizing drink.

- **Servings:** 2
- **Preparation Time:** 5 minutes
- **Cooking Time:** None

Ingredients:
1/4 cup (30 g) raw almonds
2 dates, pitted
1/2 banana
1/2 cup (120 ml) unsweetened almond milk
1/2 cup (120 ml) water
1/4 tsp (1.25 ml) ground cinnamon

Directions:

1. In a blender, combine all the ingredients and blend until smooth.
2. Pour into glasses and serve immediately.

Nutritional Facts (per serving):
Calories: 150
Carbohydrates: 28 g
Protein: 3 g
Fats: 4 g
Sugars: 18 g
Salt: 20 mg

19. Iced Matcha Latte

A refreshing iced latte made with matcha green tea and almond milk, offering a delicious and antioxidant-rich beverage that's perfect for a midday pick-me-up.

- **Servings:** 2
- **Preparation Time:** 5 minutes
- **Cooking Time:** None

Ingredients:
1 tsp (5 ml) matcha green tea powder
1 cup (240 ml) unsweetened almond milk
1/2 cup (120 ml) cold water
Ice cubes
1 tsp (5 ml) honey or maple syrup (optional)

Directions:

1. In a shaker or jar, combine the matcha green tea powder, almond milk, cold water, and honey or maple syrup if using.
2. Shake or stir vigorously until well combined.
3. Pour over ice and serve immediately.

Nutritional Facts (per serving):
Calories: 50
Carbohydrates: 7 g
Protein: 1 g
Fats: 2 g
Sugars: 4 g
Salt: 40 mg

20. Beetroot and Berry Smoothie

This vibrant smoothie combines the earthy sweetness of beetroot with the tartness of mixed berries, creating a nutrient-packed and heart-healthy drink.

- **Servings:** 2
- **Preparation Time:** 5 minutes
- **Cooking Time:** None

Ingredients:
1 small beetroot, peeled and chopped
1/2 cup (75 g) mixed berries (blueberries, strawberries, raspberries)
1/2 banana
1/2 cup (120 ml) unsweetened almond milk
1/2 cup (120 ml) water
1 tsp (5 ml) honey (optional)

Directions:

1. In a blender, combine all the ingredients and blend until smooth.
2. Pour into glasses and serve immediately.

Nutritional Facts (per serving):
Calories: 90
Carbohydrates: 22 g
Protein: 2 g
Fats: 1 g
Sugars: 15 g
Salt: 35 mg

These twenty refreshing smoothie and beverage recipes offer a range of flavors and nutrients, ensuring that you can enjoy delicious and heart-healthy drinks throughout the day. Whether you're looking for a quick breakfast, a midday pick-me-up, or a hydrating treat, these recipes will help you stay on track with your heart-healthy lifestyle.

60 Days Meal Plan

	Breakfast	Lunch	Snacks	Dinner
Day 1	Scrambled Eggs with Smoked Salmon	Edamame and Quinoa Salad	Dark Chocolate Avocado Mousse	Mushroom and Spinach Stuffed Chicken Breast
Day 2	Berry Green Smoothie	Quinoa and Black Bean Salad	Almond Butter Apple Slices	Lemon Herb Grilled Chicken with Steamed Broccoli
Day 3	Tropical Smoothie Bowl	Baked Salmon with Quinoa and Asparagus	Baked Apple with Cinnamon and Walnuts	Thai-Inspired Chicken Curry with Brown Rice
Day 4	Edamame and Quinoa Salad	Mediterranean Chickpea Wrap	Greek Yogurt with Berries and Chia Seeds	Baked Cod with Garlic and Tomatoes
Day 5	Savory Quinoa Breakfast Bowl	Mushroom and Spinach Stuffed Chicken Breast	Chia Seed Pudding with Berries	Spinach and Feta Stuffed Salmon
Day 6	Grilled Veggie and Hummus Wrap	Grilled Chicken and Avocado Salad	Roasted Chickpeas	Quinoa-Stuffed Bell Peppers
Day 7	Pear and Almond Smoothie	Spinach and Feta Stuffed Chicken Breast	Banana Oat Cookies	Herb-Roasted Chicken with Root Vegetables
Day 8	Roasted Beet and Goat Cheese Salad	Lentil and Vegetable Soup	Avocado Toast with Cherry Tomatoes	Salmon with Asparagus and Lemon-Dill Sauce
Day 9	Ricotta Toast with Honey and Almonds	Grilled Veggie and Hummus Wrap	Greek Yogurt Parfait with Granola and Honey	Spaghetti Squash with Pesto and Cherry Tomatoes
Day 10	Strawberry Banana Smoothie	Baked Salmon with Quinoa and Asparagus	Veggie Sticks with Hummus	Lentil and Vegetable Stir-Fry
Day 11	Chia Seed Pudding with Mango	Spinach and Feta Stuffed Chicken Breast	Avocado Chocolate Brownies	Grilled Chicken with Mango Salsa
Day 12	Grilled Portobello Mushroom Sandwich	Chickpea and Spinach Curry	Baked Sweet Potato Chips	Baked Salmon with Quinoa and Asparagus
Day 13	Veggie-Packed Frittata	Farro Salad with Roasted Vegetables	Coconut Macaroons	Moroccan-Spiced Chickpea Stew
Day 14	Scrambled Eggs with Smoked Salmon	Turkey and Avocado Sandwich	Cottage Cheese with Pineapple	Baked Cod with Lemon and Garlic
Day 15	Apple Walnut Oatmeal	Grilled Chicken with Mango Salsa	Baked Pears with Honey and Almonds	Baked Tofu with Stir-Fried Vegetables
Day 16	Tropical Mango Smoothie	Zucchini Noodles with Pesto and Cherry Tomatoes	Peanut Butter Banana Bites	Baked Chicken with Sweet Potatoes and Brussels Sprouts
Day 17	Avocado and Egg Breakfast Sandwich	Lemon Herb Grilled Chicken with Steamed Broccoli	Dark Chocolate-Covered Strawberries	Turkey and Vegetable Meatloaf
Day 18	Blueberry Almond Smoothie	Grilled Veggie and Hummus Wrap	Whole-Grain Crackers with Avocado and Tuna	Spinach and Feta Stuffed Salmon

	Breakfast	Lunch	Snacks	Dinner
Day 19	Whole-Grain Banana Pancakes	Baked Chicken with Sweet Potatoes and Brussels Sprouts	Mango Sorbet	Grilled Shrimp Skewers with Quinoa
Day 20	Baked Sweet Potato with Black Beans and Avocado	Baked Cod with Lemon and Garlic	Edamame with Sea Salt	Salmon with Asparagus and Lemon-Dill Sauce
Day 21	Peanut Butter Banana Toast	Chicken and Vegetable Stir-Fry with Brown Rice	Banana Ice Cream	Baked Eggplant Parmesan
Day 22	Scrambled Eggs with Smoked Salmon	Farro Salad with Roasted Vegetables	Oat and Nut Energy Bites	Lentil and Vegetable Stir-Fry
Day 23	Veggie Omelette with Tomatoes and Spinach	Grilled Shrimp Skewers with Quinoa	Almond Butter Chocolate Cups	Chicken and Vegetable Stir-Fry with Brown Rice
Day 24	Spinach Pear Smoothie	Shrimp and Avocado Salad	Carrot Sticks with Tahini Dip	Moroccan-Spiced Chickpea Stew
Day 25	Blueberry Almond Breakfast Smoothie	Grilled Chicken with Mango Salsa	Berry Crumble	Whole Wheat Spaghetti with Tomato Basil Sauce
Day 26	Shrimp and Avocado Salad	Tofu Stir-Fry with Broccoli and Carrots	Frozen Yogurt Bark with Berries	Baked Salmon with Quinoa and Asparagus
Day 27	Cottage Cheese and Berry Bowl	Herb-Roasted Chicken with Root Vegetables	Zucchini Chocolate Cake	Spinach and Feta Stuffed Salmon
Day 28	Pineapple Mint Smoothie	Spinach and Feta Stuffed Chicken Breast	Spiced Pumpkin Seeds	Baked Cod with Roasted Cherry Tomatoes
Day 29	Sweet Potato Breakfast Hash	Baked Cod with Roasted Cherry Tomatoes	Raspberry Chia Jam	Baked Chicken with Sweet Potatoes and Brussels Sprouts
Day 30	Avocado Green Smoothie	Baked Sweet Potato with Black Beans and Avocado	Cucumber Slices with Feta and Olive Oil	Turkey and Vegetable Meatloaf
Day 31	Avocado and Tomato Toast	Mushroom and Spinach Stuffed Chicken Breast	Oatmeal Raisin Cookies	Lentil and Vegetable Stir-Fry
Day 32	Turkey and Avocado Sandwich	Cauliflower Rice Stir-Fry	Mixed Berry Smoothie	Grilled Shrimp Skewers with Quinoa
Day 33	Apple Cinnamon Quinoa	Grilled Chicken with Mango Salsa	Peanut Butter and Banana Quesadilla	Salmon with Asparagus and Lemon-Dill Sauce
Day 34	Cherry Vanilla Smoothie	Grilled Portobello Mushroom Sandwich	Dark Chocolate Almonds	Whole Wheat Spaghetti with Tomato Basil Sauce
Day 35	Spinach and Mushroom Breakfast Wrap	Edamame and Quinoa Salad	Lemon Blueberry Muffins	Quinoa-Stuffed Bell Peppers
Day 36	Almond Date Smoothie	Roasted Beet and Goat Cheese Salad	Apple Nachos with Peanut Butter and Nuts	Spinach and Feta Stuffed Salmon
Day 37	Greek Yogurt Parfait with Walnuts and Honey	Baked Salmon with Quinoa and Asparagus	Strawberry Banana Smoothie	Baked Cod with Garlic and Tomatoes

	Breakfast	Lunch	Snacks	Dinner
Day 38	Grilled Chicken and Avocado Salad	Spaghetti Squash with Marinara Sauce	Cherry Tomato and Mozzarella Skewers	Chicken and Vegetable Stir-Fry with Brown Rice
Day 39	Oatmeal with Fresh Berries and Almonds	Mediterranean Chickpea Wrap	Cinnamon Baked Apple Chips	Lemon Herb Grilled Chicken with Steamed Broccoli
Day 40	Spinach Pear Smoothie	Edamame and Quinoa Salad	Banana Oat Cookies	Baked Eggplant Parmesan
Day 41	Avocado and Egg Breakfast Sandwich	Mediterranean Chickpea Wrap	Dark Chocolate-Covered Strawberries	Mushroom and Spinach Stuffed Chicken Breast
Day 42	Chia Seed Pudding with Mango	Grilled Veggie and Hummus Wrap	Almond Butter Apple Slices	Salmon with Asparagus and Lemon-Dill Sauce
Day 43	Apple Walnut Oatmeal	Lentil and Vegetable Soup	Whole-Grain Crackers with Avocado and Tuna	Thai-Inspired Chicken Curry with Brown Rice
Day 44	Peach Basil Smoothie	Zucchini Noodles with Pesto and Cherry Tomatoes	Greek Yogurt with Berries and Chia Seeds	Lentil and Vegetable Stir-Fry
Day 45	Veggie-Packed Frittata	Grilled Chicken and Avocado Salad	Peanut Butter Banana Bites	Baked Cod with Roasted Cherry Tomatoes
Day 46	Veggie Omelette with Tomatoes and Spinach	Turkey and Avocado Sandwich	Roasted Chickpeas	Thai-Inspired Chicken Curry with Brown Rice
Day 47	Chia Seed Pudding with Mango	Farro Salad with Roasted Vegetables	Cinnamon Baked Apple Chips	Herb-Roasted Chicken with Root Vegetables
Day 48	Beetroot and Berry Smoothie	Chickpea and Spinach Curry	Avocado Toast with Cherry Tomatoes	Turkey and Vegetable Meatloaf
Day 49	Ricotta Toast with Honey and Almonds	Herb-Roasted Chicken with Root Vegetables	Frozen Yogurt Bark with Berries	Spaghetti Squash with Pesto and Cherry Tomatoes
Day 50	Mediterranean Chickpea Wrap	Baked Salmon with Quinoa and Asparagus	Veggie Sticks with Hummus	Moroccan-Spiced Chickpea Stew
Day 51	Pear and Almond Smoothie	Baked Cod with Lemon and Garlic	Spiced Pumpkin Seeds	Grilled Chicken with Mango Salsa
Day 52	Sweet Potato Breakfast Hash	Lentil and Vegetable Soup	Baked Sweet Potato Chips	Whole Wheat Spaghetti with Tomato Basil Sauce
Day 53	Savory Quinoa Breakfast Bowl	Baked Sweet Potato with Black Beans and Avocado	Dark Chocolate Avocado Mousse	Moroccan-Spiced Chickpea Stew
Day 54	Shrimp and Avocado Salad	Grilled Chicken and Avocado Salad	Almond Butter Apple Slices	Mushroom and Spinach Stuffed Chicken Breast
Day 55	Tropical Smoothie Bowl	Spaghetti Squash with Marinara Sauce	Baked Apple with Cinnamon and Walnuts	Lemon Herb Grilled Chicken with Steamed Broccoli

	Breakfast	Lunch	Snacks	Dinner
Day 56	Oatmeal with Fresh Berries and Almonds	Mediterranean Chickpea Wrap	Greek Yogurt with Berries and Chia Seeds	Thai-Inspired Chicken Curry with Brown Rice
Day 57	Scrambled Eggs with Smoked Salmon	Grilled Veggie and Hummus Wrap	Chia Seed Pudding with Berries	Baked Cod with Garlic and Tomatoes
Day 58	Ricotta Toast with Honey and Almonds	Quinoa and Black Bean Salad	Roasted Chickpeas	Baked Cod with Roasted Cherry Tomatoes
Day 59	Strawberry Banana Smoothie	Lemon Herb Grilled Chicken with Steamed Broccoli	Banana Oat Cookies	Quinoa-Stuffed Bell Peppers
Day 60	Chia Seed Pudding with Mango	Grilled Veggie and Hummus Wrap	Avocado Toast with Cherry Tomatoes	Mushroom and Spinach Stuffed Chicken Breast

Conclusion

Reflections on Your Journey

As you reach the end of this book, I want to take a moment to reflect on the incredible journey you've embarked on. When you first picked up *The Science-Backed Heart Healthy Diet for Beginners*, you took a significant step toward improving your heart health and overall well-being. This journey has been about more than just changing your diet; it's been about embracing a new way of living—one that prioritizes your heart, your health, and your future.

You've learned about the critical role that diet plays in cardiovascular health, from understanding the essentials of a heart-healthy diet to mastering the art of cooking nutritious meals that support your heart. You've explored the science behind the foods you eat, debunked common diet myths, and discovered practical strategies for making heart-healthy choices every day. Whether you were learning how to navigate social situations with confidence or exploring the vibrant flavors of heart-healthy recipes, every chapter in this book was designed to equip you with the knowledge and tools you need to succeed.

But beyond the information and the recipes, you've made a commitment to yourself. You've chosen to take control of your health, to make conscious decisions about what you eat and how you live, and to prioritize the well-being of your heart. This commitment is no small feat. It requires dedication, perseverance, and a willingness to change habits that may have been ingrained for years. You should be incredibly proud of the progress you've made.

Remember that every small step counts. The changes you've implemented—whether it's swapping out processed foods for whole grains, incorporating more fruits and vegetables into your diet, or finding joy in heart-healthy snacks—are all victories that contribute to a stronger, healthier heart. It's easy to overlook these small wins in the pursuit of bigger goals, but I encourage you to celebrate each one. They are the building blocks of long-term success.

Looking Ahead

As you look ahead, I want to encourage you to continue on this path with confidence and determination. Maintaining a heart-healthy lifestyle is not about perfection; it's about consistency and balance. Life will always present challenges—busy schedules, social events, and moments of temptation—but with the knowledge and strategies you've gained, you are well-equipped to navigate these situations while keeping your heart health in mind.

One of the most important things to remember is that this journey is ongoing. Heart health is not something you achieve once and then forget about; it's a lifelong commitment to taking care of yourself. This means continuing to make informed choices, staying curious about new research and trends in heart health, and being open to adapting your diet and lifestyle as your needs change over time.

To keep your heart-healthy lifestyle sustainable, I recommend setting realistic and achievable goals. These goals don't have to be grand; they can be as simple as trying a new heart-healthy recipe each week, incorporating an extra 10 minutes of physical activity into your daily routine, or taking time each day to practice mindfulness and reduce stress. The key is to make these goals a natural part of your life, rather than a chore or an obligation.

Another vital aspect of maintaining your heart-healthy lifestyle is seeking support when you need it. Surround yourself with people who encourage your efforts and share your commitment to health. Whether it's family, friends, or a community of like-minded individuals, having a support system can make all the difference. Don't be afraid to ask for help, share your successes, or lean on others during challenging times. Remember, you're not alone in this journey.

As you continue to explore new ways to support your heart, stay open to learning and experimenting with different foods, exercises, and wellness practices. The field of nutrition and heart health is ever-evolving, and there's always something new to discover. Perhaps you'll find that you enjoy a particular type of exercise, or you'll stumble upon a new favorite recipe that becomes a staple in your diet. Embrace these opportunities for growth and enrichment.

One of the most rewarding aspects of maintaining a heart-healthy lifestyle is the ripple effect it can have on those around you. By modeling healthy behaviors, you may inspire your family, friends, and even coworkers to make positive changes in their own lives. The impact of your journey can extend far beyond your own health, contributing to a culture of wellness in your community.

In moments of doubt or difficulty, revisit the reasons why you started this journey in the first place. Whether it was a desire to improve your health, reduce your risk of heart disease, or simply feel better each day, these motivations are powerful reminders of why your efforts matter. Keep these reasons close to your heart, and let them fuel your determination to stay on course.

As you move forward, I want to leave you with a few final pieces of advice:

1. **Be Kind to Yourself:** It's important to approach this journey with compassion and understanding. There will be days when you slip up, and that's okay. What matters most is that you get back on track and continue making progress. Don't let setbacks discourage you; instead, view them as opportunities to learn and grow.

2. **Stay Informed:** The world of nutrition and heart health is full of information—some of it helpful, some of it confusing. Continue to educate yourself, but always be critical of the sources you trust. Look for evidence-based advice and consult with healthcare professionals when needed.

3. **Enjoy the Journey:** Heart health is a serious matter, but that doesn't mean it has to be a burden. Find joy in the process, whether it's discovering new flavors, enjoying the benefits of regular exercise, or simply feeling good about the choices you're making. A positive attitude can make all the difference.

4. **Keep It Simple:** Don't overcomplicate things. Healthy living doesn't require elaborate plans or strict rules. Focus on the basics: eat a balanced diet rich in whole foods, stay active, get enough rest, and manage stress. Simplicity is often the key to sustainability.

5. **Celebrate Your Successes:** No matter how small, take time to acknowledge and celebrate your achievements. Whether it's a week of consistent exercise, a new favorite recipe, or a noticeable improvement in your energy levels, these successes are worth celebrating. They are the proof of your hard work and dedication.

Finally, I want to express my sincere gratitude for allowing me to be a part of your journey. Writing this book has been a labor of love, and my hope is that it has provided you with the knowledge, inspiration, and tools you need to take control of your heart health. Your decision to invest in your well-being is one of the most important choices you can make, and I'm honored to have been able to support you along the way.

Remember, your heart is at the center of everything you do. By nurturing it with care, you're not only enhancing your health but also ensuring that you can live a vibrant, fulfilling life for years to come. Keep going, stay committed, and never forget that every step you take brings you closer to a healthier, happier you.

With warmest regards and heartfelt encouragement,

Dr. Emily Reynolds
Nutritionist and Heart Health Advocate

Made in the USA
Las Vegas, NV
11 January 2025

16014335R00083